MODERN LEGAL STUDIES

Diversion in the Criminal Process

AUSTRALIA
LBC Information Services
Sydney

CANADA and USA
Carswell
Toronto—Ontario

NEW ZEALAND
Brookers
Auckland

SINGAPORE and MALAYSIA
Thomson Information (S.E.) Asia
Singapore

MODERN LEGAL STUDIES

Diversion in the Criminal Process

Professor Christopher Harding
University of Wales, Aberystwyth

Gavin Dingwall
Lecturer, University of Wales, Aberystwyth

London
Sweet & Maxwell
1998

Published by
Sweet & Maxwell Limited of
100 Avenue Road London NW3 3PE.
http://www/smlawpub.co.uk
Typeset by Selwood Systems, Midsomer Norton
Printed by Butler & Tanner Ltd, Frome and London

A CIP catalogue record for this book
is available from the British Library.

ISBN 0421 586907

No natural forests were destroyed to make this product,
only farmed timber was used and re-planted.

PREFACE

The idea of "criminal law" conjures up a powerful image in both the popular perception and formal and academic discourse of crime control: a landscape occupied by police, courtrooms and (often) prison walls and bars. For the majority of people, who are never involved in seriously delinquent behaviour, there may be a reassuring sense of inevitability about the process of criminal law. Textbooks on criminal law assume in their presentation of the subject an ordered world of legal accountability. And official statements about crime are usually based on counts of formal processing of offenders which serve at the same time both to exaggerate and to scale down the actual nature of the phenomenon of criminality. In this book we have set out to probe systematically the reality of this conventional sense of crime regulation, by saying something about the amount and the kind of conduct that is dealt with fully and finally—or not, as the case may be—by the formal processes of the criminal law. We have used in our title the now widely accepted term "diversion", to conveniently summarise the ways in which criminal law is not used, as the easiest way of indicating to the potential reader the thrust of our discussion. But the argument which emerges from this discussion suggests in fact that the vocabulary of diversion may be misleading. Rather, it would seem, the process of formal criminal law is itself a kind of diversion, from a realm of social control within which there exist a range of motives, both public and private, for not resorting to the formal methods of prosecution, trial and punishment.

In discussing the subject in these terms we have necessarily taken a wide sweep across a range of subject divisions: on the one hand, having to be descriptive about a number of aspects of criminal justice and criminal procedure, while also on the other hand analysing in both a jurisprudential and a sociological manner the nature of criminal law and its analogies in the more "private" and less visible spheres of social control. The book should therefore serve, hopefully, as a companion volume for a wide range of existing literature on criminal law, criminal justice and the penal system. But primarily we hope that it will help those engaged in the discussion and study of these subjects to appreciate more fully and even to re-interpret the relationship between the conventional ideas of crime, law and society.

The ideas informing a work of this kind inevitably have a somewhat imprecise genesis in a longer period of teaching, research and informal discussion. But the idea for a single monograph on the subject of "diversion" came about quite spontaneously and suddenly and we are grateful to the editorial staff of Sweet and Maxwell and the editorial board of the Modern Legal Studies series for enabling us to bring our work to fruition so speedily. Once we were into the business of collecting and examining material specifically for the book and writing it, we benefited of course from the assistance of a number of people, most notably our colleagues and former colleagues in the Crime and Law Research Group at the University of Wales, Aberystwyth who were kind enough to take time to discuss our early ideas and refine our arguments, as were those who listened to us giving papers on diversion in Aberystwyth, Gregynog and Utrecht. Gavin Dingwall would also like to thank Andrea Blackhurst for her encouragement and her continual willingness to debate issues of crime and crime control. We are also grateful to the staff at the Hugh Owen Library at the University of Wales, Aberystwyth, the National Library of Wales, Aberystwyth, the Law Library at the University of Edinburgh, and the National Library of Scotland, Edinburgh, who facilitated our research. Finally we wish to thank our students, past and present, whose interest in the area and willingness to challenge our views has, we hope, been mutually beneficial.

We have striven to be as up-to-date as possible in our discussion of contemporary events and developments and research activity and hope therefore that we have reported fully and accurately on the state of law, society and research as it stands at the beginning of 1998.

GAVIN DINGWALL
CHRISTOPHER HARDING

CONTENTS

Table of Cases

Table of Statutes

Chapter 1

The Concept of Diversion

Ideal belief or naive assumption, or perhaps a mixture of both, may suggest that in a system of prohibitory rules, especially one characterised as "criminal law", all breaches of such rules should be dealt with in a way that is both formal and consistent. Clearly the effectiveness of the system of rules itself depends upon a certain minimum level of response, but there are also considerations of fair treatment and popular support which may be urged in favour of a full and consistent policy of dealing with all breaches in a like manner. Some legal systems do indeed base themselves on such an idea of "legality" or "compulsory prosecution" (Ashworth (1984)) whereby the relevant official agencies are expected to deal formally with all breaches of criminal law which come to their notice. It is clear, however, that such a principle of "legality" is in practice subject to important exceptions (Van Den Wyngaert (1993)), while other legal systems are openly based on a discretionary and selective policy of enforcement. This work is concerned with an important feature of this problem of enforcement of rules of criminal law: the extent to which breaches of criminal law are *not* dealt with by the normal agencies of enforcement according to the conventional methods of criminal procedure but are nonetheless subject to responses which are less visible and less easily recognised while still amounting to a significant social reaction to law-breaking. Such alternatives to formal criminal proceedings act as an instructive barometer of a society's perception and tolerance of problems of delinquency and in quantitative terms account for a sizeable segment of enforcement activity.

"Diversion" is the term which has been increasingly used to describe in a shorthand fashion the collection of enforcement strategies outside the boundaries of conventional and formal criminal procedure. This term is pleasingly and usefully concise and does possess some explanatory force, but it is also a concept which needs to be handled carefully and its definition is a matter of some importance. In particular, it suggests a certain norm and prioritisation as regards responses to criminal offending: that is, a formal and official process of prosecution, trial and sanctioning. Implicit in this idea is the role of state machinery, officials and power. Indeed, popular image and official rhetoric probably coincide in a vision of police investigations, public justice in courts of law and a system of imprisonment and other formal modes of punishment. But this idea of the centrality of formal criminal justice may be misleading, not only because many rule breakers do not experience that process but also because in many instances its use would not have been seriously contemplated in the first place. "Diversion" may be an appropriate description of what happens to those offenders for whom there is a conscious decision not to use the formal process of prosecution and trial in cases where there is a fair expectation that it would otherwise have taken place. But it is less properly applied to convey the idea of what happens to those offenders who are customarily and as a matter of principle dealt with outside the conventional parameters of formal criminal justice, for instance by non-State agencies or by non-repressive procedures and measures. "Diversion" begs the question of the norm: from what is the offender being diverted? The study being undertaken here is concerned with a wide range of social processes which have in common the fact that they are responses to delinquency of a kind which may be characterised as "criminal". While "diversion" is a useful shorthand term, in the present context it is being used advisedly to convey the idea of a system of different responses, without wishing to imply the centrality or priority of formal criminal justice within the overall scheme of reaction to criminal rule-breaking. It should also be noted that "diversion" is not being used here in the sense of "crime prevention" (see Pease (1994)). Preventive or security measures may be referred to as a means of diverting crime itself, but diversion of crime is a different matter from diversion of process, and "crime prevention" is probably a preferable term to describe the former.

The concept and the practice of diversion

It should be appreciated that much of what may now be described as "diversionary" activity has for a long time been a feature of social organisation. As will be seen, the concept of diversion now has a fashionable resonance among both officials of the criminal justice system and its critics. Yet it has always been an inescapable though less trumpeted fact of life. The principle *de minimis non curat lex* as commonly applied to trivial offences or defects in procedure—do not expend resources on trivial infringements—has a long pedigree in most systems of law, as an article of common sense. Moreover, many of those who have had it in their power to respond in some way to acts of wrongdoing have tempered their decision by reference to ideas of justice or mercy with the result that action may be deflected away from the very young, the infirm, the mentally unfit or even the socially disabled, in which case the strict letter of the code gives way to the moderating force of compassion and fair treatment. Or, then again, there may be more strategic or calculating reasons for not using the full force of the law. For instance, a prescriptively severe law may be laid down in legislation but applied with selection and mercy in order to achieve both deterrence and social support at the same time, as is thought by some social historians to have been the function of the notorious "Bloody Code" of English criminal law during the eighteenth century (Cockburn (1977), Sharpe (1984), Beattie (1986)). There is nothing very new about diversion except perhaps the term itself.

Discussion and study of diversion and alternative enforcement procedures have come to the fore in the last twenty years, but the term itself is still some way from being one of textbook art. Discussion of the subject may appear under a number of headings, such as "informal justice" (*e.g.* Matthews (1988)), "gatekeeping" (Ashworth (1984, 1994)) and "enforcement", with varying degrees of attention being given to official processes (*e.g.* cautioning by the police, settlement agreed with regulatory agencies) or less formal processes (*e.g.* mediation, resolution by "private" agencies such as employers, educational institutions or professional bodies), although typically and predictably the more informal and less official processes are not so well investigated and much interesting work remains to be done in that context. What is of general importance, however, is the burgeoning interest in both the theoretical and practical aspects of diversionary and informal processes of dealing with delinquency. There may be a number of reasons for this increased attention. The familiar and visible formal procedures have been subjected to greater critical analysis, both as regards their inherent desirability (for instance, the critique presented by labelling theory (Taylor, Walton and Young (1975)) and in relation to their penal and corrective effectiveness (for instance, as regards the possibly counter-productive effects of stigmatising certain types of offender in criminal proceedings). From an official perspective, as recorded crime rates have increased in many countries and public expectations of crime control have also risen, time-consuming and costly proceedings have presented a crisis in resources, prompting an interest in speedier, simpler and less costly alternatives. From more than one point of view, therefore, the existing collection of informal and diversionary processes and their possible further development have become a topic for debate and analysis.

Such discussion, with its inevitable comparison of the formal with the less structured, and of the official with the less visible, has brought the salient features of both main models into sharper focus, clarifying their perceived strengths and weaknesses. In very broad terms the principal advantage of formal criminal justice is often seen as lying in its open and public quality which is more likely to guarantee fair dealing and accountability and thus public confidence. Conversely, the lower level of visibility of informal processes, although they are likely to prove less costly and more flexible, may give rise to concerns about unstructured discretion and possible arbitrariness. In addition, there is the fear that, as official discourse embraces the ideology of alternative processes and diversion, alternative may not remain alternative but instead become additional, as a field of colonisation by the state system of social control; in short, the spectre of "net-widening" enters the debate. Any critical discussion of the subject should therefore take on board these pervasive themes: the question of transparency and its implications for justice; the balancing of cost, effectiveness and respect for individual autonomy; and a grasp of the wider dimensions of the subject—is there some point of overall control in what is happening, or any overarching strategy, are these developments spontaneous and un-coordinated, or is there a more sinister process of direction and ultimately a phenomenon of net-widening?

This is not to assert in any way that these are new problems. As already stated, most alternatives to formal criminal justice are in fact well-established. It is the sense of awareness and its concomitant critical perceptions which have emerged more definitely in recent years, prompting an interest in revealing and understanding more about that previously more opaque zone of enforcement activity and perhaps also in harnessing its forces to the service of more structured policy. As a concept, diversion is still in its infancy; the processes to which it refers, however, have a history and in many instances may be seen as mature practice.

Constructing a map of diversion and alternatives to formal criminal justice

It is important to realise that the opportunities for diversion from formal criminal justice exist at a number of different points in that process, from the earliest stages of reporting the offence to (at least in some senses of the term) the stage of sentencing. Viewing matters in terms of points along the conventional process of criminal justice provides perhaps the most convenient map for discussing the whole field of diversion. Moreover, much else depends upon the particular location of a diversionary policy within the overall context of criminal justice, and also on the persons on whose initiative the diversionary action takes place. As a starting point in discussion, the following main points of diversion may be identified.

1. The victim of the offence decides to take no formal action ("victim waiver" or resolution of the issue by his or her own action).
2. The offending conduct is dealt with alternatively by another agency (for instance, a professional body or association, an educational institution, within a family).
3. The official investigating agency deals with the matter itself or refers the matter to another official agency (for instance, police cautioning, health and safety warning notices, referral to hospital).
4. The prosecuting authority decides to proceed no further or deals with the matter itself finally (prosecution waiver, penalty or deal).
5. Before the trial, the issue of guilt and the sanction are negotiated and fixed (plea negotiation). In this situation, the offence is diverted from any real trial, while the offender remains very much within the criminal justice process.
6. During the course of the trial process a mentally disordered offender may be diverted to hospital.
7. At the sentencing stage the offender may be officially diverted from a sentence (discharged) or (stretching the vocabulary of diversion further) from a particular type of sentence—typically a custodial measure, diversion then meaning much the same as "decarceration".

This scheme of analysis makes it clear that diversion may occur on the initiative of a number of different persons and may range from the very unofficial and informal (for instance, victim waiver) to the very formal and legalistic (for instance, referral to hospital, discharge by a sentencing court). The middle area is occupied for the most part by less formal and less visible activity on the part of official bodies (for instance, cautioning, out of court settlement). A useful metaphor to apply to this range of activity, employed by Ashworth (1984, 1994), is to see what is happening in terms of "gatekeeping", in the sense that there are a number of gates into and from the formal route of criminal justice. The victim may choose not to open the gate at the very beginning; the prosecutor may to decide to let the offender out of a gate half way down the road; the offender, lawyers and sentencer may agree that the offender passes through an internal gate which skirts around the area of contested trials and then takes the offender into a particular penal area. In this way a global map of diversion may be drawn, using the metaphor of gates and fields.

Figure 1

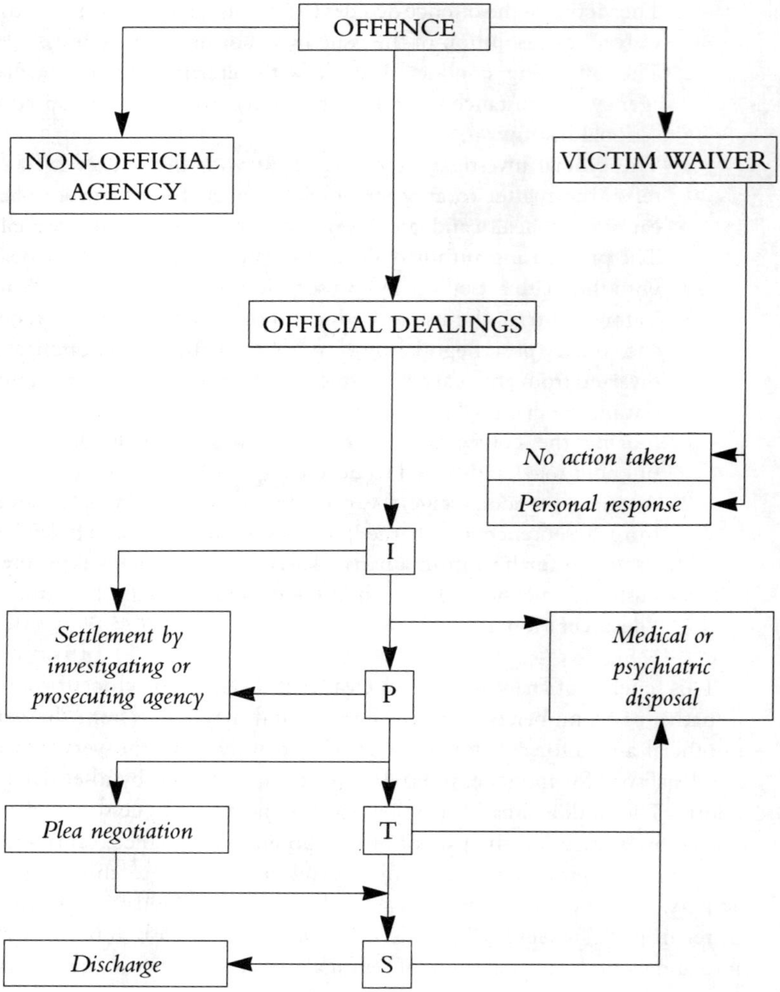

KEY

I : Investigation
P : Prosecution
T : Trial
S : Sentence

Diversion and sentencing

It would be useful at this point of the discussion to clarify further the concept of diversion by considering its relation to sentencing decisions. It is certainly possible to talk in terms of some kind of diversion at the post-trial stage—for instance, from sentence to discharge, from prison to hospital, or from custody to a community-based sentence. But it is probably more useful to regard such diversionary tactics for the most part as aspects of sentencing. Moreover, the whole issue of choice of sentence is clearly a major subject in its own right with a vast critical literature and it would be impractical to subsume it within a discussion of diversion. Therefore, while it may be a sensible use of language to talk about a diversion from custody or from penal to non-penal measures (such as supervision or psychiatric treatment), the subject-matter in such cases is more properly one of choice of sentence or disposal and to a large extent will fall outside the scope of this work.

On the other hand, care should be taken not to foreclose entirely discussion of what happens at this later stage of the criminal justice process, especially in so far as some decisions or policies may be inter-related with earlier events. A significant example of this would be the decision to discharge (see generally Wasik (1985)), which may in many cases be a belated recognition that the case should not have been prosecuted or tried in the first place: that, despite the existence in technical terms of a criminal offence, the matter would have been more appropriately dealt with through another process. In England and Wales there seems to have been clear evidence that certain decisions to prosecute rather than, in particular, to caution offenders have led to a kind of judicial reversal of that decision through the use of absolute discharge. Wasik has commented:

> ". . . there is a quite clear statistical relationship between the decision to prosecute and the use of the discharge on sentence. This emerges from investigation into the widely differing rates of use of the discharge from one part of the country to another. Research [Ditchfield (1976)] has indicated that this variation can be attributed to a corresponding variation in the police cautioning rate and prosecution policy generally. This correlation appears to hold good for both adult and juvenile offenders." (Wasik (1985), p. 222.)

In certain types of situation courts will clearly be trying to bring about an *ex post facto* diversion. For instance, in relation to a prosecution under food and drugs legislation, Lord Dilhorne stated in a House of Lords speech:

> "What this litigation has cost I dread to think. A great deal of the time of the

courts has been occupied. I cannot see that any advantage to the general body of consumers has or will result, apart, perhaps, from the exposition of the law. In cases where it is apparent that a prosecution does not serve the general interests of consumers, the justices may think fit, if they find that the Act has been contravened, to grant an absolute discharge." (*Smedleys Ltd. v. Breed* [1974] 2 All E.R. 21, 33.)

It would therefore seem to be helpful to consider sentencing decisions or arguments of this kind in the context of a discussion of diversion since they may embody an important critique of prosecution policy. An example of a similar device which ought for the same reasons to be brought within the scope of a discussion of diversion is the provision in section 662.1 of the Canadian Criminal Code which provides for absolute discharge in place of conviction. In effect this is a kind of diversion by acquittal, in order to avoid the stigma or other consequences of a criminal record (Wasik (1985), p. 213; Bobiasz (1974)).

Of a rather different order are those decisions on sentence which are effectively taken at an earlier stage as part of a negotiation as to plea. In such cases the choice of sentence is compromised through the prospect of a certain outcome being used as an inducement to the offender to divert him or herself from the process of a contested trial. This is of course a different kind of diversion, though one of importance, but it illustrates again the intertemporal relationship which may exist in the decision-making process. The issue of plea negotiation as a route of diversion is considered more fully in Chapter Nine below.

Generally, therefore, sentencing issues will not be considered in this discussion of diversion, except in so far as they inter-relate with or refer back to earlier points in the process when some kind of diversion has or could have taken place.

Diversion in the unofficial realm

Some important decisions taken in response to criminal offending are located in civil society as distinct from the official criminal justice system; in such a context the significant actors are private individuals and do not represent state authority. As stated above, the term "diversion" is of more doubtful application in this context since there may be no assumption about using formal criminal proceedings in the first place; indeed, in what may be regarded as some of the standard cases of "unofficial" action, a decision to use formal criminal proceedings *instead* may be regarded as a kind of diversion. The study of unofficial responses to criminal activity is more difficult in view of the sometimes informal and less fully recorded character of these processes.

Within the general field of unofficial responses there are two main but very different kinds of situation. In the first place, many cases are in effect resolved by the victim's own decision to settle the matter him or herself or to do nothing: either "private settlement" or "victim waiver". It is of course difficult to be precise about the extent of such responses, but victim report studies (such as the *British Crime Surveys* carried out by the Home Office in the U.K.—see Chap. Three, below) provide at least some idea of the circumstances in which they are likely to occur. The reasons for such victim settlement may range from a clear preference for dealing with the matter privately (for instance, crime in the context of close personal relations, the family or a tightly knit community, in which outside or "official" intervention is not welcome) through to a lack of confidence in the effectiveness of any official response (Hough and Mayhew (1983)). It then becomes evident that different policy questions arise. On the one hand, for example, there is the issue of the desirability, in both moral and public policy terms, of allowing this kind of settlement to take place, especially if serious offences are involved, in a closed or private environment, which may lack the levels of consistency and due process associated with formal criminal proceedings. Certainly, it should not be assumed that private or community justice represents a "softer" option: the responses of families or closed ethnic groups may be relatively severe (for instance, as regards resort to corporal chastisement). On the other hand, there are important questions about the actual and perceived effectiveness of official agencies, and the interaction between the public, individuals and certain groups and those agencies which result in such perceptions. This is still relatively uncharted territory and much interesting work remains to be done.

In the second place, some offences may in the natural course of events be dealt with by an authority outside the legal system, typically educational institutions, professional disciplinary bodies and employers. A number of points arise in this particular context. A distinction should be drawn between criminal offences and other "internal" or "domestic" breaches being dealt with by such authorities; for instance, as between theft of a book from a university library (criminal offence) and infringement of the borrowing regulations of the library (domestic offence). It is conceivable that both could be and are dealt with by the university itself, but in the first case the university may be seen as a kind of agent for the system of criminal law. (Or is that the correct way to view the matter? Why should the state claim prior jurisdiction over the theft, a basic question which only arises if the conventional priorities are themselves questioned?) In so far as the unofficial authority is dealing with behaviour which qualifies as a criminal offence, to what extent is this appropriate or desirable? To use the lawyer's terminology, this is a problem of choice of jurisdiction. And, if unofficial authorities are customarily dealing with certain types of criminal offending, this may give rise to the risk of double jeopardy (subject to proceedings more than once in relation to the same offence) and consequential questions about the relationship between these authorities and the agencies of formal criminal justice.

Ultimately the central question in relation to such unofficial responses to criminal offending concerns the extent to which it is appropriate for the matter to be in the hands of victims or unofficial agencies (see the discussion in Chaps Three and Four). This in turn involves the issue of the role of the state in dealing with delinquent behaviour and whether the characterisation of such delinquent conduct as "criminal" implies that it is the primary or even the exclusive responsibility of the state. At one end of the spectrum of debate, critics of the exercise of state power have attacked both the right and the desirability of the state "taking over" "criminal disputes" from victims, offenders and those most closely affected by offending behaviour (Christie (1982), de Haan (1990)). Another line of argument, a version of subsidiarity, would stress the advantages of dealing with infractions at a more local level by bodies with a special interest in the conduct of the offender, so legitimating the role of educational institutions, professional bodies and the like in this respect. In effect such arguments are concerned with no less than the proper scope of the criminal law, but not so much from the angle of what conduct should be criminalised, but rather as regards who should deal with particular offenders in particular circumstances. Behind these arguments of theory and policy, and whatever their outcome, it should be remembered as a basic social fact that a large number of offences are in practice resolved by victims themselves or by non-state agencies acting in an environment of relatively low visibility.

Diversion and questions of responsibility

A significant segment of diversionary practice in relation to the criminal justice process concerns the situation of those considered in some way to be without responsibility for their actions. Such diversion is in part based upon moral considerations and the retributive argument that the process of blame and punishment cannot be justifiably used in relation to those who could not have acted otherwise and were not offending as autonomous actors (Hart (1968)). There is also a more pragmatic argument that little is achieved by using criminal proceedings in such cases, when a more socially appropriate and constructive response would be, for instance, some kind of psychiatric treatment or welfare programme. There are two main categories of person who come within this field of diversion: the very young; and the mentally disordered. The former, in many modern legal systems, are automatically diverted until a certain age of legal responsibility (10 years in the case of English law, under the Children and Young Persons Act 1933, s. 50, in which case other legal processes (for example, care or supervision) may be used). Beyond that point any diversion may be less predictable and depend upon circumstances and the character and background of the offender. This more discretionary area of activity is exemplified by the practice of police cautioning of juvenile offenders in England and Wales, which has become an increasingly significant response in recent years to offences committed by those between the ages of ten and eighteen (see Chap. Seven, below). In this context there appears to be in general terms an inverse relationship between age, maturity and capacity, and diversionary practice: the older the offender, the less justification for diversion from criminal proceedings (leaving aside the position of the very elderly offender). But the matter is also dependent on shifts in policy and this can result in important differences both over time and from place to place. For instance, compared with England and Wales, Scotland has a much more significant diversion of juvenile offenders from formal criminal proceedings through the system of children's hearings set up under the Social Work (Scotland) Act 1968, which provides for a substantially welfare-based approach to most cases of juvenile offending (Murray and Hill (1991)). In England and Wales, proposals regarding the diversion of young offenders reached a high point during the 1960s (see for instance the Government White Paper, *The Child, the Family and the Young Offender*, Cmnd. 2742 (1965)), and were partly reflected in a number of provisions (though some of these were not implemented) in the Children and Young Persons Act 1969. Since then the pendulum has swung away from such a determinedly welfare approach in England and Wales, and the more recent preference for police cautioning keeps the offender within the more repressive field of action of criminal justice (Gelsthorpe and Morris (1994)). The diversion of mentally disordered persons is increasingly important in terms of official policy and available legal procedures (principally under the Mental Health legislation), yet is not always easy to achieve in practice (Fennell (1992), Peay (1994), and see Chap. Six, below). Thus, although it is legally possible to transfer mentally disordered "offenders" at several points in the formal criminal justice process, a number of problems can be identified. In the first place it may not be easy to identify clearly and convincingly the existence of mental disorder, which itself may be a matter for argument, even among experts. Secondly, there are some significant borderline conditions in relation to which questions of responsibility and treatability are far from settled (the situation of the psychopathic offender is very much in point here (Prins (1991)). In the third place, the agencies or institutions which normally have to take over responsibility for such disordered persons may object and not provide the necessary resources, especially in the context of a measure such a hospital order, in respect of which the relevant institution must certify that the resources for accommodation and treatment are available. Finally, in so far as some mental disorders are also potentially dangerous conditions, considerations of public safety and security may also limit the options for diversion and work to keep certain offenders within the confines of the criminal justice (and more especially the prison) system. Thus the potential for diversion may not be fully realised, despite the rhetoric and official policy in its favour.

Diversion in the context of cases of mental disorder may mean a number of different things in practice depending upon the nature of the problem. "Mental disorder" is a very wide term which encompasses a number of very different conditions: some are considered to be treatable by psychiatric methods, others may be more appropriately dealt with by some form of training or alternatively some kind of welfare provision. In practical terms there may be a considerable difference as between institutional responses and community-based measures, as regards the level of compulsion and security, and consequently the degree of need for legal protection for those subject to such diversion. Indeed, in this area, diversion from criminal justice may lead to an equally or more restrictive and subjectively unpleasant regime and it is well recognised that compulsory treatment requires justification as much as the imposition of punitive sanctions (Peay (1994)). There is also a number of agencies who may be involved in receiving diverted offenders of this kind, ranging from medical and psychiatric services, through to probation and welfare agencies and even voluntary and unofficial support services. But for the most part the diversion of both young and mentally disordered offenders presupposes an alternative system of responses by state-based agencies and leads to a welfare or treatment-oriented approach to dealing with situations of deviant or unacceptable behaviour.

Settlement by investigating and prosecuting agencies

This is a major area of diversionary activity combining an "official" character with an adherence to repressive sanctions and represents a significant alternative to conventional criminal justice. The official nature of this kind of process derives from the involvement of investigating and prosecuting agencies: the police, public prosecutors and other specialised agencies such as tax and customs authorities, transport authorities, local government bodies, health and safety regulators, and finance and competition regulators. The dichotomy between investigating and prosecuting bodies may not exist in all of these contexts and is most important in practice in the realm of conventional criminal procedure, where police investigations are customarily coupled with a distinct system of public prosecution (for example, the Crown Prosecution Service in England and Wales, the Procurator Fiscal in Scotland). In the case of specialised agencies the process of investigation and prosecution may be continuous, although perhaps using different personnel for these two purposes within the same agency. However, the investigating body's decision not to take the matter further (most notably the police caution) is effectively a decision not to prosecute and may be conveniently dealt with as part of the subject of prosecutorial diversion, the important questions then being the extent to which such matters as police cautions are regulated by policy worked out by public prosecutors and what the relationship may be between police and prosecutorial decision-making (see Chaps Seven and Eight, below).

There is a significant convergence of negotiated settlement and penality in this area. The penal sanction remains part of the process, although it may take more or less obvious forms, ranging from the more explicit prosecution fines and "compounding" penalties to the less tangible element of reprimand inherent in a caution. It is necessary for the offending conduct to be established and admitted to so as to constitute a real and attractive alternative to formal prosecution and conviction. At the same time there is a clear advantage for the enforcing agency: the case is "cleared" with a lesser expenditure of resources yet the offender is not "let off". A caution in itself may have an important dissuasive effect and the offender experiences, objectively at least, the discomfort of a reprimand. Compounding involves the recovery of unjustified gains (tax or duty owed must be paid over) and a financial penalty introduces a repressive element into the sanction. At the same time, there is throughout this area of activity an important element of discretion and negotiation—a "deal" is being made to ensure a cost-effective clearing up of offenders' conduct, a lower visibility sanction in return for a quick admission of guilt. The process embodies a seductive cocktail of expediency and penal effectiveness and represents a major challenge to the concept of full and formal criminal procedure.

It is therefore in this area that the prospect of diversion amounts to a major policy choice for the official agencies of law enforcement and diversion in this context is in some important respects distinguishable from processes such as victim waiver, action by unofficial agencies or the non-prosecution of the young or the mentally disordered. For here the offender is kept within the realm of state-based criminal justice but there is a conscious and informed decision to use different procedures and different sanctions. The role of state agencies and the resort to a penal and dissuasive response is still seen as appropriate and there is an analogy with the formal process of investigation, trial and punishment. Yet there are also important differences in this method, most notably as regards the levels of discretion and transparency and in the fact that the responsibility for conventionally distinct functions (investigation, determination of liability and choice of sanction) are concentrated in the hands of one authority. There are risks, therefore, in relation to the values of "legality", as comprised by a consistent and predictable response, accountability, division of powers and due process for defending parties. Up to a point, this is a problem of balancing expediency with the requirements of legal protection, but it would be too simplistic to present the arguments only in those terms. For one thing, there may also be vested professional interests which may provide a resistance to any shift away from formal criminal proceedings. On the other hand there may also be a genuine belief in and persuasive argument as regards the penal effectiveness of processes such as cautioning, compounding and the use of prosecution fines. There is clearly an important emergent debate in both official and academic contexts on the merits of moves towards less formal responses within criminal justice. For present purposes it would be sufficient to point to just two official statements in this regard. In the first place, the Report of the Royal Commission on Criminal Justice (the Runciman Commission) considered with enthusiasm the existing system of "fiscal" (prosecution) fines in Scotland and recommended in definite terms that "prosecution fines on the Scottish model be introduced in England and Wales for use instead of prosecution in appropriate cases" (Runciman Commission (1993), Chap. 5, para. 63). At the same time the Runciman Commission was attracted by the idea of combining cautioning with a requirement to co-operate with social work agencies or the probation service or to submit to medical supervision (Runciman Commission (1993), Chap. 5, para. 60), which would effectively extend the "sentencing" element in the caution along the lines of a "caution plus". This more ambitious approach to cautioning had already gained the support of the House of Commons Home Affairs Committee in a 1990 report on the Crown Prosecution Service (Home Affairs Committee, 1990). But the Government demonstrated considerable reservation in its response to the latter report, stating: "the police do not wish to become involved in sentencing, believing that this would be contrary to the basic principles of the criminal justice system . . . the Government endorses this position" (*Reply to the Fourth Report*, HMSO, 1990). In reality, however, this would seem to be a debate about *the extent* to which other agencies may take over the functions of trial and sentence, not so much whether they should do so. The caution *is* a kind of sentence, a disposition with its own penal and dissuasive potential. Even on a minimalist reading of the situation, it is a negative sentence, depriving a court of the power to decide on the matter. The crucial question of policy and principle to be addressed in this context is how far to move along this path.

Justifying diversion: a calculus of benefits and risks

The main perceived advantages and disadvantages associated with the use of diversion in criminal justice and the reasons for enthusiasm or restraint in its use have been outlined above. In a discussion of this kind it is important to have a critical yardstick which may be employed to assess the operation of diversionary practice and policy in a number of contexts of criminal justice. There would appear to be three principal elements of critical discourse which taken together may determine whether a diversionary approach may be justified; two of these elements are positive, while the other is negative in the sense of providing a restraining force.

The first positive element may be termed penal effectiveness: the question of what is the most effective way of achieving social control in relation to particular forms of undesirable conduct. In this way, certain major categories of behaviour—the "delinquency" of the young or the mentally disordered, offending of a trivial nature, offences in the context of economic or technical regulation as distinct from those which threaten basic human security and well-being—present themselves as candidates for diversion, as not being appropriate for resolution through the full and formal procedures of criminal justice. In such cases, not only is a conventional criminal proceeding arguably not necessary, but it may also be counter-productive (for instance, in terms of overstigmatisation) and therefore ineffective. Such discussion of effectiveness raises questions about appropriate agencies, procedures and sanctions. In a sense, this is the most basic aspect of the question of justification for diversion: without the possibility of enhancing the effectiveness of social control the question is unlikely to arise as one of positive policy in the first place.

The second positive element is the other main reason for opting out of full criminal proceedings: financial constraints and consequently the optimum use of scarce resources. For theorists, the issue of resources may appear to be mundane and something which should not be allowed to determine policy. But it is a pervasive problem of criminal justice. The enforcement of criminal law and the use of penal and other sanctions is an expensive and time-consuming process which makes extensive demands on human resources. Many criticisms of the operation of criminal justice turn ultimately on the issue of inadequate resources and, in the light of this, much of what goes under the heading of diversion has the attraction of expediency. Expedience is of course also interrelated with effectiveness, and particularly "cost-effectiveness", but at the same time what is expedient and saving of resources is not necessarily the most effective in terms of social control. Much will then depend on the weighing of different objectives. It may be demonstrated, for instance, that cautioning in relation to certain types of offender or offence is effective in terms of individual deterrence; why, then, do anything more? But it may also be argued that cautioning is insufficient in terms of retributive justice or satisfying the needs of victims and that only a more formal and public process of condemnation will satisfy these latter interests. In some cases there may be a fortunate convergence of arguments relating to penal effectiveness on the one hand and optimum use of resources on the other hand. But this cannot always be presumed.

The third element in the calculation operates as a moderating force in relation to the pursuit of both penal effectiveness and resource efficiency. The formal structure and public character of conventional criminal procedure is designed to guarantee aspects of legality: consistency, accountability, proportionality and rigorous handling of evidence and argument—in short, the principal components of "due process" and justice. The main perceived risk in many instances of diversion is that of arbitrary, unfair or abusive treatment. This was a central and one of the most damning parts of the critique contained in Baldwin and McConville's seminal study of plea negotiation and trial avoidance (Baldwin and McConville (1977)), where it was alleged that considerations of expediency were allowed to prevail over those of fair treatment. Referring once more to the 1990 House of Commons Home Affairs Committee Report and its endorsement of "caution plus", it is important to note the guarded response to some of those ideas by civil libertarians. NACRO (National Association for the Care and Resettlement of Offenders), for instance, were concerned about the development of an "alternative criminal system" (*sic*), lacking the safeguards of due process usually associated with formal criminal procedure (Home Affairs Committee, 1990, evidence). Such concerns have to be taken seriously and the principal challenge is to integrate legal safeguards into diversionary processes in such a way that the advantages of flexibility and informality are not lost. Certainly, however, the principle of external legal control must be accepted as a minimum condition so that the equivalent level of protection to that flowing from Article 6 of the European Convention on Human Rights should be available in any context of "official" diversion. Such guarantees are of course much more problematical in the context of processes located within civil society.

While hardly possible in the area of victim settlement and waiver, they could nonetheless be realised through some kind of review procedure in the case of disciplinary proceedings of professional bodies, educational institutions and the like. In legal terms, these are not novel questions and the issue of legal protection has already been explored, for instance, in the area of "administrative" procedures and sanctions under national law (under the European Convention, mention may be made of the cases of *Ozturk v. Germany* ((1984) 6 E.H.R.R. 409) and *Funke v. France* ((1993) 16 E.H.R.R. 297) and also in European Community competition law (Harding (1992)), and as regards judicial review of professional disciplinary bodies under English law (see the discussion in Chap. Four, below). How best to ensure legal protection in the field of operation of diversion will therefore be a significant and inevitable aspect of the discussion which follows in this work.

A final critical theme is more speculative and fits less easily into the calculus of justification. This is the issue of "net-widening": the risk that diversion operates, not as an alternative to formal criminal procedure, but as a supplement, effectively extending the net of social control to include those who previously may not have been subject to such processes. The concept of net-widening as such begs many questions, not least about the desirability and nature of social control itself and the way in which control mechanisms may be measured and their impact assessed (see McMahon (1992) for a useful summary of these arguments and problems). In relation to diversion the task is to attempt to estimate the extent to which informal and unofficial processes have supplanted formal criminal proceedings or, alternatively, the extent to which they represent an additional incursion of social control mechanisms into previously unregulated areas. This may be a feasible research task in relation to the more official procedures such as police cautioning, but in some other areas of diversion, with little or no systematic record-keeping, the research obstacles are formidable and inquiries are necessarily based upon informed guesswork. Clearly, if net-widening concerns are to be intelligently addressed a great deal of research needs to be carried out and the available evidence handled carefully and rigorously; in particular, the temptation to make gloomy or even apocalyptic assumptions should be resisted (McMahon (1992), Chap. 4). In the context of diversion, the net-widening debate would benefit in particular from a more penetrating historical analysis and the issue of social control via the more opaque processes within civil society should be properly investigated (see, *e.g.* Thompson (1993)). Only if such "unofficial" mechanisms of social control are taken into account is it possible to construct a convincing argument one way or another about net-widening tendencies. Moreover, it is unclear what kind of time-scale should be used in constructing such arguments. Given the extensive real history of diversionary measures, it may be argued that such studies should be over a longer rather than a shorter period of time.

It is beyond the scope of a work of this kind to include any full research into the potentially net-widening effect of any particular diversionary processes, but the general issue will be taken on board where appropriate and the broader lines of what may be useful further research will be suggested. This issue is likely to remain one of the most intriguing yet also less easily penetrable aspects of the whole subject.

Chapter 2

Diversion in a Historical Perspective

A search for and study of historical congeners and antecedents of present day diversionary practice in criminal justice soon raises problems with the concept of diversion itself. As has been pointed out in Chapter One, the term diversion has entered contemporary parlance to refer to the choice not to employ the formal and paradigmatic legal procedure as a way of dealing with delinquent conduct. Any doubts as to whether this is really a "diversion" are likely to be reinforced when earlier practice is considered. This may be especially true in the case of the English legal system, which retained an allegiance to a process of private prosecution largely dependent on the initiative of victims of offending conduct up to a later date than occurred in many other legal systems.

Research into the history of crime and criminal justice suggests for the most part that in England and Wales, prior to the middle of the nineteenth century, the crucial decision of the victim whether or not to initiate legal proceedings was influenced by a number of factors and that resort to formal prosecution was just one of a number of possibilities and was by no means always viewed as the most natural or advantageous course of action. Admittedly, some of the research in this field seems to be imbued with the assumption that prosecution should be, and was, viewed as the norm. Samaha, for instance, in his study of crime in Elizabethan Essex, remarks at one point that "the escape of prospective convicts began with the failure of many, perhaps most, victims to use the criminal justice system to redress their injuries ..." (Samaha (1974), p. 45). The term "failure" suggests a deviation, voluntary or not, from a course of action which was both expected and desirable. Also, there has sometimes been a suggestion that enforcement of criminal law, prior to and without a system of public prosecution, was haphazard and without much sense of strategy. Writing recently, for example, Malcolm Gaskell states: "Before the nineteenth century, the English criminal law depended on informal and amateur policing, privately initiated suits and trial by jury; as a consequence its enforcement was often random, inefficient and unfair" (Gaskell (1996), p.

342). But such language begs a number of questions: inefficient and unfair from which point of view? And randomness may depend on context. Much of the other research, however, into criminal justice during the early modern period and later tends to reveal a more conscious and strategic choice on the part of victims in favour of methods other than formal prosecution, as will be discussed below.

Indeed, it may be necessary in placing the discussion in a historical context, to adjust the perspective on the choice whether or not to prosecute. During a period when this choice was very much in the hands of victims of offending conduct and there was little official intervention in the activation of criminal procedure, it seems that the decision to "go to law" was very much strategic in character. In the first place, victims appeared to be actively considering whether it was in their own best interests to prosecute or to use self-help or some other means of resolving the matter. The range of alternative means—some of them very significant in practice—will be considered below. Secondly, the decision to prosecute, when taken, could well have been motivated by considerations well outside the simple enforcement of criminal law. The evidence of malicious prosecutions and proceedings taken as a component of a wider dispute suggest a strategic manipulation of the formal legal process for private ends in some cases. This point is made succinctly by Hay:

> "Once we remind ourselves that the law is used for the furtherance of disputes as much as their resolution, we can free ourselves from the moral fallacy that describes courts simply as places where criminals are brought to be dealt with by judges, juries or the state." (Hay (1989), pp. 347–8.)

What follows in the rest of this Chapter is an examination of material relating to responses (mainly by victims) to offending behaviour, from the beginning of the early modern period through to the end of the nineteenth century in England and Wales. The context of this discussion should be borne in mind. An important point is that, at least until the middle of the nineteenth century, this was a legal system characterised by the absence of anything like a system of public prosecution (in contrast to contemporary developments in many other legal systems: see Hay and Snyder (1989). Another significant point of context was that, certainly during the early modern period, and also for many areas during the later eighteenth and in the nineteenth centuries, responses to crime were taking place within the framework of relatively small, local communities and a set of interpersonal relations different from those prevailing in modern urban societies. If the offender was a neighbour or relative of the victim (as was often the case during the earlier period), this would inevitably affect the reaction to the offending behaviour. This is not to suggest that modern criminality is of a wholly different character. Indeed, a good deal of crime is still committed against persons well-known to the offender, and this continues to influence some victims' reactions (see the discussion in Chap. Three, below). But in a twentieth century context it has been much less exclusively a matter of the victim's response and official concerns about law enforcement have been much more intrusive.

Early modern and eighteenth century reactions to offending behaviour

(A) Elements in the decision whether or not to prosecute

In addressing the issue of how criminal law was enforced in seventeenth century England, Sharpe has commented:

> "What is immediately apparent, and what must modify any conclusions that the historian might draw from the study of 'crime' as revealed in formal prosecutions is that the agents of law enforcement had many alternatives to indictment or presentment at hand. In fact, it appears that when dealing with the local, resident malefactor, court action was conceived of as a fairly remote sanction, normally one to be resorted to only when other means of control had failed." (Sharpe (1980), p. 107.)

It must be appreciated therefore that the central role played by the victim of offending behaviour, and often also the issue of the victim's relationship with the offender, was a key determinant of how to proceed. In so far as the victim was in a position to make an informed and reflective decision, the kind of calculus and criteria employed may have been in some senses analogous to that of the twentieth century public prosecutor, comprising a mix of factors: cost, evidential problems, seriousness of the offence, public or community interests. On the other hand, the victim's response may have been in some situations instinctive, unreflective, fatalistic or helpless (which would also be surely true of some latter-day cases of offending). But the absence for the most part of any central public authority interested in the enforcement of criminal law rendered the situation of the victim, and to some extent also the local community context, so much more decisive during the seventeenth, eighteenth and earlier nineteenth centuries. Indeed, it may be both meaningful and helpful to present much of the subject as being concerned with the role of the victim-enforcer. Moreover, in relation to offending which was in a sense "victimless" (typically, for instance, offences against church order or some regulatory offences) and where action would then be taken by ecclesiastical authorities or local constables, there were sometimes significant community disincentives to prosecution. For instance, in discussing the possibility of formal action being taken to deal with alehouse disorder and drunkenness in the early seventeenth century, Wrightson and Levine remark:

> "It was the possibility of activating networks of personal connection ... and of touching off a small explosion of conflict within the village that made prosecution of any but the most notorious of offenders so dangerous to local harmony. This factor, above all, made the presentment jurymen and petty constables of the period so notoriously unwilling to prosecute petty offence." (Wrightson and Levine (1979), p. 139.)

A similar reluctance to contemplate legal proceedings has been noted in research considering the situation in different parts of Wales during the nineteenth century (Jones (1992), pp. 5–6).

In such a context, then, there were clearly a number of key considerations which would influence the decision-making process of victims and other interested parties either towards or away from formal prosecution. One of the most obvious factors (and one of great practical importance) was trouble and cost. To put the matter simply, the cost of the formal process had to be met by the prosecution, who in a large number of cases would have been the victim. Such expense would include typically: subpoenas to witnesses and the warrant to the accused, for either to be summoned for examination by magistrates; recognisances to be bound over to give evidence at trial; the drawing up of the indictment; and the fees of various court officers during the trial. In addition to formal fees, there may well have been the costs of travel and accommodation for both the prosecutor and witnesses, and perhaps the necessity to pay compensation to witnesses for their trouble and loss of earnings. From the middle of the eighteenth century some prosecutors began to employ lawyers to represent their cases, a further expense even if only for a minority during that period (Beattie (1986), pp. 41, *et seq.*). The problem was well recognised at the time. For instance, Henry Fielding, at the start of the 1750s, was a notable critic (Fielding (1751) and legislation in the 1750s provided for some costs of prosecution to be met from county treasuries (Beattie (1986), p. 42). But it is not easy to assess the impact of such measures of public support. It is clear that only part of the total costs would have been met so that much would have still depended on the means of individual prosecutors. On the other hand, Beattie argues that by the later eighteenth century criminal prosecutions were not completely out of the question for persons of modest means (Beattie (1986), p. 47).

A measure of self-help was also developed to deal with this problem: the formation of prosecution associations (often by groups of land-owners), one function of which was to meet the costs of actually mounting a prosecution from a common fund contributed to by the members. (There are a number of studies of the problem of meeting the cost of prosecution in the pre-police era in England and Wales—see, for instance, Shubert (1981); Hay (1975a); King (1983); Philips (1983). Suffice it to say for present purposes that the issue was undoubtedly an important consideration for victims in deciding on their response to offending behaviour.

A related problem was the collection of evidence and apprehension of offenders. Witnesses might need to be persuaded to testify and perhaps also be compensated but there was also the problem of the resources necessary for both collecting further evidence and apprehending the offender. Prosecution associations and a widely used system of rewards were responses to some of these difficulties, especially for purposes of securing evidence which might otherwise not easily have been obtained (Beattie (1986), pp. 48, *et seq.*). From 1692, a statutory system of publicly funded rewards was also in operation. But an important and undesirable outcome of the reward system was the emergence of the occupation of "thief-taker"; some of the latter were serious criminals (thief-makers) in their own right. Statutory rewards as such were abolished by legislation of 1818, by which time there were signs of an emergent police and detective force. All this serves to illustrate further the degree of difficulty faced by victim-prosecutors.

But the cost and practical difficulty of "private" prosecutions were essentially problems of resources which could be remedied or mitigated by state intervention (as would eventually be the case) or the pooling of resources. While such problems were naturally important, they should nonetheless be placed in a broader psychological context in which prosecution would often still not have been seen as a desirable response even if there had been no practical or economic difficulties. In particular, the significance of local and community attitudes towards delinquency and their decisive impact on individual cases ought to be borne in mind when considering the techniques of social control in pre-industrial society. Such attitudes reveal a sense of the exceptional aspect of formal prosecution and a strong, almost natural preference for local solutions. For instance, in respect of seventeenth century Essex, Sharpe comments:

> "Many of those indicted for stealing had a whole career of petty larceny and a growing reputation for thieving behind them; finally, their delinquencies grew so persistent that the parish became tired of them, or they irritated an individual into prosecution by stealing something of unusual value . . . The presence of the persistent offender must have created considerable problems for the community,

but in many cases his presence seems to have been accepted as part of the natural order of things." (Sharpe (1984), pp. 79–80.)

Similarly, Underdown, referring to incidents of unruly behaviour in a Wiltshire village in 1612–13, states in summary:

> "The incident exemplifies attitudes to order typical of many traditional communities: a preference for persuasion rather than legal process; informal mediation by the clergy; official connivance ... at failure to punish a law-breaker; finally a resort to direct action to counter the authorities' neglect of community feelings." (Underdown (1985), p. 17.)

There are a number of points to note about this evident preference in many cases for informal and non-legal responses to offending conduct of different kinds. The first point concerns perceptions of delinquency and the seriousness of offending behaviour. This is a subject which may be both variable and opaque, and context is likely to be all-important. To take the example of larceny: this was an offence which was during the early modern period and the eighteenth century increasingly subject to severe legal penalties (whipping in the case of petty larceny; grand larceny was a capital offence). Yet it seems that the offence was often tolerated or dealt with informally at a local level. Perceptions of delinquency would in turn depend upon other factors, either local or more general, including class and economic relations. As Beattie argues: "there was no general attitude towards 'crime' or 'the law', either among the propertied or the poor, but rather attitudes towards particular offences with particular sanctions attached to them" (Beattie (1986), p. 73). Individuals, and local communities, were in a position to make up their own minds about the seriousness of offending conduct and the appropriate response. The measure of discretion in this respect may appear startling to twentieth century notions of criminal justice and the initial reading of what had happened in many cases may suggest a sense of the arbitrary and the random. That may be one way of interpreting individual and local preferences, but it should also be remembered that seventeenth and eighteenth century society was much more governed by those preferences.

This point leads to another of explanatory force. There appeared also to be in many pre-industrial communities a tendency to distinguish between local, "native" offenders and those who were outsiders, in that the latter were more likely to be prosecuted. Sharpe, for instance, contrasts the likely reactions to the "itinerant thief" as compared to the "resident pilferer" (his own vocabulary reinforcing the different perceptions) (Sharpe (1984), p. 82) and research generally confirms this impression of indulgence towards local, known offenders (see, for instance, Ingram (1977)). Nor is this, upon reflection, particularly surprising. In close-knit communities, with a low level of social mobility, people have to continue to live with each other and this fact would argue against the use of formal procedures and sanctions.

Another point concerns the effectiveness of responses. For reasons already mentioned, in a pre-mid-nineteenth century context, dealing with offending behaviour should be seen from the perspective of the victim rather than that of a wider public interest. Modern preoccupations of crime control by the state are much less relevant for the seventeenth or eighteenth century victim of crime. A more individualised preoccupation with personal satisfaction or recovery of stolen property was likely to predominate. Therefore the successful resolution of the "dispute" from the victim's standpoint might well comprise quickly and personally administered chastisement or the easiest method of recovery of property or money. This again may help to explain what in many cases would appear to the late twentieth century observer as a preference for and tolerance of "self-help". Such considerations of effective resolution would also of course interrelate with issues of cost, perception of the offence, and community cohesion. Thus Beattie notes:

> "In trespass and assault cases in which the public interest was not thought to be deeply engaged, magistrates were themselves encouraged to arrange agreements that would settle the matter privately and keep it out of the courts." (Beattie (1986), p. 39.)

Another instance cited by Beattie (1986), p. 39) from a report in *The Gentleman's Magazine* ((1784) Vol. 54, p. 635) illustrates how what would qualify as a serious offence in legal terms was dealt with informally and very speedily:

> ". . . a gentleman gazing at a print shop in the Strand, had his pocket picked of his purse, in which were bank notes to the amount of £1,700. A poor woman who stood by observed the transaction, gave notice, and the fellow was pursued and taken, and the purse recovered. The fellow, after being rolled in the kennel, and had undergone the discipline of the mob, was permitted to escape; and the woman who discovered the theft rewarded with five guineas."

A twentieth century observer might have reservations about the agency of the "mob" in this example, but would otherwise doubtless concede that this was a highly cost-effective response to the offence. This example also leads to a discussion of the common preference for recovering stolen property by treating informally with the offender and paying for the return of money or goods, often under the guise of a "reward". The victim's overriding interest in recovery in such cases would thus compromise a more objective enforcement of the criminal law and resulted in legislation in 1717 and 1752 which criminalised different kinds of involvement in such "compounding". Nonetheless, it seems that such settlements remained common in practice and there are some traces of this approach in both the contemporary version of compounding (as employed by tax and customs and excise officials—see Chap. Five, below) and in the latter-day practice of plea and charge bargaining (see Chap. Nine, below).

A final point to consider in relation to the decision whether or not to prosecute concerns—in contrast to much of what has gone before—a motive in favour of rather than against prosecution. This was the use of prosecution maliciously as a measure of hostility or in furtherance of an ongoing dispute. Ingram comments (as regards his study of early seventeenth century Wiltshire) that "among certain classes of prosecution, cases involving blatant malice are not hard to find, while the business of the courts always included an undercurrent of near-vexatious or unreasonable litigation" (Ingram (1977), p. 122). During the early modern period it was a function of the grand jury to assess complaints and accusations and so act as a key to the door of criminal procedure (Herrup (1987), pp. 93, *et seq.*). Again, this is not to assert that malicious prosecution was a large-scale problem during the period but rather to point out its more significant role in the context of a system of private enforcement initiative, particularly as an element in decision-making which could be weighed against considerations of cost, trouble, tolerated delinquency and community cohesion.

(B) Alternatives to prosecution

The discussion has already touched upon some of the alternative, "non-legal" responses to offending. These may be usefully grouped under a number of headings.

(i) Tolerance and/or informal warnings

There is ample evidence that much delinquency was subject to informal admonition, often to a large extent, before prosecution would become a seriously considered strategy (Sharpe (1980), pp. 108, *et seq.*; Jones (1992), pp. 4, 8). The way in which this process of informal negotiation and admonition is described in contemporary accounts is often instructive. For instance, mediation and not prosecuting may be presented as "fayer meanes" (*Colchester Examination and Recognizance Book*, 1647–84, March 14, 1670: cited in Sharpe (1980), p. 111) and formal prosecution may be viewed as "trouble in lawe" (*Archbishop of York's Consistory Court Cause*

Papers, C.P.G. 2738: cited in Sharpe (1980), p. 111). Underlying such descriptions in the concern that formal legal proceedings would be disruptive of community relations (Sharpe (1980); Underdown (1985), p. 16; Ingram (1977), pp. 125–7). This approach might well include therefore methods of mediation and arbitration on the part of friends, neighbours, or persons of authority in the local community. Both process and sanctions could be informal and extra-legal: Ingram ((1977), pp. 125–7) refers to mediators professing a "quasi-moral concern to minimise strife" and the sanction behind the mediation being the disapproval of neighbours (for examples of such mediation in a Welsh context, see Jones (1992), p. 8). It is probably correct, then, to think in terms of a spectrum of informal processes, including diverse but related techniques such as admonition, mediation and arbitration, all of which were sustained by informal expressions of community disapproval.

(ii) Personally administered or community sanctions

To some extent a distinct response may be identified in terms of definite sanctions being employed by the victim ("self-help") or, in a way which might now be categorised as informal, by a local community. Beattie's example, quoted from *The Gentleman's Magazine* in 1784 and referred to above, would supply a good example of informal community chastisement. The extent of such reactions is naturally difficult to measure, and there will still of course be instances, perhaps severe instances, of this in the late twentieth century. But in a social context lacking organised police or other enforcement agencies, its significance must have been all the greater. At the same time, the existence of systematic community penality during much of this earlier period ought to be taken into account. Certain types of delinquency, some of which would qualify as criminal offending, were regularly visited by "informal" community justice, now often referred to as "rough music" (see in particular, Thompson (1991), Chap. 8; Alford (1959); Ingram (1984); Jones (1989); Jones (1992)). Although a twentieth century reading of "rough music" would emphasise its function as a sanction for breach of *community* norms, it should be remembered that very often, especially during the early modern period, these would overlap with rules enforceable by either ecclesiastical or secular courts, relating to such matters as unruly behaviour and verbal abuse, illicit sexual conduct, adultery, and ill-treatment of wives, including physical violence. The rough music itself could take a number of forms, but in general would comprise a public, processional shaming ritual, either involving the actual offender or a proxy or effigy. The immediate object was usually either ostracism or expulsion of the offender from the community. Thompson ((1991), pp. 485–6) suggests that there was a move away from directly physical rough treatment towards a more ritualistic acting out of the punishment; this may parallel the shift away from corporal punishment in the formal legal system, from the later eighteenth century.

The important point is to recognise the opportunity and in many cases the preference for informal responses and sanctions, either by individuals or collectively. Such responses could be either swift or summary, typically at the time when the offence was committed, or could follow a longer period of tolerance or deliberation. Either way, they comprised an important alternative to "formal" justice.

(iii) Church, manorial and "domestic" regimes of discipline

Delinquency could also be subject to other disciplinary processes distinct from criminal prosecution, although the possibilities under this heading vary in the degree of formality employed. At one end of the spectrum was the jurisdiction firstly of the ecclesiastical or church courts, and secondly of the local manorial courts, functioning until the middle of the seventeenth century. Both were significant court jurisdictions during the earlier part of the early modern period and dealt with a wide range of petty offending which from a present-day standpoint might bear comparison with some aspects of magistrates' courts criminal jurisdiction, such as minor disorderly behaviour and "regulatory" offending. But there were also matters which, at the time, would not have been dealt with in any case through criminal prosecution in the usual sense, and therefore could not have been diverted in any sense; they were quite simply subject to a different formal system of discipline (for a study of these jurisdictions, see Sharpe (1977)). It is interesting, however, to trace the subsequent regulation of these areas of conduct after the demise of the special jurisdictions, either by magistrates (on the development of magistrates' summary jurisdiction and powers of binding over, see Sharpe (1980)) or otherwise. Thompson, for instance, speculates on the shift from ecclesiastical to community regulation:

> "Since the church courts in England were in decline from the late seventeenth century, and were exercising less effectively their powers to inflict penalties for domestic and sexual offences, it is tempting to suggest that the vigour of eighteenth century rough music indicated a shift from ecclesiastical regulation to community self-regulation ..." (Thompson (1991), p. 482.)

On the other hand, discipline could be administered less formally through the economic "authority" of employers and land-owners, and a good deal of delinquency and criminality would in practice have been regulated by such domestic authority. Sharpe comments that "the employer's power to punish his servants physically or by dismissal must have resulted in many instances of indictable behaviour being dealt with other than by prosecution" ((1980), p. 113; see also Jones (1992), p. 6) and also points to the opportunities for major land-owners to impose their own sanctions against poachers and other criminal trespassers (see also Hay (1975b)).

(iv) Labour discipline and economic controls

Throughout the early modern period there was a perceived association between delinquency as a moral and social malaise and economic dysfunction, the latter usually described in the vocabulary of idleness, vagrancy and poverty. The late sixteenth and early seventeenth centuries were notable for a widespread fear and distrust of a growing vagrant population (this may also be related to the more vigorous response to offending by "outsiders", referred to above). The house of correction, or "Bridewell", was developed during this period, and in practice came to provide a means for dealing with a certain proportion of vagrancy-associated delinquent behaviour which might in theory have been the subject of criminal proceedings. Thus Sharpe notes:

> "The inmates of the house of correction at Chelmsford for example, included vagrants, poachers, disorderly or runaway servants, parents of bastards, disorderly alehouse-keepers, and persons described as being of "ill fame", "ill repute" and "lewd behaviour", or as leading a disorderly life, pilfering, or having no calling . . ."

and adds:

> "Detailed records of persons entering a house of correction, unhappily a somewhat rare class of archive, thus provide yet more evidence of the dimensions of petty crime, delinquency and disorder." (Sharpe (1980), p. 117.)

There is also evidence of the operation of "poor law" controls within the community itself. Levine, for instance, reports on the economic controls exercised in the Essex village of Terling in the earlier seventeenth century, through a system of "badging" poorer members of the community. A charity had been established by a yeoman of the village, with the condition that relief from its funds be distributed only to those people in the parish who were obedient and subservient: those who frequented alehouses, were notorious blasphemers or regularly broke the Sabbath were formally excluded (Levine (1977), p. 119). Such controls, of course, later evolved into the workhouse system governed by poor law legislation. It is clear, therefore, that there existed for some time a network of regulation, directed formally at problems of poverty and vagrancy, yet in effect managing a range of perceived delinquent, not to say criminal conduct, and no doubt regarded as more appropriate and effective than criminal prosecution (note, for instance, Sir Edward Coke's favourable view of the house of correction as compared to the use of imprisonment—*Institutes of the Laws of England*, (1841)).

(v) Binding over

Binding over by justices was another significant response to a wide range of offenders and others who aroused suspicion. Sharpe cites a contemporary author, Michael Dalton, writing in the middle of the seventeenth century, who refers to the justices' discretion to use binding over to deal with persons disposed to acts of violence at one extreme and those who "live idly, and fare well" at the other (Michael Dalton, *The County Justice* (1677), pp. 263–86; Sharpe (1980), pp. 116–17). Sharpe also comments:

> "... binding over to keep the peace or to be of good behaviour must have seemed an attractive alternative to indictment for assault. It was cheaper, more immediate, less troublesome, less risky, and, given that the assailant risked financial loss if he persisted in his conduct, probably more effective." ((1980), p. 117.)

It was probably therefore a significant means of regulating violent and disorderly behaviour, with also the advantage of providing some prospect of continuing control rather than exacerbating bad feeling locally, which may well have been an outcome of criminal prosecution.

(vi) Negotiating the return of stolen property and compromise generally

Focusing on a particular area of offending, albeit one of both social and legal significance, larceny (theft), leads to a consideration of another important option: treating with the offender to return stolen goods in return for a payment. The incentives for such "compounding" would have been to some extent similar to those that operate today—avoiding the cost, uncertainty and delay of formal proceedings and more readily satisfying the victim's need to recover stolen property. However, there is a distinction in that there was no penalty necessarily arising from such accommodations; indeed, the offender made a net gain in that payment was received for the goods in question. For this reason, compounding a felony was itself a serious offence under legislation of 1717, and a further concern was that the practice was being exploited by the organised criminal networks of "thief-takers", such as Jonathan Wild (Howson (1970)). Nonetheless, this remained a popular method of dealing with thefts, under the guise of paying "rewards", and was further supported by the development of advertising columns in newspapers. Jones, in his study of crime in nineteenth century Wales, reveals a strong tendency towards settlements of various kinds, even after legal proceedings had begun, and despite the laws against compounding:

> "... many people looked for compensation, compromise, and apologies rather than strict punishment. At every point of the legal process, compromises could be reached. to give force to these agreements, they were sometimes written down and witnessed ..." (Jones (1992), p. 7.)

This profile of "diversion" or recourse to processes and solutions beyond the limits of formal prosecution and punishment can be summarised in the scheme set below.

Self–help	• tolerance • personally administered punishment • treating for the return of stolen property
Community mediation of disputes	• arbitration • reference to person of authority
Informal regimes	• community sanctions (especially "rough music") and informal warnings • sanctions used by employers and land–owners
Other jurisdictions	• ecclesiastical and manorial court sanctions • binding over by justices • committal to house of correction

A glance at the range of possibilities is likely to recall Sharpe's question: were those who *were* prosecuted in some ways atypical (Sharpe (1980), p. 118)?

The later nineteenth century and the advent of national policing

The nineteenth century in England and Wales may appear as a period of transition between the *ancien régime*, during which responses to criminal offending depended so much on the initiatives and reactions of victims and of local communities, and the "modern" period, during which enforcement has been largely given over to a national agency (until the 1980s, the police and a number of specialised agencies). To what extent and in what ways was there a change in the pattern of responding during the nineteenth century?

Historians of policing generally assert that major changes occurred in Britain in the third to sixth decades of the nineteenth century as the old system of unpaid constables was superseded by a new regime of paid professional officers operating a policy of "regular patrols, co-ordinated surveillance, and the discriminating use of force" (Hay and Snyder (1989), p. 5). The change was brought about in particular by legislation in 1829, setting up the Metropolitan Police, and in 1856, requiring county forces to be set up. However, it should be noted that the emergence of the "new police" was not associated happily in the minds of most contemporaries with a shift in responsibility for prosecutions; indeed, there was a strong resistance towards such a notion on the part of the politically influential landed gentry, as an unacceptable constitutional revision. In fact, police acquisition of the prosecutorial role was very much an incremental process, nor was it always very transparent: for instance, pragmatically taking over the role of prosecution associations, prosecuting offences in their own names as "private" prosecutors and being brought further into the picture by local initiatives, such as that in Leeds, where magistrates bound over the Chief Constable to prosecute a large proportion of cases. And there was still, in the middle years of the century, a significant Parliamentary objection to the police acting as prosecutors, expressed clearly for instance in the view of the Attorney-General, Sir Alexander Cockburn, in 1855, that prosecutions by the police were not "consistent with the proper administration of public justice" (Select Committee on Public Prosecution, 1854/55, p. 186, Q2396—see Hay and Snyder (1989), p. 44). But at the same time, there was little support for an independent system of public prosecutors and the police assumed their prosecutorial role almost by default, and also aided by some modifications to the process, in particular through entrusting the conduct of the case in court to lawyers (see generally the discussion in Hay and Snyder (1989), pp. 40–44).

Within this rather opaque process it is difficult to assess the impact of the new police on earlier and existing prosecution practice. There are important questions: whether the police supplanted or supplemented the traditional participants in the process of criminal prosecutions; whether police involvement changed in any way the flow of cases towards the courts; and what were the relative decision-making powers of the police and of victims and other interested parties over time. While it may be true that by the end of the nineteenth century the police had achieved a commanding role in relation to prosecutions, how exactly that compares to what had gone before is less easy to establish.

For one thing, it seems that a preference for not going to court survived in some contexts and was realised when official involvement could be kept at bay. Indeed, it is striking that throughout the nineteenth century—a period during which formal prosecution was generally considered to be becoming easier—many victims continued actively to choose not to prosecute, for a range of reasons (Jones (1992), Chap. 1). In particular, Davis' research into prosecution patterns in later nineteenth century London reveals a significant reluctance, or at least selectivity, as regards the resort to criminal proceedings, on the part of three different groups—employers, working class victims, and the police themselves (Davis (1989), Chap. 5).

There is evidence that during the nineteenth century depredations by employees were rife in a variety of commercial contexts. Yet, as Davis comments: "None the less, employers apparently overlooked vast quantities of law-breaking by employees before they took legal action" (Davis (1989), p. 401). One reason appears to have been the perceived effectiveness of sanctions; at a time when the labour market was plentiful, dismissal, or the threat of it, could in itself have more serious long-term consequences than even a sentence of imprisonment. When used, criminal prosecutions (or "pilferage campaigns") often coincided with periods in which labour was in demand or the labour market buoyant, or were employed for exemplary purposes. For the most part, employers such as dock companies or market gardens appeared to wish to retain control over the disciplining of their own labour force as much as possible (Davis (1989), pp. 401–8). A related point was that employers may have been unwilling to initiate legal proceedings against valued skilled employees who might have been difficult to replace, or long-serving employees, for reasons of sentiment. In some cases also, an employee detected in theft might have been encouraged to stay in that employment and work off the value of the theft—a kind of set-off, providing for the employer a more effective recovery of losses, and the opportunity to maintain discipline, than might arise from using prosecution.

It is also clear that in some contexts, employee theft or fraud was actually tolerated for clear economic reasons: for instance, bus conductors' fare fraud, or the watering or "bobbing" of milk by milkmen was not only difficult to prevent or detect but was effectively condoned by employers as an economic justification for lower wages. Then, prosecutions would only make sense to the employer if the theft or fraud threatened the latter's economic interests in some way—for instance, if the poor quality of bobbed milk had an impact on sales (Davis (1989), pp. 409–13). Altogether, this material evidences an impressive reluctance to use formal legal process, and in effect a redefinition of the scope of the criminal law.

Davis' research (1984) has also demonstrated the complexity of "working class" prosecutions during the course of the nineteenth century. Admittedly, as such prosecutions became easier in both legal and practical terms, their number increased; but the motives for involving the police and seeking a legal solution were varied, and informal sanctions were not by any means thereby displaced. As regards both property offences and offences of violence, prosecution was not necessarily the first choice for the working class victim. As in the earlier period, prosecutions frequently occurred only after a period of tolerance or after failure to resolve the matter by informal means. Moreover, a number of cases were started but not followed through, with the victim withdrawing from prosecution—for instance, believing that a sufficient "lesson" had been administered by arrest and a night in the police cells, or, in the case of ill-treated women, unwilling to face the consequences (family destitution, later revenge) of a husband's imprisonment. In addition, and very interestingly, it seems that some working class prosecutors were using the legal process for essentially non-punitive purposes: for example, to settle neighbourhood disputes, especially in a situation of cramped and difficult living conditions, or, in a very different kind of case, to transfer the responsibility for unmanageable juveniles to the new reformatory and industrial schools by prosecuting their own children (Davis (1984, 1989)). In summary, Davis argues:

> "The business of the courts demonstrates, in particular, that historians have underestimated the extent to which informal sanctions against wrongdoers applied within the community survived alongside official law enforcement as applied by the police and the courts at least until the end of the nineteenth century; while historians have similarly overestimated the extent to which the nineteenth century state was either able or willing to intervene in the everyday affairs of its subjects through the agency of the newly organised police and police courts in order to systematically suppress law breaking." (Davis (1989), pp. 314–5.)

Similar considerations apply to the role of the police in relation to both arrests and prosecutions. During the second half of the nineteenth century police involvement in the enforcement process became more extensive, yet there is evidence of both a continuing informal enforcement activity and selective enforcement, as was the case with other categories of prosecutor. Verbal cautions, physical "cuffing" (Emsley (1985)) and admonitory "nights in the cell" were frequently employed, especially when dealing with drunk and disorderly behaviour (Davis (1989), p. 420). Equally, however, a consciousness of resistance to or suspicion regarding the police role on the part of law abiding as well as law breaking members of the community made the police careful to focus their attention on that group of offenders considered to be a priority for purposes of law enforcement by the law abiding public. In particular, a consensus emerged on the part of the police and the public that police enforcement of the criminal law should concentrate on the casual (and consequently recidivist) working class. Certainly, there were political risks for the police in taking action against any of the upper middle classes suspected of offending, and similarly in relation to the "respectable" working class. Thus a vicious circle of perception and enforcement confirmed the prevailing belief in a distinct "criminal class" located primarily within the ranks of the casual working class (Davis (1989), pp. 421–4).

Signposts from the past

A number of the analytical themes which emerge from this historical view of "diversionary" activity over a period of some three hundred years serve to anticipate some of the discussion which follows regarding successive stages in the criminal law process in the contemporary legal world. First and foremost, it is clear from the research surveyed above in relation to both the early modern period (the late sixteenth to early eighteenth centuries) and the eighteenth and nineteenth centuries that there was a striking and in many respects consistent preference for not using formal legal procedures as a response to offending behaviour. This was true of a range of victims, in a range of contexts, and for a variety of reasons, over virtually the whole period. Considerations of cost, perceptions of effectiveness and notions of what would be appropriate in social terms combined to make "alternative" processes very often the "natural" choice rather than a kind of "diversion". What strikes the historian is the rich repertoire of process and sanctioning available to both victims and communities in judging their own response to instances of delinquency. Such opportunities may be located within a spectrum of degrees of formal structure and of public visibility, but from the evidence there can be little doubt of the awareness and consciousness on the part of contemporaries of the choices being made during these periods. In so far that what is revealed by such research may surprise the modern observer, this perhaps indicates the extent to which, during the twentieth century, society has "lost sight" of the phenomenon of refraining from the use of formal legal process. What is revealing in this respect is the concern expressed by a number of writers in recent years that the state has "taken over" or even "stolen" disputes from the real parties and is casting its net of control ever wider (see, for instance, Christie (1977); Bianchi and Van Swaaningen (1986); de Haan (1990); and the discussion at the beginning of Chap. Four, below). Partly this position may reflect a hankering after earlier models of social control which appear more decentralised. But partly it may also be missing the point, to be argued in the following chapters here, that alternatives to formal criminal justice have remained alive and well during the twentieth century.

A number of other points of argument may be flagged at this stage for purposes of the following discussion. In the first place, there is the fact that victims and others, in deciding not to make use of formal criminal proceedings, in effect redefine the scope of what counts as criminal. To describe this as a form of "decriminalisation" may be misleading since the alternative response would often have comprised a method of consciously dealing with delinquency as delinquency. But the actual scope of *the criminal law* may be significantly altered. For some, this may in itself be a matter for concern. An official statement on this subject from the earlier part of the nineteenth century, for instance, raises constitutional agonies—the Royal Commission on the Constabulary Force, reporting in 1839, commented:

> "To give to private individuals the power of determining whether the law shall be enforced or not, is in effect to give them a *veto* on the acts of the legislature—to give them more than the power of pardoning, and abandoning to them the prerogative of mercy." (Royal Commission, P.P., 1839, XIX (169), p. 99; see also Philips (1977).)

Such a view of the matter provokes interesting questions, for the present as much of the past: *is* it a matter of concern that victims have such a power, and, if so, what can be done in practice to change this situation?

This state of affairs has in turn implications for both official and public perceptions of the "crime problem". On the one hand, if delinquency is routinely and (in a sense) happily dealt with by other means, to what extent may it still be described as a "crime problem", with all the rhetorical connotations entailed in that kind of vocabulary? On the other hand, it sends a warning signal about reliance on perceptions of official process and on official records in drawing conclusions about the extent and nature of delinquency, crime and social problems. This point is made in a very telling way by Jones in his study of crime in nineteenth century Wales.

He firstly quotes Lord Justice Brett from an address to the grand juries of Cardiganshire and Pembrokeshire in 1883:

> "Gentlemen, I would willingly congratulate you on the non-existence of crime in your several counties *if* it did not exist; but as I believe it does exist, though, by some means, it is not brought before me, my congratulations must assume a modified form."

And Jones continues with the remark:

> "This comment raised important questions about the evidence of criminal activity and the manner in which the legal code was considered and administered in Wales. Much law-breaking went unseen or unreported." (Jones (1992), p. 3.)

The general point is that responses to and concern about crime depend inevitably on how the subject is perceived and understood and a useful understanding of the subject requires an appreciation of the full range of responses to crime and delinquency rather than being based solely or mainly on a knowledge of the official process and data therefrom.

A further point to consider as the discussion proceeds is the emergence of the paradigm of state managed prosecution and penality in the general consciousness of the twentieth century. Why has this paradigm become dominant and what lies behind the contemporary view that this is the standard response to delinquency, so that the alternatives then appear as "diversion"? In turn this leads to the question: are there compelling reasons for asserting that "official" and "formal" methods should be preferred (the implied view, for example, of the Royal Commission on the Constabulary Force in 1839, mentioned above)? In other words, what informs the presumption in favour of formal criminal justice? These issues, then, will be considered on the basis of the evidence of contemporary practice presented in the following chapters.

Chapter 3

Victim Waiver

In practice, victim waiver is a significant, although a somewhat "dark" and therefore inaccurately comprehended area of diverting offending behaviour from the process of formal prosecution. "Victim waiver" is being used in this context to refer to the decision, however motivated, of those directly or primarily affected by offending conduct not to report the matter to any official agency and thus rule out in effect the possibility of any formal process of prosecution. The discussion in Chapter Two showed that, historically, there had been a significant preference in a number of situations for "not going to law" in this way. The purpose now is to explore the extent to which such a preference has survived into the late twentieth century on the part of victims, bearing in mind the present-day ("modern") interest and role of the state in mounting formal prosecution via its range of enforcement and prosecution agencies.

Two major arguments will inform this discussion and determine its framework. First, there is the obvious but nonetheless crucial point to be made—that the police and other official agencies are highly dependent on victim reporting for there to be any official action in relation to many instances of offending behaviour. Writing in 1985, Hough and Mayhew substantiate this observation by stating:

> "The vast majority of crimes known to the police are brought to their attention by the public. In line with much other research ... the 1984 BCS [British Crime Survey] found that 91 per cent of crimes known to the police had been reported to them—mostly by victims or their families ... The police rarely discovered crimes for themselves, and were at the scene of the crime when it happened in only three per cent of cases known to them. Clearly then, reporting is the critical factor in determining the number and nature of crimes coming to police attention." (Hough and Mayhew (1985), p. 19.)

The second argument, again obvious upon short reflection, but one that has massive theoretical implications, is that in deciding whether or not to report crime, victims (and friends, families and witnesses) contribute significantly to definitions and perceptions of criminality. At the crudest level, such victim decision-making has a bearing on statistics of crime and thence upon official policy-making and public and media perceptions of offending. In other words, it affects the raw material for much discourse on the problem of crime. But also, in a more subtle way, victims are in this way redefining the broad sense of what is criminal and this then raises questions about the very understanding of that word. Even if a crime has been undoubtedly committed in a technical and legal sense, a victim's view that it is, for instance, too trivial to justify any kind of response amounts to a redefinition of the "real" criminality of the event. This then becomes an aspect of the well-known but difficult-to-document gap between law "in theory" and law "in practice".

Reference has already been made to the "dark" nature of victim diversion. For fairly clear reasons, it is a phenomenon which is not in its nature going to be very easy to penetrate, quantify or analyse. Its extent will necessarily remain a matter of rough estimate and the reasons and motivations of victim decision-making are likely to be only imperfectly recorded and open to analysis. Nonetheless, the extensive development of crime surveys based on victim reports over the last 20 years in a number of legal systems has produced valuable data relating to the phenomenon of victim waiver and the choice whether or not to report and so perhaps trigger a prosecution. Much of this data confirms intelligent guesswork about the categories of offending behaviour which is commonly not reported and the categories of victim who regularly do not report offences. But such research has also revealed a certain amount of information about the motivations for reporting or not reporting offences and some of the conclusions in this respect have perhaps been less predictable. Some of the findings from crime surveys and research based on such surveys will be discussed in more detail below.

But the fact of victim waiver leads to further questions concerning its consequences, turning on the basic question: what happens if the victim decides not to report an offence to the police or other relevant authority? There are clearly a number of possible outcomes, from nothing more happening at all (the victim's decision is the end of the matter) at one end of the spectrum, through a range of self-help actions (personal reprisal or resolution) and informal sanctioning processes. This is an area ripe for further investigation and much interesting work remains to be done, although the collection and interpretation of such material present both methodological and theoretical challenges to the researcher.

Finally, it should be asked—what are the implications for the theory and policy of criminal justice of data on victim waiver as it emerges? In theoretical terms, this kind of data should enable a reassessment of established concepts of what is criminal or delinquent and of methods of responding to such behaviour; as already pointed out, victims may be involved in a significant process of redefining law. Policy arguments are also likely to be affected by concerns generated by data relating to victim waiver. For instance, if consistent patterns of non-reporting suggest that certain categories of victim are systematically disadvantaged and denied real opportunities for legal redress, this will become a matter of both public and official concern. Alternatively, a regular resort to informal sanctioning processes may raise questions about both the rigour and the justice of such methods viewed as solutions to social problems, and also about the relationship between informal and official processes as concurrent or competing means for dealing with either the same or comparable offending conduct.

This chapter will therefore consider in turn what is known at present about the phenomenon of victim waiver; the outcomes of such waiver in practice; and then the theoretical and policy issues arising from the debate on this subject.

The nature of victim waiver

Total enforcement in formal terms of criminal law or other systems of prohibitive rules is of course unrealistic for a number of reasons. Nor is it reasonable to expect the victims of breaches always to activate official and formal processes in response to their having been offended against. But the extent of waiver will always be difficult to assess (if not impossible in exact terms), and a more sensible line of enquiry would relate to instances of what is generally agreed to be more serious offending behaviour, but which is not put forward for official action. Again, the question of how often this happens is of interest, but difficult to answer, whereas the questions of why and with what result may be more realistically explored with profit. In this way, certain questions relating to offence reporting have become established features of recent crime surveys.

(A) The victim's cost-benefit analysis

British research into the reporting of crimes has been (as in other jurisdictions) largely based upon victim report surveys and has been regularly included in the British Crime Surveys since 1984 (Koffman (1996)). The crime surveys have shown consistently that a major factor in the decision not to report was the perceived triviality of the offence—low on a scale of seriousness, either as regards the kind of offence in itself or the actual loss or damage caused to the victim. This perception accounted for 58 per cent of the unreported offences in the 1984 Survey (Hough and Mayhew (1985), p. 19); just under 50 per cent in the 1988 Survey (Mayhew, *et al.* (1989), p. 24), and 55 per cent in the1992 Survey (Mayhew, *et al.* (1992), p. 26). Skogan's international survey of victim studies, covering a number of different countries, repeats this finding:

> "Victims' expressed reasons for not reporting can usually be summarized using a cost-benefit metaphor. The most commonly reconstructed motive for non-reporting is that the crime was 'not serious enough'. A variant of this rationale is highest or next to the top on the list of victims' reasons for non reporting in virtually every survey that has been constructed." (Skogan (1984), p. 120–1.)

Other significant reasons for not reporting offences—the police would not be interested (7% in the 1984 BCS; 10% in the 1988 Survey; 13% in the 1992 Survey); and that the matter was inappropriate for the police (11% in 1984 and 1988, 12% in 1992) may be related to some extent to a view of offence seriousness, assuming a perception that it was the role of the police to deal with serious crime. On the other hand, distrust of the police or inconvenience appeared only as marginal reasons for non-reporting. However, lack of confidence in the police or pessimism as to what they could achieve was a greater disincentive (17% in 1985, 25% in 1988; and 24% in 1989). The cost-benefit analysis combines a pragmatic and predictive decision-making (will anything useful be achieved?) with a kind of threshold criterion of offence seriousness. The significance of the latter aspect supports the idea of a process of offence revaluation being undertaken by victims, whereby lesser offending is "written off" for purposes of any legal action.

This informal *de minimis* classification is not a straightforward determinant, however, since some trivial offences do get reported while some serious offences go unreported. Such "oddities" of reporting are usually explicable in more specific terms relating to the kind of offence. Perhaps most significantly, burglaries and vehicle and bicycle thefts are more likely to be reported since reporting is necessary for purposes of insurance claims; on the other hand, the existence of closer victim-offender relationships may act to decrease the chances of reporting. Pease (1988) refers to these two situations as respectively "strange reports" and "curious silences". The strange or anomalous reports identified by the 1984 BCS were predominantly thefts, especially from a motor vehicle, leading Pease to comment: "It becomes clear that insurance brings into the net of crimes known to the police offences which would not otherwise be reported by reason of their triviality" (Pease (1988), p. 22; see also Skogan (1984), p.

121). But it should be noted that if insurance claims are a prime motive for reporting such offences, this reflects not so much a wish to prosecute, but the desire to recover the value of the property. It is also likely that such reporting is not accompanied by any real expectation of apprehension or prosecution of the offender but is regarded more as a formality in the recovery process. In that case, reporting to the police can itself be viewed as a kind of diversion from or adjunct to the victim's primary purpose.

"Curious silences" are less easy to analyse. These relate to offences regarded as serious by victims in a general sense (above the median in terms of seriousness and police priority) yet sometimes reassessed by victims *in the event* as not serious (28% of Pease's "anomalous non-report" sample from the 1984 BCS were said to be "too trivial" to report, and seven per cent involved no loss or damage (Pease (1988), p. 24)). To some extent these may comprise objectively serious offences which in such cases have caused little perceived or actual harm. It is not surprising that an absence of personal loss or harm would disincline some victims from the trouble of taking the matter further. A distinction may then be drawn between "normative" and "real" injury which reflects the gap between a wider objective and public interest in responding to offences generally and the more personal interest in doing so. To put the matter another way, victims are (unsurprisingly) more likely to be law enforcers when they are closely and personally affected by breaches. Other significant reasons for non-reporting within Pease's sample included the belief that the police could have done nothing (21%) or would not be interested (13%). This again reflects the cost-benefit calculus based upon an assessment of police energy or ability (and may also derive from views as to resources as much as police attitudes). Skogan's international survey also emphasises this predictive factor. He reports a general correspondence between the solution rate for various types of crime and the frequency with they are reported (Skogan (1984), p. 121) and cites earlier research (Schneider *et al.* (1976)) which found that the belief that police would be able to apprehend offenders and that the courts would convict encouraged reporting, while conversely a widespread belief that not much can be done to recover stolen property was a disincentive to report. On the whole, this data suggests a significant and constant threshold for victims to cross for purposes of initiating the formal criminal law process—combining a perception of sufficient seriousness of the matter with a judgment of return-for-effort (is it worthwhile to become further involved?) One other significant area of non-reporting relates to offences committed by persons well known to the victim, and/or also sexual offending, which raises questions of a rather different nature and is discussed below.

(B) VICTIMS WHO WAIVE: THE INTIMATE OFFENCE

A growing body of research suggests that some offences of personal violence, especially against female victims, go unreported when the assailant is well known to the victim; and also that sexual offending has been historically more likely than not to fall outside the net of reporting (Worrall and Pease (1986); Skogan (1984), pp. 126, *et seq.*).

Two important factors may be identified in such cases. First, "non-stranger relations" or "relatedness" complicates both the immediate response and the future situation for the victim. If the offender and victim are personally close, emotional ties will naturally affect the decision as to whether to take the "dispute" to outsiders. Thus the United States National Crime Survey found that in rape cases, over 20 per cent of the instances not reported were held back on grounds that it was a "private or personal matter" (Skogan (1984), p. 126). Close personal relations also imply *continuing* relations and so increase the prospect of reprisal in some form, another reason for not reporting. Again, in rape cases fear of reprisal accounted for over ten per cent of non-reported rapes in the United States Department of Justice's 1979 study of victimisation (U.S. Department of Justice (1981)), and an Israeli study of incidents of personal violence between relatives and neighbours found fear of revenge to be the second most common reason for not reporting the offences (Fishman (1984)). As the historical material reported in Chapter Two demonstrates, generally close and continuing relations can provide compelling reasons not to prosecute.

A second important point relates to the way in which sexual offending and violence may effectively be reinterpreted as non-offending behaviour. Redefinition of an offence-situation as "domestic" or "matrimonial", so taking it out of the "public" sphere of interest, whether by victims themselves (usually women or children) or by others is an important instance of diversion from formal criminal proceedings of objectively serious offences. Official reluctance to interfere in the domestic sphere will be considered in Chapter Four, but it is also clear that a number of women and children have been or continue to be either conditioned into or intimidated from raising the matter of domestic violence for purposes of legal proceeding. It is now widely accepted (Freeman (1979); Dobash and Dobash (1981); Doggett (1992)) that violence against children and wives is firmly rooted in both Western and other cultures and there may be significant practical and psychological restraints on the reporting of domestic violence. Freeman argues, for instance:

> "But wives are reluctant to report assaults by their husbands ... They may expect to be degraded and humiliated. They may know ... about police attitudes

> towards what are euphemistically designated 'domestic disturbances'. If they are frequent victims they may tend to refrain from reporting because the burdens of such reporting and follow-up actions may be intolerable. They may believe that, without a husband to support them, they will be in a worse position. They may sense that initiating police action is likely to cause them even greater distress: greater poverty, worse beatings-up etc. The publicity involved may also act as a deterrent. They may not wish to be instrumental in the imprisonment of their husbands; they may believe he needs 'help, not punishment'." (Freeman (1979), p. 184.)

This list of interrelated restraining factors usefully encapsulates the sense of psychological trap in which victims of matrimonial and family violence may find themselves: a mix of emotional and material dependence and fear of wider, less controllable disruption. It is of course arguable that this situation is itself the result of centuries of patriarchy (Dobash and Dobash (1979), (1981)) and such an argument would be relevant to working out any solutions, but the point to note for purposes of immediate discussion is the extent of victim-diversion which occurs in this context (to the point, for example, where it may be considered relatively dangerous for the police to intervene in marital disputes—over 20 per cent of police deaths on duty in the United States have been estimated to result from domestic disturbance calls (Parnas (1967)). In effect, what are in terms of criminal law very serious offences, committed with some frequency, are not appearing as such in the criminal justice system. No doubt a similar point could be made about violence towards and sexual abuse of children, which has been the subject of more recent discovery (Freeman (1979), Chaps 2, 3).

The question of what happens in practice to such cases of diverted violent offending (whether just helplessly tolerated or responded to in some informal manner) will be discussed below. More immediately, a point of policy should be emphasised. Victim waiver of "intimate" and violent offending is morally a very different matter from that of "non-serious" offending, as discussed earlier. Battered women and children do not choose not to report their plight on the basis of a rational cost-benefit calculus, but rather because they are trapped within economic and social structures and processes which, at least until very recently, have involved a reinterpretation of the nature and reality of the offending behaviour (typified in the classic statement by the nineteenth century lawyer magistrate Edward Cox: ". . . the conclusion of my experience is that I do not believe in rapes" (Cox (1877), p. 82)). The problem is concisely stated by Dobash and Dobash when they argue that female victims of domestic violence, for a number of reasons, experience feelings of shame and guilt which "become internal controls that contribute to women's reluctance to seek outside assistance despite their rejection of the violence" (Dobash and Dobash (1981), p. 574). The resolution of this situation is therefore a moral imperative but also involves a considerable policy dilemma which would require dedicated action at a number of levels; in fact, nothing less than social restructuring (Freeman (1979), p. 213).

(c) Victims who waive: demographic patterns

Crime surveys have allowed some analysis of patterns of victim reporting or non-reporting in terms of categories of victim. With the important exception of the category just discussed (victims of "intimate" offending), factors such as socio-economic status, gender and race appear on the whole to make relatively little difference (sometimes contrary to popular assumptions about community-police relations).

The 1984 British Crime Survey analysed reporting patterns according to social class (manual and non-manual). This revealed a small but consistent difference as regards property offences: a slightly higher rate of reporting among the non-manual victims, but this may in part be explained by a higher rate of insurance cover and level of loss as regards the victims in that class (Hough and Mayhew (1985), p. 23). There was a rather more significant difference in relation to offences of violence, since non-manual victims were more likely to report such offences, including those which could be regarded as minor on the scale of seriousness (Hough and Mayhew (1985), p. 24). This finding begs some interesting questions about the resort to self-help (more common in the case of manual victims?) and access to legal services (probably greater for non-manual victims), which would need to be addressed by further research.

Other comparisons extrapolated from the 1984 sweep related to age (those under the age of 26 were less likely to report—unsurprising); levels of education (those with more education were more likely to report); and gender (no significant differences, except in relation to female victims of violent and sexual offences, as discussed already) (Hough and Mayhew (1985), p. 25). The 1988 survey produced data relating to different ethnic groups and this revealed little differences in patterns of reporting as between white, Afro-Caribbean and Asian victims (Mayhew, Elliot and Dowds (1989), Chap. 5).

Many of these findings are replicated in Skogan's international survey of reporting patterns, which on the whole confirms that reporting tends to be independent of demographic variables (Skogan (1984), p. 124, *et seq.*). This also applied to comparisons between different types of community; thus Laub found no significant differences between reporting rates in urban, suburban and rural areas (Laub (1981)). One of the most significant demographic factors in this context, as revealed in a number of different national studies of offence reporting, appears to be age. Elderly victims seem on the whole to be much more ready to report offences, and younger males constitute an important category of low-level reporters (Skogan (1984), pp. 125–6). Again, the extent of victim waiver among younger males raises interesting questions about self-help, the impact of peer group culture and the way in which some offending behaviour on the part of young people is addressed through school or family discipline rather than the criminal law (see Chap. Four, below).

(D) Victims who waive: business and corporate actors

A significant aspect of victim waiver relates to the situation of a distinctive category of victims—corporate actors and businesses. As a group, such victims are not affected in such a direct or personal manner as most of the other victims already considered. Businesses as victims suffer in an economic rather than a personal sense and are often able to redistribute or pass on the loss via subsequent business dealing or absorb it without very much immediate noticeable effect. This will naturally have some impact on their response to offending behaviour but there are also other considerations which may lead them away from formal prosecution. Such responses can be examined with reference to two main categories of business and corporate victims: employers who suffer from employee theft and related offences; and businesses prone to shoplifting.

Employee theft is a large area of offending, but Marshall comments: "Nearly 8,000 cases of 'theft by employee' came through the courts in England and Wales in 1981, but this is thought to be the minute tip of a large iceberg" (Marshall (1985), p. 30). What research has been carried out in this area suggests a strong tendency not to prosecute, and this follows a well-established tradition of non-prosecution by employers in earlier periods, as discussed already in Chapter Two (and see Robin (1967); Metzger-Preziger (1978); Institute of Personnel Management (1979)). Findings from research in the United States, Britain and Europe are consistent in showing that a minority of detected employee offences are reported to the police: an early British study found that large firms contacted the police in only 31 per cent of cases, and small firms in only 21 per cent of cases (Martin (1962). The situation is neatly encapsulated in Ditton's aphorism " 'caught' for the employee thief rarely means 'court' " (Ditton (1977a), p. 181). Although there is a dearth of more recent, post 1980s research into this phenomenon, employer-victim preferences seem well-established and widespread and are explicable in terms of both tolerance (in one research sample for half the firms questioned theft only began when the goods were worth £5 or more (Martin (1962)) and commercial expediency. The latter issue appears very significant, especially in that employers may resort to a range of sanctions, the most severe of which is dismissal, and these are often likely to appear more cost-effective than formal prosecution. The implications of this preference for "private sanctions" will be considered below (see also the discussion by Henry (1978), Chap. 7, and (1982)).

Shoplifting is another extensive category of property offending in relation to which much depends on the response of the business-victim, since virtually all such offences are discovered by shop staff and reported by the latter, if at all, to the police. Research which has been carried out into shoplifting and the way in which it is dealt with shows that retailers have different practices and policies as regards the reporting of apprehended offenders. Walsh, in a survey based in Exeter in the 1970s, found that among self-service shops the average reporting rate was around 44 per cent (Walsh (1978)). A survey by the Home Office in 1985 discovered a reporting rate of 65 per cent (Home Office Working Group on Shop Theft (1986)), while more recently it was found that of 60, 322 apprehended shoplifters in 1990, for whom outcomes were known, 61 per cent were reported to the police (Farrington and Burrows (1993)). The latter research also explored company policy on reporting among large retailers. Five companies had a policy of reporting all offenders, but these accounted for only two per cent of the national total of apprehended shoplifters. All of the others exercised a discretion, taking into account in particular the age of the shoplifter and the value of the stolen property. In some cases, such a policy was based on liaison with the police, who themselves recommended criteria taking account of age, mental state, pregnancy and property value, and were partly intended to anticipate Crown Prosecution Service decisions (Farrington and Burrows (1993), p. 64). These findings reveal a degree of co-operation and integration of policy which goes some way to meet the concern expressed earlier by Marshall that shops are not well placed to exercise discretion on this issue (Marshall (1985)) in that they may lack the appropriate expertise or information. Much may depend on the size of the retail outlet and the kind of staff employed to deal with shoplifters. The reasons for not reporting are often likely to be bound up with resources and calculations of cost-effectiveness and it may be that retailers will sometimes consider on-the-spot warnings to be effective, and immediate recovery of the goods to be an important objective. Although, therefore, this is another significant area of victim waiver in a business context, it has different features compared to the response to employee offending.

Victim settlement

(A) "TOLERATION" AND "SELF-HELP"

There would appear to be two main outcomes of victim waiver. Firstly, nothing further happens: a "simple" waiver, or "exiting" (Marshall (1985), p. 28; Black (1989), pp. 76–77, where the term "toleration" is employed). An important question arising from such a situation is whether, in moral and social terms, this is an acceptable outcome. Clearly the answer will depend largely on the nature of the offence and the circumstances of those concerned, offender and victim. For instance, such cases which involve a minor financial or property loss, when the victim is in effect "writing off" a small injury, are of less concern than instances of serious and persistent domestic violence, which are simply tolerated by victims with no attempt to seek any kind of relief. Black identifies some of the main concerns about victim "exiting" or "toleration": ". . . it is more likely in some social situations and directions than others, such as when the offender is socially superior to the aggrieved party or when both are socially marginal or unrespectable" (Black (1989), p. 76).

But in a second kind of situation the victim may waive the possibility of formal legal proceedings but seek another resolution, largely by his or her own means. This may be categorised as a form of "self-help" or "personal settlement" and may encompass a variety of techniques, from an immediate return of violence at one end of the spectrum to more sophisticated and institutionalised employer sanctions at the other extreme. But once again the resort to self-help raises both moral and social questions.

Self-help in the form of personal retaliation, especially if it involves violence, gives rise to interesting problems of legal theory. This is because such a response to offending behaviour is in itself, from the standpoint of the state's legal system, criminogenic ("taking the law into one's own hands", responding to crime with further crime, often condemned in formal legal pronouncements). Yet, in anthropological as distinct from legal terms, such dispute resolution has a significant history and remains in some contexts the social reality of the situation. As Black argues:

> "There is a sense in which conduct regarded as criminal is often quite the opposite. Far from being an intentional violation of a prohibition, much crime is moralistic and involves the pursuit of justice. It is a mode of conflict management . . . Viewed in relation to law, it is self-help. To the degree that it defines or responds to the conduct of someone else—the victim—as deviant, crime is social control." (Black (1983), p. 34.)

Although it is a phenomenon which is naturally difficult to quantify and does not lend itself to very exact typologies, self-help is clearly a significant reaction to delinquent behaviour and dispute situations, not only in earlier and "traditional" societies but also in a modern social context. Despite the difficulty of estimating its extent, its existence and typical incidence have been identified confidently enough by sociological studies (for a useful overview of such research, see Black (1983)).

There is a spectrum of self-help responses which, if brought to official attention, will appear as criminal offences in their own turn. At one extreme, many homicides arise from quarrels or may be seen as acts of self-defence or responses to provocation: Lundsgaarde's research in Houston in 1969, for instance, found that only just over 10 per cent of homicides there occurred in the course of "predatory" behaviour (such as burglary or robbery) (Lundsgaarde (1977)). American research has also demonstrated that many assaults and non-fatal acts of violence result from quarrels, often between people who know each other well (Vera Institute of Justice (1977); Merry (1981)). Thirdly, the taking of property or acts of destruction of property may have a "moralistic" or retributive character and from the offender's point of view may be seen as measures of reimbursement or retaliation in the context of another grievance (Vera Institute of Justice (1977)). Similarly, acts of vandalism and malicious damage of property may in effect be acts of retaliation; as Black phrases the matter, "whereas ... a Plains Indian may kill a horse, a modern agent of justice may damage the offender's automobile" (Black (1983), p. 37). In some situations, self-help responses may not be simply retributive in nature but also complicated by sub-cultural norms of "manliness" or "honour", which may lead to an even more deliberate steering of the matter away from the purview of the legal system as gang members go into battle (Matzu (1964), p. 155, *et seq.*) or duelling rituals are engaged in (Baldick (1965)). At the far end of the spectrum, however, there may also be instances of self-help which do not amount to criminal offences in any form, but are more in the nature of negative acts of avoidance or denial, such as acts of ostracism or withdrawal of support. These are much less problematical from the point of view of the formal legal system, yet at the interpersonal level may be very effective in some situations.

The general point to note is that victim settlement through some form of personal retaliation is both widespread and, for a number of victims, a tempting strategy. It is, however, socially problematic in that is, without the controls of formal criminal justice, generative of long-term indefinite disputes (feuds). It is legally problematic in that, lacking official authority, it often replicates offending behaviour and so undermines the formal authority of the criminal law. Small wonder, then, that courts frequently deliver strictures about individuals "taking the law into their own hands".

(B) Action taken by employers

One particular area of victim settlement deserves further consideration in view of the range of sanctions which may be privately utilised—action taken by employer-victims. Such action taken against employee-offenders may be distinguished from other "closed" fora, such as educational institutions, the military, or professional regulatory bodies, in that these latter employ relatively formal, quasi-legal disciplinary procedures which are usually subject to some kind of external scrutiny (and will be therefore considered separately in the following Chapter). Employers are closer to conventional victims in terms of their responses to offending behaviour affecting their own interests. But they occupy a distinctive position through their ability to make use of a range of (sometimes potentially severe) sanctions located within the employment relationship, especially the sanction of dismissal from employment.

As noted above, employers may often prefer to use their own sanctions rather than institute criminal proceedings. Research findings in this area suggest that employers are frequently motivated by a desire to maintain control themselves over the matter and to maximise the flexibility of their responses. The employers' interests are outlined by Martin in his earlier study of employee offending:

> "... it is clear, from the high dismissal rate of men not prosecuted, that employers do not treat these offences lightly. Their policy may be described as a mixture of humanity and expediency ... It is humane because the man concerned does not appear in court ... he does not become a man 'with a record' ... It is not surprising ... that the employer, faced by an offence committed by a man possibly well-known to him, should when possible take the lenient course ... leniency, however, may also be expedient. The matter is dealt with once and for all, no time is wasted going to court, nor is the firm's name brought undesirably into the public eye ... The police are kept out of the premises so that there is no risk of the employer losing control of what happens in the case ..." (Martin (1962), p. 104.)

From the employers' point of view this approach comprises an attractive mix of appearing "soft" while being rigorous in protecting their own interests. There is also a sense of mutual benefit in a "negotiated" settlement—for instance, the employer agreeing to refrain from prosecution and not to make any further mention of the offence if the employee agrees to go quietly and restore stolen property (cost-effectiveness on both sides—the mutual advantages are summarised by Henry (1978), p. 129). Ditton has indicated the prevailing attitude in this situation very concisely by saying that "... as far as employers are concerned, there is no room for civic sentimentality in business" (Ditton (1977b), p. 7).

It would seem that employers can make use of a tariff of sanctions, ranging from warnings, "docking" of pay (a kind of fine), suspension for varying periods of time with or without pay, demotion, transfer and loss of promotion, through to dismissal, with or without references. This has led some commentators to express concern about the way in which such sanctioning discretion is exercised, in particular as regards the risk of arbitrary or inconsistent responses on the part of employers (see, *e.g.* Henry (1978), pp. 129, *et seq.*; Marshall (1985), pp. 31–33). Marshall especially argues that dismissal without references is a severe sanction and may well be more devastating than the outcome of legal proceedings in a number of cases. Moreover, there may also be a juridical concern that in some situations there may not be sufficient evidence to secure a conviction, yet the employer does not necessarily have to worry about niceties of procedure and evidence in order to dismiss the suspected employee-offender. Marshall questions whether unfair dismissal rules would provide any protection in the absence of criminal proceedings resulting in an acquittal (Marshall (1985), p. 32). On the other hand there is evidence in recent decades of a move towards formalisation of rules and procedures within companies for dealing with employee delinquency, and that this has been in response to governmental and legislative pressure (Institute of Personnel Management (1979); Henry (1982), p. 369). This indicates some incorporation of due process values into employer-administered penality so that this area of "private" discipline or justice may in fact be converging with models of professional and institutional discipline discussed in the following chapter. Also of interest is Henry's identification of a trend towards "corrective" as distinct from punitive sanctions (which may be seen as replicating criminal justice trends). This tendency was seen by Henry, writing in the early 1980s, as partly:

> "a product of the attempt to overcome the difficulty of securing swift dismissals in the face of the growing collective strength of trade unions, the general increase in the scale of company operations, and the general trend towards pluralism in industrial relations" (Henry (1982), p. 376).

The point of wider interest is that the employer-victim appears to occupy an intermediate position between the conventional less powerful victim and agencies (whether part of the criminal justice system or not) with clearly defined prosecutorial roles. In analytical terms this suggests that it is useful to view the whole phenomenon of responses to offending, and diversion as one aspect of that phenomenon, as a *continuum* which proceeds from directly affected victims to that of other parties who represent a broader interest in dealing with the offending conduct. To see the subject in these terms may also provide some insight into the "modern" character of criminal law, whereby the state has appeared to acquire greater responsibility for dealing with delinquent behaviour *vis-à-vis* those more directly affected by such action.

Chapter 4

Unofficial Systems of Discipline

In considering the well-known critical stance of recent years that it would be desirable to move away from formal criminal justice to more informal and negotiated responses to crime and delinquency (see, *e.g.* Danzig (1973); Christie (1977); Matthews (ed.) (1988), generally for a critical re-evaluation of "informalism"; Nergard (1993)), Stuart Henry puts the argument:

> "... such a critique ... overlooks the very important area of informal disciplinary procedure ... the majority of 'judicial' decisions within our society take place *informally* and privately within particular social institutions. In some ways this renders the decentralisation critique misplaced since we already have decentralised criminal processing ..." (Henry (1981), p. 180.)

This statement alerts the reader of criminological debate to the important point that a good deal of offending and delinquent behaviour is dealt with by disciplinary procedures that have an unofficial character, in that they are to a large extent separate from the formal legal system. The typology of such disciplinary modes is not neat and reveals varying degrees of integration with the state system of law. A historical congener of this kind of system might be the separate jurisdiction of the ecclesiastical or church courts which exercised control over a wide range of delinquent behaviour until well into the seventeenth century in England and Wales (Ingram (1987); Shoemaker (1991)). Notable present day instances of distinct disciplinary systems include those of educational bodies, professional bodies, trade unions and sporting authorities—all of which have a largely "private" or "domestic" character—and military and prison authorities, these last two being much more closely integrated into the structure of state authority as "public" bodies. But even the justice meted out through "private" systems of discipline may be subject to some external legal scrutiny via such procedures as judicial review.

The general point of relevance here is that these disciplinary systems are concerned with a range of delinquent conduct, some of which may be legally defined as "criminal" under the "outside" rules of the legal system, but some of which comprises conduct which only offends against the "inside" norms of the system—university or school regulations, standards of professional conduct, prison rules or whatever. Thus an act of personal violence may be both a criminal offence and a breach of school or prison rules, but an unfair practice in an examination or an act of mutiny (at least until recently—see the discussion below on the transformation of prison mutiny into a criminal offence) will not as such be criminal offences. The main interest of the present discussion is not so much in the offences specific to disciplinary systems (interesting and important though they may be in their own right), but in breaches of criminal law which may be diverted into another disciplinary system from the state's jurisdiction. It is also important to distinguish two diversionary situations of this type: first, where there is total diversion (the legal system takes no action); and secondly, where the diversion is partial in that the legal system maintains an interest at the same time as action is being taken elsewhere. This second sub-category of case gives rise to issues of "double jeopardy".

The double jeopardy problem can be simply illustrated by the statement of a senior British judge in a criminal appeal, relating the case of an unfortunate man convicted of criminal damage, having caused minor damage to the receiver of a public telephone through loss of temper and feelings of frustration. (Incidentally, this is also an example of minor offending which would normally present itself as an obvious candidate for diversion from formal prosecution and would also effectively be decriminalised by most victims according the findings of the British Crime Surveys—see Chap. Three, above.) The defendant, having been convicted and fined, Scarman L.J. made a special point of saying, when the case was heard on appeal:

> "The Court was disturbed ... by what we were told as to the possible attitude of the professional body which governs the appellant's professional life and ... I wish it to be on public record that we see in the facts of this case no reflection on the integrity or honesty of the appellant and that there is nothing here which would lead this Court to think that he is unfitted for his profession. We hope that these observations will be drawn to the attention of the professional body." (*R v. Parker* [1977] 2 All E.R. 37 at 40.)

This, then, is an example of a conviction for a criminal offence itself becoming a breach of a code of professional conduct and so begetting a further possible sanction. Admittedly, there may be a semantic argument that the "professional" offence, as a failure to adhere to a general standard of behaviour, is in some sense a breach distinct from the act of criminal damage, but the Court of Appeal was clearly of the view that for practical purposes the two issues were so closely interrelated as to give rise to concerns about double jeopardy. This is likely to be true of many examples of this type of problem and care should be taken that policy questions and moral concerns should not be defined away by using fine juridical distinctions.

The possible definitional and procedural routes are illustrated in Figure 1, which could serve as a framework for discussing many examples of generic offending conduct such as personal violence or damage to or the taking of property. The principal point of interest for purposes of the present discussion lies in the question: to the extent that conduct could be dealt with in both systems, what are the arguments in favour of it being one rather than the other and are there compelling arguments against it being considered under both? Again, a simple example should suffice to make the point clear. If a student steals a book from a university library, should the matter be dealt with as a breach of the university's library regulations (in which case the sanctions might conceivably include a ban from using the library, suspension from the university or disqualification from taking a degree) or as the criminal offence of theft (with a statutory maximum penalty of a term of imprisonment under English law)? The university and the general legal system will of course to some extent be acting to protect different kinds of interest (respectively those of the university and of the wider community). But there is also in this example a core common interest (respect for the property of others) which is being served and this does present the possibility of a genuine choice of process. The same issue has already appeared in the context of employers taking action against employee offending (see Chap. Three, above), although, as already noted, in a somewhat less institutionalised setting. The answer to the question will usually depend upon notions of both appropriate forum (a kind of "subsidiarity" argument) and of justice.

Excursus: the problem of "cheating" behaviour—"reverse diversion"

Before pursuing the main theme of diversion from formal criminal proceedings in this context, it may be useful to test the rationale for separate disciplinary systems by probing further one of the main forms of delinquency which is dealt with by such disciplinary authorities. The justification for special systems of discipline is often membership of a group or organisation which by its nature requires a code or standard of conduct embodying special obligations not imposed on members of the community

Figure 1

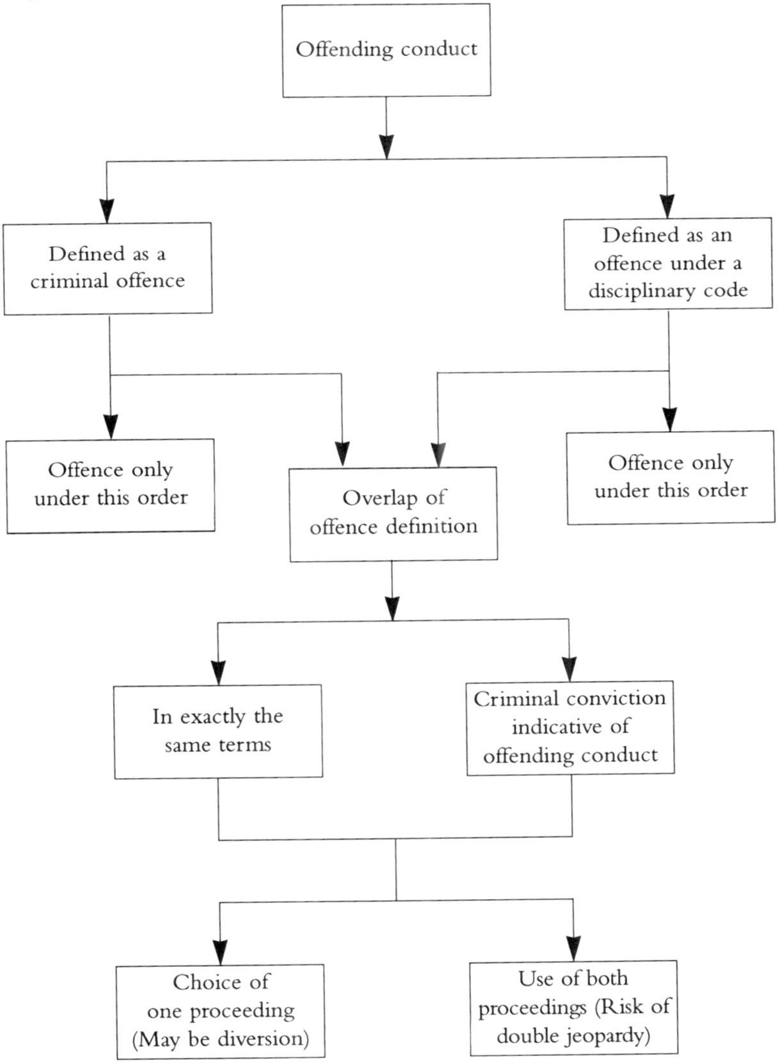
Offending conduct
Defined as a criminal offence
Defined as an offence under a disciplinary code
Offence only under this order
Overlap of offence definition
Offence only under this order
In exactly the same terms
Criminal conviction indicative of offending conduct
Choice of one proceeding (May be diversion)
Use of both proceedings (Risk of double jeopardy)

at large. Such obligations and their possible breach naturally relate to the specific activities of the group or organisation—typically, education, the conduct of a trade or profession, or a sporting activity. What many of these breaches have in common is not just a failure to adhere to a special group standard of conduct (in general terms, for instance, a "professional" or "sportsmanlike" way of behaving) but more particularly a kind of dishonesty or violation of trust, often summed up in the idea of "cheating". In an educational and academic context, unfair examination practices and plagiarism are significant examples of cheating; sporting bodies regulate a wide range of underhand tactics which lead to an unfair advantage and would also qualify broadly as cheating. In a commercial and professional context the exploitation of a position of confidence or access to information for purposes of private gain may also be regarded as a species of cheating. Generally, all of these situations comprise instances of private or personal advancement, by means which are regarded as unfair, deceptive or unduly exploitative. This sense of cheating behaviour was expressed in a legal context by Devlin J. in the following terms:

> "If a man joins a profession in which the use of trade weapons is barred, and then proceeds to employ them, he is taking an unfair advantage over his fellows. They restrain themselves, believing rightly or wrongly that such restraint is essential to the good health of the profession as a whole; he gets the benefit of their restraint and fills his purse at their expense. He is defaulting on the obligation, by which explicitly or implicitly, he undertook to be bound, when they made him of their company." (*R v. Hughes* [1957] 2 All E.R. 436 at 442.)

Sometimes there may some linkage or even overlap with criminal offending, especially in the area of deception and fraud. But frequently the matter is clearly outside the ambit of criminal law and for that reason the subject of specialised regulation. In the context of the present discussion, it may be pertinent to ask to what extent it is appropriate to leave such matters to "private" or "domestic" regulation.

At this point it may be helpful to take some common examples of this kind of delinquency. First, in the context of educational qualifications, rules have been developed to deal with the deceptive of unfair gaining of such qualifications, by methods such as copying from other candidates, using prohibited material in examinations, and plagiarism (see generally Farrington and Mattison (1990), pp. 75, *et seq.*). (Plagiarism does not have a legal definition, but is commonly understood to comprise the deliberate "passing off" of another's work as one's own for purposes of academic gain.) These unfair practices may be subject to procedures of investigation, hearings and sanctions and the latter commonly range through warnings, deduction of marks, disqualification from the particular test and complete exclusion from the course leading to the qualification, with concomitant degrees of stigma and personal impact. Secondly, in the increasingly commercialised and lucrative context of sporting activities, there exist a wide variety of potential unfair tactics, such as the use of drugs which distort performance, poaching of rival team members and using ineligible team members, to name just a few. Again a range of disciplinary procedures and sanctions may be applied (Grayson (1994), p. 286, *et seq.*), sometimes with extremely severe effects (for example, a ban from sport, with consequent loss of livelihood, not to mention reputation; demotion of the team to a lower division or league, entailing a considerable loss of revenue). Thirdly, in the professional and commercial field, there are a number of examples of "misconduct" which would fall into the looser category of cheating behaviour: in the case of solicitors, for instance, over-charging clients (Abel (1988), p. 255) or improperly lending money to a client. A number of professions in Britain have their own disciplinary procedures which are actively and frequently used to deal with improper conduct (notably, the medical and related professions, the legal profession, chartered accountants and architects) and may impose a range of sanctions, typically reprimand, suspension and total disqualification (for a detailed study of the operation of such professional disciplinary proceedings, see (in relation to the medical profession) Smith (1994)). Finally, in the financial services sector in Britain, "self-regulation" has been recognised as an important regulatory method under the Financial Services Act 1986, section 114 of which delegates regulatory powers to the Securities and Investment Board (SIB), actually a private company, which in turn is empowered to recognise other self-regulating bodies (SROs) to deal with particular aspects of investment business (for instance, the Securities Association, the Investment Management Regulatory Organisation (IMRO)). The SIB and SROs have powers to institute disciplinary proceedings and employ disciplinary sanctions such as reprimand, fines, censure, suspension and expulsion (see generally Rider, Abrams and Ferrar (1989), Chaps 3 and 12). A great deal of commercial misconduct in this sector is dealt with by such disciplinary methods (Levi (1993), p. 79), although the SIB, along with the Department of Trade and Industry, also has a role in the criminal prosecution of serious financial fraud.

Whether the context is higher education, sport or professional activity, a persistent point of concern relates to the rigour and fairness of such procedures and the extent to which they should for that reason be subject to external scrutiny. In view of the specialised nature of the kind of activity being regulated, it is on the one hand understandable that judgments about improper or deviant conduct may be viewed as being best made by peers or others with a close knowledge and acquaintance with the issues in question (the common justification for self-regulation or "keeping your own house in order", and once again a species of subsidiarity argument). For instance, Farrington and Mattison comment, in relation to cheating in examinations: "The law in general is much less suited to intervention in cases which are wholly related to the academic nature of a university" ((1990), at p. 78). On the other hand, the closed or "domestic" character of such disciplinary proceedings will inevitably lead to concern about safeguards against arbitrariness, bias or over-harsh judgments and, even if it may not be feasible to review the substance of disciplinary decisions, at least elements of natural justice may be assured through some process of external review. For this reason, whatever the legal basis of the disciplinary jurisdiction itself and despite its apparently private character, educational, sporting and professional disciplinary decisions in Britain have gradually come within the ambit of judicial review under the general legal system.

Arguments in favour of such intervention are convincing in the light of what is revealed in some of the case law. In 1957, for example, the High Court overruled a decision of the Architects' Registration Council that to combine the practice of architect and house agent amounted to "disgraceful" conduct justifying removal from the register of architects—in other words, disqualification from practice—(*Hughes v. Architects' Registration Council* [1957] 2 All E.R. 436) as a manifestly disproportionate reaction. In 1965 the Scottish High Court granted a declaration in favour of the St Johnstone Football Club against the Scottish Football Association; the latter had censured and fined the Club for arranging a benefit game for one of its players without formal authorisation, but gave no notice of its decision or opportunity to appear before the disciplinary authority (*St Johnstone Football Club v. The Scottish Football Association Ltd* [1965] S.L.T. 174). In 1966, the Court of Appeal allowed an appeal against a decision of the Stewards of the Jockey Club refusing to grant a trainer's licence to a woman simply on account of the applicant's gender, as being contrary to public policy (*Nagle v. Feilden* [1966] 2 Q.B. 633). Finally, in an Australian case relating to treatment for drug addiction, the Supreme Court of Western Australia allowed an appeal against the Medical Board of Western Australia's finding of "infamous or improper conduct", since there was a reputable minority view which approved the manner of treatment adopted by the defendant practitioner (*Cranley v. Medical Board of Western Australia* [1992] 3 M.L.R. 94). Such examples across the spectrum of disciplinary proceedings illustrate decisively the value of monitoring through the process of judicial review.

As a matter of English law, the willingness of courts to intervene and scrutinise the operation of "domestic" disciplinary systems is not absolutely clear and free of inconsistency (Cane (1996), pp. 20–21), but the rationale of such external control is sufficiently cogent and convincing. As Cane states: "... bodies of this sort exercise great, and often monopoly, power over some area of social and economic activity in which not only participants in the activity but also the wider public have an interest" (Cane (1996), p. 21).

These may therefore be regarded as distinct regulatory systems whose operation is of public concern. In terms of diversionary theory, those persons subject to such regimes are of course at the beginning outside the scope of legal rules, but their cases may be diverted *into* the legal system for their better protection—a kind of "reverse diversion" compared to the usual sense of the term.

This phenomenon of "reverse diversion" differs in some important respects from diversion in the usual sense and in the normal direction (that is, away from formal legal proceedings). Most importantly, it does not represent a substitute process, nor is it motivated by expediency; on the contrary, it is more like an appellate process and so prolongs and complicates the system of regulation. But in some ways it serves as a warning of the potential risks inherent in the standard version of diversion: the possibility of less rigorous, less transparent procedures, and of a lower level of due process safeguards. This is the main concern relating to separate disciplinary systems and can perhaps be summarised in the question—to what extent are such procedures analogous to criminal proceedings? The offending conduct in question may relate to a special rather than a broader public interest (although this point may be arguable), but the nature of the proceedings, method of control and types of sanction on the one hand recall features of the criminal law process and on the other hand may result in a material impact and stigma comparable to, if not more significant in some instances, than a criminal conviction. As Smith remarks about the proceedings before the Professional Conduct Committee (PCC) of the General Medical Council:

> "Although the PCC does not have power to fine or imprison, the sanctions which [it] is able to impose can have equally significant effects upon a practitioner's livelihood, career, and reputation. Hence, its procedure is subject to rules similar in effect to those which apply in the criminal courts." (Smith (1994), at p. 67.)

Taking such a view, importation of the standards and controls of the legal system may be seen as an appropriate means to guarantee fair treatment. As was said quite famously by another senior judge:

> "These bodies which exercise a monopoly in an important sphere of human activity, with the power of depriving a man of his livelihood, must act in accordance with the elementary rules of justice. They must not condemn a man without giving him the opportunity to be heard in his own defence." (Denning L.J., in *Abbott v. Sullivan* [1952] 1 Q.B., 189 at 198.)

The possibility of diversion to unofficial discipline

(A) EDUCATIONAL INSTITUTIONS

Naturally enough in view of the amount of time spent by children and young persons in schools and by other students in institutions of higher education, a certain amount of delinquency, some of it qualifying as criminal in a legal sense, is likely to occur in educational contexts. Schools in particular may seek to regulate some types of delinquent conduct (typically behaviour described as "disruptive", fighting between children and bullying) by their own regulations and systems of sanctions, although very serious criminal offences would almost certainly be "referred on" to the legal system. It is difficult to estimate the amount of delinquency and criminal behaviour which in practice is regulated by educational discipline; the patterns and extent of such regulation have not been systematically researched. But it is clear, for instance, that within Britain the main types of response (use of measures such as detention, suspension and expulsion) and also the policies of control do have a fairly standard character (Graham (1988), p. 32). Some research has been carried out into the use and impact of sanctions within schools (Clegg and Megson (1973); British Psychological Society (1980); Maughan and Ouston (1979); Topping (1983); Marshall (1987)). The findings of such research do not reveal very much about the relative effectiveness of particular sanctions, apart from suggesting that corporal punishment (whether formally or informally administered) and frequent tellings-off tend to show a negative correlation with good behaviour (Clegg and Megson (1973); British Psychological Society (1980); Maughan and Ouston (1979)).

For present purposes, two main questions present themselves. First, how appropriate is it for educational bodies to deal with such behaviour rather than the authorities of the state legal system? Secondly, in so far as the matter is addressed by educational discipline, how should the approach taken in that context relate (if at all) to that of the legal system? The first question will no doubt be answered to a large extent by common-sense. On the one hand, a good deal of "playground violence" would most appropriately be handled by school authorities. At the other end of the scale, serious instances of violence and intimidation or activities involving dangerous drugs or offensive weapons would probably be widely regarded as matters for the police. But inevitably the dividing line may not always be drawn easily or consistently. A relevant factor is the question of resources and, linked to the latter, morale, since the willingness of schools to be involved in the disciplining of conduct which could qualify as criminal may be affected by such pragmatic considerations.

The second question has a bearing on the conduct of disciplinary procedures and the nature and objectives of the sanctions employed. The effectiveness of disciplinary action will depend upon a sense of its own legitimacy and the cogency of its goals. Legitimacy is likely to be undermined if requirements of due process and fair treatment are not respected; Topping's review of research on school sanctions suggests, not surprisingly, that an effective regime of sanctions depends upon a regime which is systematic, predictable and consistent (Topping (1983)). There is also some evidence that long-term goals of compliance may be better achieved through constructive approaches rather than more negatively punitive sanctions. Thus, while corporal punishment may have counter-productive consequences, as noted above, there have also been arguments put forward recently in favour of more pre-emptive strategies, building on the perception that low achievement and disruptive behaviour at school is a contributing factor to later criminality and that an integrated and holistic approach by schools in dealing with the former may then become a valuable component of criminal justice strategy (Utting (1996), p. 83). Similarly, Marshall has referred to the use of school mediation projects in presenting a similar argument. Resolution through mediation, rather than official punishment, is seen as promoting greater self-management by young people of situations of conflict: a community boards programme in San Francisco was claimed:

> "to teach people new skills in communication and conflict resolution, give them a chance to exercise responsibility for improving their school environment, build a sense of peer co-operation and community at school and decrease tensions, hostility and violence among students." (Marshall (1987), pp. 40–41.)

The thrust of much recent research has therefore been to explore the interrelationship between reactions to delinquency in an educational context and within the legal system and to suggest the benefits of a more integrated strategy whereby an effective management of delinquency at school can help to minimise the extent of criminality in a legal context. The value of such a holistic approach to delinquent behaviour is that it reveals the cumulative and interdependent impact of a number of socialising institutions such as the school and the family in addition to the formal legal system and also the need for mutual awareness on the part of those different disciplinary orders.

(B) Professional bodies, clubs and associations

In the case of disciplinary action taken by professional organisations, clubs, sporting authorities and other "private" regulatory bodies, the issue is less one of complete diversion of criminal offending thereto than the way in which the latter may be taken into account in such distinct disciplinary procedures. As has been argued above, in this context an important issue is procedural rigour and the guarantee of due process in such proceedings, and a specific aspect of this is the possibility of double jeopardy (Harding and Ireland (1989)). If a member of a profession, occupational group or club is convicted of a criminal offence and this fact is then the basis of or an element in disciplinary proceedings within that organisation, is there thereby in effect a double punishment? This is not diversion in the usual sense, but a kind of "supplementary diversion".

The issue comes about primarily because conviction for a criminal offence may often provide evidence of unfitness as regards membership of the professional or other group: it is in itself a species of professional or "member" misconduct. A significant example of this equation of criminal conviction and professional misconduct is in relation to the medical profession (although it should be noted that there are similar provisions in relation to other professional groups, such as lawyers, dentists and architects, so that what is said about the medical profession may usually be applied by analogy also to the situation of some other professions). Section 36(1)(a) of the Medical Act 1983 provides the Professional Conduct Committee of the General Medical Council with jurisdiction to rule on cases of professional misconduct arising from the fact of a criminal conviction (although not in cases where conviction has been followed by a probation order or discharge, or where the conviction has been quashed on appeal, or if the conviction is of a trivial nature (Smith (1994), pp. 31–33)). Is there any sense of double penalty if an individual is firstly convicted and dealt with for a criminal offence and then disciplined by the professional body in relation to the same matter? The prevailing view as a matter of English law is that the criminal court and disciplinary body are carrying out distinct functions (the one is concerned with a criminal charge, the other with the issue of fitness to engage in a profession); as such, there is no double punishment (Smith (1994), pp. 69–70; see also the ruling by Lord Lane C.J. in *R v. Committee of the Pharmaceutical Society of Great Britain, ex p. the Pharmaceutical Society of Great Britain* [1981] 2 All E.R. 805). This is true enough up to a point: the two tribunals are dealing with violations of different interests, the wider public interest embodied in the criminal law and the narrower professional interest in fitness to practise. Yet at the same time, both responses are triggered by a single event and looking at the matter for purposes of deciding on appropriate sanctions, it is at least arguable that any decision on the use of sanctions should take into account the whole possible range of responses which may follow from the original offending conduct. One way of resolving this moral dilemma may be to accept that in some cases professional disqualification may be necessary in order to guarantee professional standards, in which event a way should be found of incorporating this into the overall penal calculus employed by the criminal court. A practical problem lies in the fact that a criminal court will decide on the matter prior to any professional disciplinary proceedings. But it is not impossible to envisage some closer liaison between sentencers and disciplinary bodies in such cases; for instance, such liaison could be triggered by arguments presented in mitigation of sentence. In other words, taking in this way a wider view of the issue of sanctions could lead, usefully, to a more integrated process of decision-making on the part of the criminal courts and disciplinary bodies. In moral terms it does not seem unreasonable for a criminal court to incorporate an outcome such as professional disqualification into its own penal calculation.

Returning to the central issue of diversion, an underlying question remains: is there any justification for diverting some alleged criminal conduct to be dealt with as a question of professional or other discipline (in the same way that educational institutions or employers respond to conduct which may be technically criminal in character)? The argument could be presented in the following way. If an employee commits a theft and the matter is dealt with by his or her employer (for instance, by dismissal from employment), or a student or pupil commits an act of criminal damage which is then disciplined by a school or college, why should some offences committed in the course of professional activity not be dealt with solely as a matter of professional discipline (such as the defrauding solicitor, or the assaulting sports person)? The answer lies partly in the fact of the more closed environment of some forms of employment and educational process, which may render the employers' or schools' system of control inevitable, especially in so far as the latter may also be the direct victims of the offending conduct. Moreover, the most compelling arguments in favour of diversion to "unofficial" agencies may be based much more on expediency than on considerations of either the public interest or the offender's interest in such a process being used. Put another way, some "unofficial" regulation and sanctioning of delinquent behaviour may be an inevitable fact of life and may to some extent be justified by the need to protect distinct interests such as the maintenance of professional or other occupational standards. But a conscious and systematic policy of diversion is another matter. In practice of course a good deal of less serious criminal offending will ordinarily not be prosecuted within the legal system, but may well be taken up within a process of unofficial discipline. What would be more controversial, and less easy to justify, would be a deliberate transfer of serious offending conduct to the unofficial sphere of discipline (for instance, an alleged rape being dealt with exclusively by university authorities), at least, not without a rigorous process of scrutiny by the legal system, which is unlikely to prove cost-effective.

"Semi-official" disciplinary systems: the armed forces and prisons

There are also distinct disciplinary systems of contemporary importance which have a close relationship with state authority, in that they are themselves very much emanations of state power and have a formal basis necessarily within the state's legal order. The internal disciplinary systems of the armed forces and the prison system are perhaps the most notable examples, since both members of the armed forces and prisoners are largely subject to a separately regulated mode of life, although in very different circumstances. Both groups are subject to distinct codes of behaviour which supplement and, to some extent, supplant the regulation of their position as ordinary citizens of the state. As a result, some criminal offending on the part of members of the armed forces and of prisoners may be dealt with respectively by courts-martial and the prison disciplinary proceedings and to that extent is diverted, as a matter of legal principle, from the "regular" legal system.

As far as the British armed forces are concerned, the division of jurisdiction is stated succinctly in the *Manual of Military Law*:

> "The general principle is that an offence, whether committed on Ministry of Defence premises or not, which affects the person or property of a civilian should normally be dealt with by a civil court, but that an offence which involves only service personnel, their property or service property, should normally be dealt with by the military authorities." (Ministry of Defence (1972), Chap. 7, para. 4.)

(In this terminology, "civil court" includes, in fact means, "criminal court".) Therefore, unless there is a civilian connection with the offence in question, it will come before the military authorities in order that the latter "may have effective control over persons who are subject to military law" (Chap. 7, para. 1(a) of the *Manual*). This "military jurisdiction" comprises two main categories: the system of "courts-martial" and a system of summary disposal applied to servicemen below a certain rank and carried out within the offender's unit (Lyon (1998), pp. 109–10). It should be noted that this is an example of diversion in a very full sense: it operates as a matter of principle (there is no discretionary element, such as characterises many other instances of diversion) and, with the exception of the appellate process, the infrastructure of prosecution, trial and sanctions is wholly a matter for the armed forces. The Courts-Martial Appeal Court is the only real point of intrusion from the legal system outside—this court has the same personnel and powers as the Criminal Division of the Court of Appeal and has jurisdiction to hear appeals against sentence (Armed Forces Act 1996, s. 17).

The military justice system in the United Kingdom has recently been the subject of a significant legal review following the application of a serviceman under the European Convention on Human Rights in the case of *Findlay v. United Kingdom* (see (1997) 24 E.H.R.R. 221). The applicant, who had been dealt with under the court-martial process, sought to complain about the impartiality of those proceedings and, having failed to obtain judicial review under English law, was successful in arguments before both the Commission and Court of Human Rights that aspects of the court-martial procedure infringed Article 6 of the Convention. The Court found that the court-martial proceedings were not sufficiently separated from the military chain of command to qualify as an impartial tribunal for purposes of Article 6. The crucial role of the Convening Officer in the procedure was highly problematical, since this officer (who was not legally qualified) not only took key prosecutorial decisions but also selected members of the court (who might be under his authority in the military chain of command) and then acted as the Confirming Officer who formally confirmed the decision and sentence of the court. Nor were there, in the view of the Human Rights Court, sufficient safeguards within the existing procedure (for instance, the availability of advice from the Office of the Judge-Advocate-General) to counteract at the very least an appearance of bias. (Neither the Commission nor the Court, however, found any evidence of actual bias in Findlay's case.) But already, following the Commission's report, there had been a review of the system, resulting in changes contained in the Armed Forces Act of 1996. Essentially, the offices of both Convening Officer and Confirming Officer have been abolished and the role of the Convening Officer has been divided between three different bodies with a clear separation of powers and personnel (Lyon (1998)).

While the example of diversion to military discipline relates to an exceptional category of offenders (exceptional through status), the situation of prisoners, although arising within a very different context, bears some analogy with the system of armed forces discipline. Prisoners inhabit a sealed-off social world (in fact even more so than members of the armed forces), which has its own code of conduct and some special types of offence, justified by the requirements of internal order. Fitzgerald has commented about the British system of prison discipline:

"The 1899 Prison Rules introduced the first comprehensive disciplinary code

> for prisons, and the 'military model' was plainly its blueprint. Efficient, centralised, institutional control called for a militaristic approach to prison discipline, with the governor as the figure of the regimental colonel, beneath him his officers and then the prisoners. Hence the language of martial law and the governor's role as summary disciplinarian endowed with powers comparable to those of a regimental commanding officer." (Fitzgerald (1985), pp 30–1.)

However, the situation inside a prison differs from that within the armed forces in an important respect—there is a natural sense of opposition between prisoners and prison authorities which inevitably colours the operation of any internal disciplinary process (Livingstone and Owen (1993), p. 180) and renders arguments in favour of some kind of external scrutiny so much more compelling. In fact, in the United Kingdom and elsewhere, prison disciplinary proceedings became increasingly open to external review, through national processes of judicial review and applications made under the European Convention on Human Rights, but right up to the 1990s criticisms continued to be made of the rigour and justice of the internal prison disciplinary system in the United Kingdom (see, for instance, Ditchfield and Duncan (1987); Woolf (1991), para. 14). The strong recommendations of the Woolf Report finally brought about important changes in the structure of the disciplinary process inside British prisons, especially as regards the handling of criminal as distinct from "internal" disciplinary offences, implemented in the Prison (Amendment) Rule 1992 (S.I. 1992 No. 514).

It is of interest to the present discussion that the new Prison Rules and Standing Orders provide for criminal offences committed by prisoners (including the new criminal offence of prison mutiny) to go before the ordinary criminal courts. The facts of a suspected criminal offence on the part of a prisoner should be referred to the police, for a decision on whether or not to prosecute by the police and the Crown Prosecution Service. If the latter decide to proceed, then there should be no parallel disciplinary proceeding, so as to avoid any claim of double jeopardy (see the European Prison Rules, r. 36(1)). If the police and Crown Prosecution Service decide against prosecution on grounds of insufficient evidence this should also bar any internal disciplinary action relying on the same evidence. Moreover, "where the resumption of internal proceedings is likely to create an appearance of unfairness out of proportion to the seriousness of the alleged disciplinary offence, the governor should consider whether the charge should be dismissed" (Standing Order 3D(7)). The effect of these legal changes therefore is to curtail significantly the "diversion" of criminal offending by prisoners into the prison disciplinary system; indeed, such offending is very largely brought back within the ambit of the general legal system. This also severs the earlier analogy between the handling of criminal offences alleged to have been committed by members of the armed forces and by prisoners.

There have been, therefore, very significant legal developments in recent years in relation to both these "closed" systems of semi-official discipline, and these may be summed up as an extension of "outside" legal control over both jurisdictions. In the case of the prison system, criminal law has "reclaimed" some of its natural territory; the military jurisdiction remains more intact, but the *Findlay* case signals a clear readiness to use the Human Rights Convention to scrutinise the way in which the process is being implemented. These tendencies have important implications for the conventional perception of diversion, operating of course in the other direction.

Diversion to unofficial and semi-official discipline: some conclusions

Two major questions arise in relation to disciplinary systems which are detached or partly detached from the state's general legal order and the relationship between the two modes of control. The first question involves a problem of justice and appears in two main aspects: the possibility of a duplication of discipline (the "double jeopardy" issue); and the level of due process in extra-legal proceedings. It is not clear that double jeopardy concerns are always satisfactorily resolved and arguably more attention should be given to this moral dilemma, which is sometimes defined away by legalistic argument. Due process concerns have often been addressed by calling upon the scrutiny of the state's legal system (typically through the process of judicial review, but there may be other methods, such as that embodied in the ombudsman principle). The development of this kind of process of review has rendered the relationship between the two types of disciplinary order, the legal and extra-legal, more explicit. But the concerns which lie behind these developments should also inform the response to the second main question—to what extent should criminal offending be diverted into an extra-legal sphere? In this respect, it would seem that the reaction has become increasingly negative, as evidenced by the growing incursion of judicial review or, even more, in the case of prison disciplinary proceedings in the United Kingdom, the recent transfer of jurisdiction to the legal order. Thus the tendency has been in the reverse direction, towards a greater element of influence and supervision on the part of the legal system over extra-legal discipline, either through the incorporation of "legal" values and principles or by explicit procedures of review and appeal.

To a large extent the crucial question in this area would seem to be not so much one of diversion as of an effective and sensible allocation of disciplinary responsibility as between legal and extra-legal authority. It would be helpful to start with a clear recognition of the fact that the same conduct may trigger the interest (and to some extent quite properly) of both the legal system and other disciplinary authorities. A first question should then be: is it necessary for both to deal with the matter? The second question is then, if not, which would be the more appropriate? But on the other hand, if it is necessary for the matter to be dealt with by both, what co-ordination would be necessary between the two, to address issues of double jeopardy and other problems which may arise from the "concurrent jurisdictions"? It may be, for example, that certain types of less serious criminal offending can be more appropriately dealt with solely by the disciplinary procedures of schools, universities and professional and sporting authorities. But, if so, the "diversion" should be on the basis of a clearly thought-out, agreed and consistent policy with provision of appropriate liaison in the interests of longer term policies of controlling delinquency (especially as regards the use of school discipline or other extra-legal resolution of delinquent behaviour). Serious criminal offending gives rise to less tractable issues. In the first place, there is clearly a strong public interest in retention of the prosecution of such offences within the formal system of criminal law. Secondly, in view of the significant consequences of conviction for a serious offence, the impact of disciplinary proceedings related to the same matter ought to be carefully addressed as an element of distributive justice.

In either situation—a possible diversion of less serious offences, or a concurrent handling of more serious offences—the important need is for co-ordination between different authorities and the working out of policy based on the perception that the different regimes have an impact on each other. This last point is illustrated by some recent argument concerning the effective control of corrupt and criminal police officers. Internal police disciplinary proceedings require the same standard of proof as criminal proceedings and cannot rely on evidence used in a criminal trial which has resulted in an acquittal. It has been argued by some senior police that these "due process" restrictions enable a number of corrupt police officers to escape both criminal conviction and disciplinary sanctions (see *The Independent*, July 10, 1997, p. 9). One consequence is said to be the practice on the part of the Crown Prosecution Service of dropping charges against police officers in weaker cases so as not to jeopardise future disciplinary proceedings (in effect, a form of diversion carried out to maximise the possibility of a sanction being applied, if it is predicted that a disciplinary measure will be more easily brought about than conviction from a jury decision). The task of balancing due process concerns against the need for effective control of police corruption and criminal activity is complicated here by the interaction of criminal and disciplinary proceedings. If it is true for instance that an internal disciplinary sanction will be more easily achieved than a jury finding of guilt, is this a matter for concern? The answer to this question will depend on the extent to which a disciplinary sanction is seen as comparable to a criminal conviction in both its function and impact. This same basic question underlies any arguments concerned with either diversion or co-ordination between different systems of discipline.

Chapter 5

Prosecutorial Settlement

Most of the discussion so far has been concerned with diversion in the sense of transferring the response to criminal behaviour to persons or authorities who are distinct from the formal legal order of the State: victims of offending behaviour, employers, and separate disciplinary authorities with a quasi-public character without being part of the general legal system. The discussion which follows here will deal with a species of diversion which operates within the scope of the state's legal order, but directs the case away from the process of prosecution and trial before a criminal court, allowing it to be resolved instead through a form of settlement with the prosecuting authority. In a sense, there is still a process of prosecuting, trial and sanctioning taking place, but this is carried out fully and finally by a single authority whose original and usually perceived role is confined to just one aspect of the process (the earlier stage of prosecution). Prosecution settlement, like many other forms of diversion, is undoubtedly motivated by expediency and perceptions of a cost-effective outcome. And, as is also the case in other contexts, concerns and objections spring from arguments relating to due process and the satisfaction of a broader public interest in prosecution and open trial.

The possibility of "prosecution settlement" in the English and some other legal systems (see the discussion Chap. Eight below as regards methods adopted in Scotland and the Netherlands) arises from the discretionary nature of the formal decision to prosecute. (In some legal systems this decision is not regarded as a matter of discretion but is compulsory for the prosecuting authority, on the basis of the principle of "legality" as opposed to that of "opportunity", although the reality of such compulsory prosecution may be open to question in practice (Van Den Wyngaert (1993)). One aspect of the decision not to prosecute—at least for some specialised agencies, not so much the police or the Crown Prosecution Service in England and Wales—is the legal power to enter into another kind of settlement instead of prosecuting or as a condition for not prosecuting. The classic model for such a process comprises the recovery of property or money and/or the imposition of a financial penalty: for instance, "compounding" by the revenue authorities in the United Kingdom (discussed below), the prosecutor fine in Scotland (see Chap. Eight below), and the Dutch transactie (see Chap. Eight also). In England and Wales, this approach is characteristically favoured in regulatory sectors concerned principally with the implementation of social, economic and financial policy and is inspired more by objectives of securing compliance with such policies rather than notions of retributive justice which characterise the enforcement of "mainstream" criminal law (offences against the person and specific property). The relevant agencies here are bodies such as the revenue collecting departments (such as the Inland Revenue, Customs and Excise, the DVLC, the NTVLRO), the Departments of Employment and of Social Security in relation to benefits fraud, and regulatory authorities such as the Health and Safety Executive and local authority environmental offices. Many of these enforcement agencies have a specific remit and a strong interest in securing long-term compliance. This often results in a flexible attitude for purposes of enforcement and a tendency to reserve criminal sanctions for extreme cases of recalcitrance. Diversion to a more consensual mode of settlement is therefore more likely to be the norm.

Much of the discussion in this chapter will thus be in the context of economic, social and environmental regulation. But there is also a rather different context of prosecution settlement, in which a prosecuting body does not so much settle the matter but refers it on to another agency for a non-criminal and non-penal resolution. This will typically be a situation of "welfare" or "health" diversion, for instance when a mentally disordered person is diverted at this stage to a medical or psychiatric regime. In some respects this is a very different kind of process and certainly involves a very different outcome as compared to a procedure such as revenue compounding, but does have something in common with the longer-term remedial approach often adopted in the context of health and safety and environmental regulation. The connecting point is the decision of the prosecutor not to use criminal proceedings and to engage instead in a more dedicated compliance or remedial strategy. However, examples of "remedial" diversion to other "expert" agencies will be considered separately in Chapter Six.

Revenue collection

Revenue collection is a crucial and necessary element of contemporary government; it is in the public interest to motivate a high level of compliance with revenue obligations, yet the task of controlling evasion is itself huge, given the number of persons subject to the range of taxation and duty regimes (Rowan-Robinson, *et al.* (1990), p. 150). Partly for reasons of resources, therefore, the use of criminal proceedings as a response to revenue evasion—a widespread option for bodies such as the Inland Revenue and Customs and Excise—has been very selective (Rowan-Robinson, *et al.* (1990), p. 150, *et seq.*; Keith Committee (1983), Chaps 16 and 17; Levi (1993), pp. 69–76). Prosecution, when it does take place, is designed to have a deterrent rather than retributive impact, by making a public example of serious offenders while enabling the majority of less culpable evaders to be dealt with by more cost-effective recovery-oriented methods. As the Keith Committee noted, in relation to Customs and Excise: "For many of those who are reluctant payers the existence of the sanctions available to the Department short of prosecution, such as warnings, compounding and seizure of goods in customs cases, is quite sufficient to ensure that they too keep within the law" (Keith Committee (1983), p. 348). But there is also in this context a perception that prosecution before a criminal court is not only unnecessary but is also ineffective from the point of the view of the objectives of the revenue-collecting body. It may be argued for instance that the level of fine imposed following a successful prosecution is so low as to encourage non-compliance and at the same time lost revenue must be recovered (if at all) through time-consuming and therefore costly civil proceedings. The Keith Committee commented in its Report:

> "It has been suggested that fraudsters should be fined substantial sums in lieu of custodial sentences, but there is no indication . . . that the courts have adopted this approach. Indeed, compared with the scale of culpable arrears, the fines imposed in the larger cases are modest." (Keith Committee (1983), p. 357.)

Furthermore:

> ". . . the recovery of arrears in prosecution cases was normally very difficult. The offender did not expect to be detected, and would have made no provision to pay the arrears. In the majority of cases, recovery depended on lengthy civil proceedings and frequently there was little prospect of full recovery, particularly from companies, which might well cease trading without assets." (Keith Committee (1983), p. 364.)

There is thus a deeply rooted sense of the inappropriate nature of criminal proceedings for purposes of dealing with revenue evasion. Court proceedings are resource intensive and the sanctions and remedies may be seen as being of doubtful effectiveness and relevance. The enforcement objective is not so much a process of publicised disapproval and condemnation as the recovery of lost revenue and encouragement of wider compliance, both of which may be more easily achieved by surveillance and negotiated "settlement" of offences.

Such settlement can be achieved by a number of methods. A significant example is the process of compounding used by the Customs and Excise authority in the United Kingdom, to deal in particular with VAT fraud (five out of every six cases of VAT fraud are dealt with in this way, according to the Keith Committee). If Customs and Excise feel that there is sufficient evidence to prosecute successfully a VAT or customs fraud they may offer not to do so (for an example of such an offer, see Note 34 of the Keith Committee's Report) in return for payment of arrears, penalties and compensation. If the offer is accepted, the terms are embodied in a written contractual agreement. The (non-) taxpayer gains a publicity and stigma-free settlement; the outcome for Customs and Excise is a cost-effective recovery of revenue coupled with a penalty. Below evasion of a certain amount (stated by the House of Commons Public Accounts Committee in 1988 to be £75,000 (Public Accounts Committee (1988)) there appears to be a presumption in favour of compounding, although generally a certain number of criteria have to be satisfied: for instance—apart from the amount of revenue evaded—the nature of the fraud, the need to deter potential offenders, the best interests of law enforcement and the revenue system, the involvement of accountants and lawyers, persistent offending, and the need to protect society from dangerous offenders are some of the factors to be taken into account (Keith Committee (1983), pp. 349–50). Compounding is therefore a well-established and regular response to VAT and customs evasion, with a clear basis in legislation (Customs and Excise Management Act 1979, s. 152) and judicial approval (*Patel v. Spencer* [1976] 1 W.L.R. 1268). In this context, it is also a good example of "presumptive" diversion. (For further details and discussion, see Buckett (1986), Mowbray (1988).)

Over the last ten years, Customs and Excise have also made significant use of civil penalties as distinct from criminal prosecution to deal with a range of VAT offences. At issue here are a number of "regulatory" delinquencies, in particular the failure to make VAT returns, to provide certain types of information, maintain documentation or pay tax by a due date. Previously, much of this conduct was classified as criminal offending but was prosecuted very selectively, partly for reasons of resources, partly through a reluctance to use the criminal sanction outside cases of persistent recalcitrance and without first providing warnings. The Keith Committee referred to a substantial international debate concerning the use of criminal sanctions in relation to such conduct and the view that "non-penal sanctions were more effective than penal sanctions in dealing with regulatory misbehaviour, and that measures such as licence suspension, forfeiture of illegal goods and civil penalties might be more drastic and more appropriate than prosecution". The Committee further suggested, in relation to "regulatory" infringements, that investigation of dishonest conduct in tax matters in a "civil" style, reinforced by inducements was generally welcome to the witnesses interviewed in its inquiries, who were also of the view that the lower civil burden of proof would not be unfair to taxpayers being dealt with in such cases (Keith Committee (1983), pp. 394–400). The Committee therefore recommended that a number of regulatory breaches be decriminalised and instead be subject to a more cost-effective and more juridically appropriate system of civil penalties. These, in the view of the Committee, would be more certain and practical in their application, being tax-geared—that is, would automatically relate the penalty to the size of the default and would take explicit account of the frequency of the default. Following this, a new civil penalty code was introduced in stages between 1985 and 1988. Section 19 of the Finance Act 1985 provided for a default surcharge as a percentage of the outstanding tax. A five per cent surcharge is payable on the first default, and for each subsequent default the surcharge is increased in stages of five per cent to a maximum of 30 per cent for the sixth subsequent default during a surcharge period. However, the imposition of any surcharge will be preceded by a warning (a "surcharge liability notice"), designed to promote compliance at an earlier stage.

The civil penalty system therefore comprises a statutory model of automatic diversion—in effect, a decriminalisation—into a process of regular and strictly graduated administrative penality. However, while this procedure shares the cost-effective character of compounding, it differs in its lack of discretion and this marks it apart from many other diversionary processes. Indeed, its automated and outline operation is more reminiscent of the way in which a great deal of minor motoring delinquency is dealt with in Britain. Sure enough, there is a clear element of penality, but the process is very predictable, uncontested and highly bureaucratic. As such it is manifestly different from the classical paradigm of full criminal procedure—time-consuming, costly, public and unpredictable—as well as from the familiar type of diversion which takes the offender into a less visible and less formal but still discretionary context of decision-making. Early estimates of the impact of the civil penalty system for VAT offences were favourable in terms of securing compliance; at the end of 1987–88 it was calculated that 80 per cent of returns and payment of VAT was being received in time and during that year the outstanding amount of VAT at any one time had been reduced by £158 million (Customs and Excise (1988); Rowan-Robinson, *et al.* (1990), pp. 165–70).

While the use of compounding and civil penalties accounts for a significant proportion of the enforcement activity of Customs and Excise, criminal proceedings (as has been noted) are still employed in a minority of cases. It is clear that the decision to prosecute in such cases is largely triggered by a number of identifiable aggravating features. Most importantly, perhaps, persistent offending will eventually bring about criminal proceedings (the notorious prosecution and conviction of jockey Lester Piggott followed a persistent failure to declare VAT liability). Secondly, it appears that collusion on the part of lawyers, accountants and officials will aggravate the perceived seriousness of the offence and criminal proceedings may well be directed against such "advisors", whose own role is important for purposes of securing compliance, as a kind of "anti-corruption" signal. Similarly, sophisticated and well-planned strategies to evade tax payments will be regarded seriously (such as the marketing of a computer system with an in-built VAT suppression facility (Customs and Excise (1987)). It also appears that certain sectors are regarded as "high risk" in relation to VAT fraud and so justify the investment of resources in large-scale criminal prosecutions to deal with "organised" criminality in these commercial contexts (especially the gold and jewellery business and the construction industry (Customs and Excise (1987)). Enforcement strategies employed by Customs and Excise can thus be presented in terms of a pyramid, combining a calculus of seriousness of offending behaviour and of cost-effective approaches to recovering or pre-empting loss of revenue (Figure 1).

Figure 1

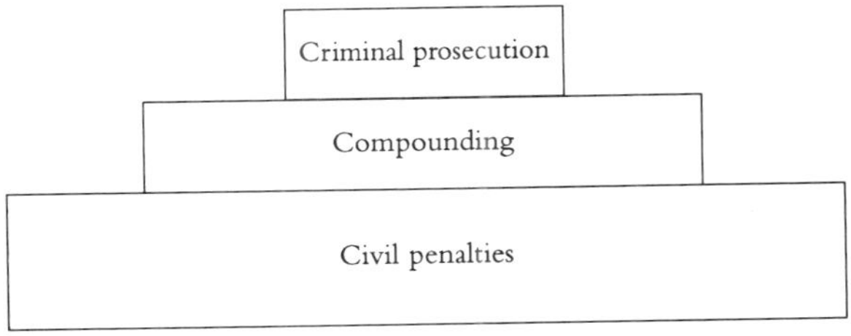

The other principal revenue collecting body in the United Kingdom, the Inland Revenue, is similarly very selective in its resort to criminal proceedings for purposes of enforcement. Statistics cited by the Keith Committee for the years 1977—1981 indicate a consistent rate of 95 per cent negotiated settlements to five per cent criminal prosecutions (Keith Committee (1983), p. 382). Levi ((1993), p. 73) gives figures for 1990—1991: 51,668 settlements, and 252 prosecutions. Cases are selected for prosecution according to criteria similar to those used by Customs and Excise: "heinous" cases (for instance, if there is evidence of collusion between the taxpayer and others; if documents were forged with intent to deceive the Revenue; using a "smoke screen" of co-operation while actually withholding significant information); "recidivists" who have previously benefited from negotiated settlements; and "status" offenders (professional advisors on tax matters and those involved in tax administration (Keith Committee (1983), pp. 457–8). Inland Revenue settlement comprises elements of Customs and Excise compounding and civil penalties—a careful negotiation in which the Revenue firstly outlines its claims against the taxpayer and the possibility of liability to pay default interest, then presents an inducement to "come clean" in a so-called *Hansard* Extract (named from the text of a Parliamentary question and answer in 1944), and finally awaits an "offer" from the taxpayer which, if and when accepted by the Revenue, forms the basis of a contractually binding settlement (for a detailed account of the process, see the Keith Committee (1983), Chap. 17). Moreover, the manner of the negotiation is deliberately non-oppressive, in order to maximise the attainment of long-term compliance (Cook (1989), p. 152).

Customs and Excise and the Inland Revenue are sometimes referred to as the "Revenue Departments" (as in the title of the Keith Committee—"Committee on the Enforcement Powers of the Revenue Departments"—whose terms of reference were confined to these two bodies). Other revenue collecting bodies in the United Kingdom have a more specialised remit, such as road vehicle licensing, TV licensing, national insurance contributions and community charges. In such contexts individual taxpayers' liability tends to be smaller and less complex than is the case with income tax and VAT; enforcement options then tend to be more cut-and-dried and there is less scope for negotiated settlement. In the case of vehicle licences, for instance, the enforcement options seem to be prosecution, mitigated penalties or no action, the last arising often on account of difficulties in tracing the owners of vehicles or because of the small amount of outstanding duty (House of Commons Public Accounts Committee (1986); Rowan-Robinson, *et al.* (1990), pp. 153–4). The complexity and scale of the particular revenue collecting process therefore appears to determine the possible extent and perceived advantages of diversion, and in particular a negotiated settlement, as an alternative to criminal proceedings.

Welfare fraud

Fraudulent claims in relation to welfare benefits (see Social Security Administration Act 1992, s. 112) fall within another specialised area of criminal prosecution, handled by the Department of Social Security. It has been customary to contrast the enforcement policy used in relation to such benefit fraud with that employed by bodies such as Customs and Excise and the Inland Revenue as regards tax evasion. A much higher proportion of the former type of offending is prosecuted: a peak figure for the United Kingdom of 20,105 prosecutions for alleged benefit fraud in 1980–1981 (Cook (1989), p. 153), as compared with the prosecution figures noted above in relation to VAT and income tax evasion. However, there occurred and interesting and significant change of policy on the part of the (then) Department of Health and Social Security after 1980. During the 1970s the number of prosecutions for benefit fraud had regularly increased (Golding and Middleton (1982); NACRO (1986a), but following the Rayner Report (the Report of the Joint Department of Employment and Department of Health and Social Security Scrutiny on Payment of Benefits to Unemployed People) in 1981, there was a shift from reactive to proactive enforcement, paying particular attention to perceived high risk areas of benefit fraud. At the same time, a greater emphasis was being placed on cost-effectiveness rather than pursuing a retributive policy of enforcement. As was stated in a DHSS internal policy document:

> "In the past, as many cases as possible were pursued to prosecution but, in the future, while the deterrent effect of successful prosecution will continue to be borne in mind, the cessation of a claim might be regarded in appropriate cases as the most effective way of dealing with the matter." (Quoted from the DHSS' *Fraud Investigator's Guide* in Moore (1981).)

In effect, this aligned enforcement policy in relation to benefit fraud much more with the approach traditionally employed by the revenue collecting departments, shifting to a preference for administrative sanctions such as withdrawal of benefits and measures of recovery, and so leaving much of the sanctioning actually in the hands of the prosecuting body. The outcome can be quantified, firstly in terms of the level of prosecutions (a decline from 20,105 to 8,090 supplementary benefit frauds prosecuted as between 1981 and 1987 (Cook (1989), p. 182)) and secondly in terms of the amount of money "saved" by persuading claimants to withdraw claims (net benefit saved rising from £11 million in 1984–1985 to £55 million in 1987–1988 (Department of Employment (1988)).

But this policy of diversion has attracted criticism. In the first place, there has been some apprehension that negotiated outcomes (benefit claims being given up) are brought about through non-prosecution interviews in relation to cases where prosecution would probably have not succeeded because of evidentiary or procedural requirements (Moore (1981), p. 138). This is the familiar concern about the lower level of legal safeguard often found in the context of diversionary practice. The DHSS appeared to appreciate this kind of criticism, since its internal *Fraud Investigator's Guide* advises officers:

> "Take care to avoid any approach which could lay [you] open to an accusation of pressuring the complainant into withdrawing his claim. For example, you should not suggest a bargain—'Admit you are not entitled and we won't prosecute'. The only justification for terminating a person's benefit . . . is that facts have definitely been established that show that he is not entitled." (Moore (1981), p. 138.)

Yet there was some evidence that DHSS investigators on the ground were not always adhering to such guidelines; for instance, the Liverpool Welfare Rights Centre reported a number of cases where it considered that benefit had been withdrawn on inadequate evidence and when it subsequently brought pressure to bear on the DHSS, the benefit payments were invariably reinstated (Moore (1981), p. 139).

Another risk associated with such non-prosecution settlement of suspected welfare abuse is the possibility of greater inconsistency than would occur in a more publicly visible context of prosecution. This is clearly illustrated by research into a related area of welfare benefit, housing benefit as administered by local authorities (Loveland (1989)). Entitlement to housing benefit would be affected by evidence of cohabitation and this therefore became an important concern for officials administering the system. Loveland's research uncovered a divergence of practice, explicable in terms of ideology. On the one hand, in a north London, Labour controlled "new urban left" authority, officials employed a non-intrusive approach: taking pains to avoid asking unnecessary questions which, if honestly answered, might reduce claimants' benefits (Loveland (1989), pp. 30–31). In contrast, officials in a Conservative controlled authority in the South Midlands and another in south London were zealously intrusive in their enquiries: "if suspicions are aroused, but no incontrovertible evidence uncovered, claimants are warned that they might face prosecution if they continue with their claim. Officers regard withdrawal as a 'victory' in such circumstances" (Loveland (1989), p.33); and "threats of prosecution are a favoured form of bluff, as is a warning of continuous surveillance of a claimant's home . . . he finds threats an effective way to reduce his overall workload, given that his primary concern is with saving and recovering money rather than with punishing offenders" (Loveland (1989), p. 36).

A second main criticism is that there remain, despite the change in enforcement policy, a significant number of welfare fraud prosecutions compared to revenue fraud prosecutions. As Cook comments: "the prosecution of a small selection of the most serious cases of tax fraud is considered an adequate deterrent to the unacceptable spread of tax evasion, yet almost twenty time that number of prosecutions seem to be required in order to deter the supplementary benefit fraudster" (Cook (1989), p. 154). These different levels of selectivity in prosecution have been widely criticised as an unjustified discrimination, especially in view of the relative estimated total loss suffered through the two types of fraud—more people are involved and more money is lost through tax fraud (NACRO (1986b)).

It may be argued that this differential response springs at least in part from different perceptions of delinquency: *failing to give* part of one's income to the state is not criminal in the same way as *taking* the taxpayers' money. To the extent that this view does inform both official and public perceptions, the differentiation is then a problem of culture and ideology. Whatever the reasons, the outcome is clearly a matter of concern in terms of distributive justice. It is true that both revenue and welfare fraudsters are subject to penalties and procedures for recovery, but these processes are likely to be very different—the courteous and business-like settlement of revenue evasion as compared to the more intrusive and threatening non-prosecution of fraudulent welfare claimants; and the widespread use of discreet, non stigmatising revenue settlements as compared to a more frequent public prosecution of welfare frauds. Whether prosecuted or diverted into informal settlement, the alleged welfare fraudster is subject to a more severe regime. Yet at the same time questions have been raised as to the real extent of the loss arising from welfare fraud. One estimate, for instance, is that the amount of underpayment of benefit to claimants entitled to it may exceed the cost of overpayment (National Audit Office (1992)).

Health, safety and protection of the environment

Public health, safety at work, and conservation and protection of the environment may be seen as to some extent interrelated fields of regulation, geared towards a broad protection of the public well-being. Within the United Kingdom a range of agencies are responsible for giving effect to such protective regulations, in particular the relevant departments of local government authorities, the National Rivers Authority (NRA), the Nature Conservancy Council and the Factory Inspectorate. However, there has been until recently a common theme to enforcement in this general field: that, despite the availability of action through criminal proceedings, there is a clear preference for the use of other processes directed towards achieving compliance and prosecution is generally perceived as a means of last resort or reserved for extreme cases. In other words, from a criminal law perspective, diversion has been far and away the norm and diversion here means some kind of resolution of the matter by the body charged with enforcement of the regulations, which is also the would-be prosecutor.

This preferred approach has been very clear in the field of health and safety and has been extensively investigated and analysed over the last thirty years. Carson's earlier study of the approach taken by the Factories Inspectorate (Carson (1970)), revealed in a sample of recorded offences a resort to criminal prosecution in only 1.5 per cent of the cases. Carson commented that the inspectors in the study "did not see themselves as members of an industrial police force primarily concerned with the apprehension and subsequent punishment of offenders . . . they perceived their major function to be that of securing compliance . . ." (Carson (1970), p. 392). The type of action taken in the majority of cases was notification of matters requiring attention. A later study carried out in the mid 1980s by Baldwin of the enforcement practice of the Factory Inspectorate, working by then under the 1974 Health and Safety at Work Act, revealed little change: "Prosecutions are comparatively rarely used in seeking compliance, largely because of resource implications, but Improvement and Prohibition Notices (which order respectively remedial actions to be taken to a time scale or work to be stopped pending such actions) are used more frequently" (Baldwin (1990), p. 323). Research undertaken at the end of the 1980s showed that prosecution is much more likely to follow an accident than result from a basic inspection, but still only about one per cent of investigations overall lead to a prosecution (Hutter and Lloyd-Bostock (1990), pp. 417–18). Health and safety is a context in which co-operation between regulator and regulated is seen, both in the United Kingdom and elsewhere, as a largely successful strategy in securing longer-term compliance and so in improving standards of safety. For that reason, any major shift in a more punitive direction (either using criminal law or a more penal approach on the part of the regulators themselves) is unlikely (Hawkins (1990).

A similar approach has customarily prevailed in relation to environmental protection and conservation. Research in both Britain (Richardson, Ogus and Burrows (1983); Hawkins (1984); Hutter (1988)) and in the United States (Hartung (1950); Kagan (1978)) has confirmed that in this context, in Hutter's words: "regulatory agencies have been found to adopt an enforcement style which relies upon negotiation, bargaining, education, and the offering of advice as the means of gaining compliance with the law, as opposed to an enforcement style which relies upon formal action and the imposition of sanctions" (Hutter (1988), pp 5–6). This is said to represent an "accommodative" or "compliance" strategy of enforcement which is co-operative and conciliatory in style and the aim of which is to secure compliance through the remedy of existing problems. Prosecution, once again, is seen as a measure of last resort. Having said that, the "accommodative" approach should perhaps be most usefully viewed as a continuum, embracing softer or harder tactics. Hutter's research, for example, compares a number of environmental health departments, all located within the same accommodative approach, but employing either "persuasive" or "insistent" strategies, the latter being less benevolent and less flexible than the former ("officers working within the insistent strategy would not be prepared to spend a long time patiently cajoling offenders into compliance: there were fairly clearly defined limits to their tolerance and they expected a more immediate response ...") (Hutter (1988), p. 157).

However, in more recent years there has been a significant shift in the attitude towards the use of prosecution in the environmental protection field. Increasing concern about the level of environmental degradation and more specifically the need to give effect to more well-defined quality objectives emanating from the E.C. have modified the traditional attitude towards enforcement (see, *e.g.* House of Commons Environmental Committee (1987)). As the environmental protection lobby has gained wider public support and participation, the level of opprobrium associated with environmental offending has increased, so altering the sense of criminality inherent in this kind of breach. Ball and Bell summarise this development in the following terms:

> "These changes have brought about a retreat from the co-operational approach to a new, more ambivalent standard. That is not to say that the enforcing agencies are ambivalent as to the difficulties faced by industrialists. However, they are now balancing the co-operational and the confrontational approaches in order to achieve environmental quality improvements." (Ball and Bell (1995), p. 115.)

During the 1990s the two principal agencies within the United Kingdom concerned with the enforcement of environmental protection rules, HM Inspectorate of Pollution (HMIP), established in 1987, and the NRA, established in 1989, have brought a greater number of prosecutions. This is especially true of the NRA (which has a larger staff) and began its operations with the expressed intention (in its Report for 1989–90) to implement a more rigorous and penal kind of enforcement. Whereas in the period 1980—1987 the regional water authorities had collectively prosecuted between 91 and 254 cases of water pollution each year, the NRA had prosecuted 592 cases in 1990, with a formal caution being issued in a further 206 cases (where the polluter admitted the offence). In comparison, the HMIP was resorting to prosecution in a much smaller, though still increasing number of cases (12 prosecutions in 1991–92, compared to ten in the preceding four years) (Ball and Bell (1995), p. 449; Hughes (1992), pp. 62–3; Rowan-Robinson and Ross (1994)).

But these developments must be kept in perspective. Despite the shifting attitude within enforcement agencies and the increasing number of prosecutions, criminal proceedings still represent a minority response overall. This is particularly so in relation to the related issue of conservation and protection of sites of special scientific interest. While more than 250 incidents of damage to such sites (at least half of which may amount to criminal offences) are reported each year, prosecutions by the Nature Conservancy Council occur on average about twice a year (Rowan-Robinson and Ross (1994), p. 211). Also, although both HMIP and the NRA are centralised prosecuting agencies who have embarked upon their enforcement tasks with clear and bullish "mission statements" there may well remain, for some time at least, a gap between rhetoric and practice, due to both culture and resources. This sense of outcome not yet matching intention is detectable for instance in Ball and Bell's analysis of recent trends in enforcement. On the one hand they comment that the traditional image of enforcement agents "collaborating with industry over a table in a room at the factory with a cup of tea while 'problem-solving' is fast disappearing". Yet it is also conceded that co-operation between the regulators and the regulated has far from disappeared: "in reality the general consensus between the two sides of the enforcement system is never likely to break down fully as detection and prosecution of every breach would be impracticable and undesirable" (Ball and Bell (1995), pp. 133–38). Indeed, it may still be questioned whether a "tougher" regime of enforcement making more use of criminal proceedings could be sensibly taken so very far in a context such as environmental protection. The central argument of the Robens Committee in 1972, in relation to health and safety at work, still appears more widely compelling—that many breaches do not have a simple causal origin nor a clear moral attribution, so raising doubts as the suitability of criminal sanctions (Robens Committee (1972), Chap. 9). It is also interesting to note that decisions to prosecute environmental protection breaches in recent years have been as much triggered by the harm caused by the breach as by any other factor; it is the "serious incident" in terms of damage that is almost inevitably prosecuted. Moreover, such prosecutions may skirt around the issue of moral culpability, especially since convictions are usually obtained on the basis of strict liability (see for instance *CPC v. NRA* [1995] Env. L. Rep. 131).

It remains very difficult to assess the relative impact of criminal proceedings and other types of response in this context of enforcement. For instance it is intriguing to note that more recently prosecution rates in the water sector seem to be falling while there is evidence that water quality has improved. The NRA considers that both outcomes may be attributable to its more confrontational policy (Ball and Bell (1995), p. 138), but this is clearly difficult to establish one way or the other. At the same time, Hawkins' earlier perception (Hawkins (1988)) should be remembered—that a high (and swelling) prosecution rate does not necessarily foster the impression that the situation is under control (indeed it may create the opposite impression). On the other hand, selective enforcement of "high profile" cases can promote a public sense of vigorous action where it is most required. For a number of reasons, therefore—limited resources, a persistent non-confrontational enforcement culture, and a natural desire to foster an impression of effective enforcement—a policy of selective prosecution may remain the norm in the context of environmental protection.

Evaluation

The instances of diversion via prosecutorial settlement discussed above—and also in other comparable contexts not specifically considered here, such as consumer protection, or building and planning controls (Rowan-Robinson, *et al.* (1990)—to a large extent have a number of features in common, most importantly perhaps the fact that these prosecuting bodies have a specialised remit and a dominant concern with achieving compliance in a cost-effective manner as distinct from a mission of bringing wrongdoers to justice. The point made by Dickens in 1970 as regards local authority regulators serves equally well for many contemporary special regulatory bodies:

> "Local authorities appear to regard their statutory duties as imposing upon them an obligation to act to achieve prescribed results, and not simply an obligation to enforce the strict provisions of the law *per se*. They are aware of being judged practically and politically by the efficiency with which they secure the purposes of the law . . . If their initiatives prove ineffective then they may consider recourse to the courts, but in general this will be a last resort." (Dickens (1970), p. 631.)

A point worth bearing in mind is that this kind of enforcement agency is part of a public body dedicated to the objectives of a particular area of policy. The achievement of those policy goals by the most effective means (and, given an inevitable limitation of resources, effective usually means cost-effective) is therefore a mission somewhat different from that of the general police force, with its concern of enforcing norms of general behaviour for the sake of those norms and ultimately a sense of public justice. Indeed, it is a recurring comment that regulators in the specialised sectors do not see themselves as police.

All of this has implications for a general theory of diversion and of the criminal process. It may even be asked in what way the phenomenon discussed in this chapter is in any sense a kind of diversion and how relevant criminal law and criminal proceedings may be considered to be in such a context. There is a striking preference for "settlement", in the interests of longer-term compliance and both recovering loss and preventing future damage. This is manifest in the enforcement strategies of the main revenue departments and in the traditional conciliatory style of enforcement in the context of health and safety and environmental regulation. In the area of welfare fraud the "non-prosecution interview" technique has been adopted with enthusiasm in recent years; and despite the confrontational approach espoused by the NRA, prosecution is still used only in a minority of cases to deal with water pollution. A range of cultural and pragmatic considerations render it unlikely that criminal proceedings will emerge as much more of a significant option for these types of enforcement agency.

This is therefore another situation in which the classic image of court process and conventional penal sanctioning needs to be revised. The significance of this last claim springs from the range of offending conduct, the number of statutory offences, the quantity of infractions, and the social and economic cost of breaches of the regulatory codes. Admittedly, this is not classic criminal behaviour which is at issue, yet by the close of the twentieth century "regulatory" enforcement represents a significant aspect of social control in everyday life.

However, simply to accept the "normality" of enforcement agency "settlement" in this area does not resolve every critical question. Two issues in particular still deserve careful scrutiny. The first may be summed up as the problem of fair treatment and this in itself comprises a number of "justice" problems: for instance, the risk of oppressive treatment of the weaker amongst the regulated, such as the welfare fraudsters, and, linked to that concern, the problem of differential treatment, for instance, as between welfare and revenue frauds or as between different kinds of polluting activity. The range of enforcement agencies involved in the regulatory field and the generally lower level of visibility of disposal by "settlement" inevitably gives rise to concerns about distributive justice and questions of how best to address those concerns.

Secondly, the specifically social, economic and environmental context of much of the offending behaviour under discussion in this chapter gives the subject a certain, though not absolute degree of homogeneity. The substantive context may be quite different from classic criminal law, but there are also different species of culpability within the regulatory field itself. In particular, there may be argued to be a moral distinction between calculated breaches leading to immediate personal gain, as exemplified by welfare and revenue frauds, and on the other hand breaches of standards which are less easily attributable to particular individuals and are sometimes more diffuse in their injurious impact, typically the environmental offence. This distinction has an impact most obviously on the question of sanctions, in that penalties may appear more appropriate in the former kind of case, and supervisory sanctions more so in the latter kind. The choice of sanction in turn has a bearing on issues of process, in that penalties import greater stigma and thus concern for due process in the proceeding leading to their imposition. It is unsurprising, therefore, to observe the resort to financial penalties and disadvantages in relation to fraudsters, albeit in an informal context, and "round the table problem-solving" in the case of health, safety and environmental breaches. But it should be reiterated that in both situations questions remain as to the desirable level of legal protection and external scrutiny for purposes of ensuring a fair outcome, both for the alleged offender and for that part of society injured by the breach.

Chapter 6

Diversion to Other Agencies: Mental Health and Mediation

The previous chapter considered a number of significant instances of prosecution settlement of criminal cases: diversion in a technical sense, by means of the prosecuting body itself resolving the matter, usually through some process of negotiation with the offending party. This chapter will consider briefly examples of diversion by prosecuting agencies in another, perhaps more conventional sense—where the matter is referred on to another agency which is perceived as being more appropriate for purposes of finally dealing with the issue. Underlying this kind of diversion is a clear sense of the unsuitability of criminal proceedings, or further criminal proceedings, usually on account of well-defined, distinctive characteristics of either the offending conduct or the alleged offender. Two particular categories of case will be considered in this context; first, the situation of persons considered to be suffering from some kind of mental disorder; secondly, a very different kind of situation, involving in essence a dispute between two or more parties which could perhaps be most effectively resolved through mediation rather than casting the matter in the form of a criminal offence to be dealt with by formal legal proceedings. But both these situations presuppose the availability of another agency with appropriate expertise to deal with the matter. In both cases also, the offending behaviour is for practical purposes re-defined, from being a criminal infraction to being a problem which requires a more constructive and pro-active and less condemnatory approach to its resolution. The discussion in this chapter does not set out to be an exhaustive account of such techniques; for instance, the use of "caution plus" by the police may be considered to fall within this category, but is dealt with in the wider context of police cautioning in Chapter Seven.

Mentally disordered "offenders"

The diversion of mentally disordered alleged offenders from prosecution, trial and certain types of disposal is now an established element of official policy in Britain and elsewhere and as such has been the subject of extensive commentary and research (see, for instance, Fennell (1991); Peay (1994)). The underlying rationale for diversion of the mentally disordered is that a substantial lack of responsibility for behaviour, in both psychological and moral terms, undermines the justification for using criminal proceedings and criminal sanctions. This is a classic opportunity for application of the principle "treatment, not punishment", in that the interests of both society and of the disordered person are likely to be best served by a response employing appropriate psychiatric approaches (including non-penal protective measures in the case of diagnosed potentially dangerous behaviour). Thus Home Office Circular 66/90, on provision for mentally disordered offenders (Home Office (1990b)), enjoins that the mentally disordered should not be prosecuted if this is not required by the public interest. It should also be borne in mind that there are opportunities for diversion at later points in criminal proceedings once a prosecution is well under way, at the remand, trial and sentencing stages, under a number of provisions laid down in the Mental Health Act 1983 and the Criminal Procedure (Insanity and Unfitness to Plead) Act 1991 (Fennell (1991); Peay (1994)). In legal terms there is thus no doubt as to the underlying principle. Its practical application is, however, more problematical.

The major difficulty arises out of the concept and diagnosis of the various categories of mental disorder; identification of somebody as being mentally disordered and the determination of the practical and moral consequences of such a diagnosis are far from straightforward. This is the point at which the caveat in Circular 66/90 enters the picture—if prosecution is not required by the public interest. On the one hand, a decision may be clear enough in the case of a severe mental illness, such as a schizophrenic condition, but any diversion pre-supposes the condition is identified and diagnosed at the appropriate time. On the other hand, a minor disorder may not present such a compelling case for diversion in terms of either the possibilities for psychiatric treatment or the lack of moral responsibility for the behaviour in question. Yet a mild disorder may lead to minor offending and so raise the question of diversion on other grounds. "Public interest" (as usual) begs a number of further questions. There is also another possible problem of whether diversion, if desirable in principle, is feasible in practical terms—for instance, is the condition amenable to treatment, and are the resources available?

Police referrals

The Mental Health legislation of 1983 clearly contemplates the possibility of diversion to psychiatric assessment or treatment at the very earliest stage, when an offence first comes to official notice. Police officers have powers under section 136 of the 1983 Act to remove to a "place of safety" any person found in a place to which the public have access, who appears to be suffering from a mental disorder and to be in need of care and control. Detention in the place of safety may be for up to 72 hours and the objective is to enable examination by a doctor and a social worker, to assess what may be appropriate for purposes of care and treatment. The Home Office Circular of 1990 urges that the place of safety should if possible be a hospital rather than a police station.

It appears that there is a significant amount of experience and willingness on the part of the police in Britain in relation to such referrals, acting either under section 136 of the Mental Health Act or more informally. The Metropolitan Police appear to make more use of the procedure under section 136 than police elsewhere in the United Kingdom, where more referrals are probably made on an informal basis (for instance, in 1986, of a total of 1521 hospital admissions under section 136, 1322 were in London (Fahy (1989))). Not surprisingly, the police are inclined to make referrals in cases of manifestly disturbed behaviour: studies of the characteristics of police-referred patients reveal a high incidence of serious mental illness (Rogers and Faulkner (1987)), and of socially disorganised and unsupported individuals. Police attention is usually alerted by bizarre kinds of behaviour, much of which could be charged as criminal offences. It also appears, in quantitative terms, to be a predominantly metropolitan phenomenon. As long ago as 1965 Rollin described the role of London as a "sump ... into which chronic psychotics from all over the United Kingdom ... are drained" (Rollin (1965)). On the other hand, care should be taken not to read too much into the urban/rural distinction as regards the qualitative aspect of such police referrals—other research has revealed few differences as between the character of urban and rural police referrals; both, for instance, have in common a high rate of psychosis among those referred (Fahy (1987)). Local organisational factors are more likely to have an impact on the rate of referrals and may help to explain apparent regional differences. For instance, in one piece of research, different referral rates as between two neighbouring London boroughs appeared to relate to different levels of psychiatric and social work help forthcoming in the respective boroughs (Bean (1986)). Other research has detected a higher probability of Afro-Caribbean persons being referred under section 136 (Littlewood (1986)).

It is difficult to evaluate the police role in making these referrals since there are no exact or reliable figures for the number not referred who might have been, nor indeed of informal referrals which appear to be more significant outside of London. A crucial question concerns the ability of police officers to identify appropriate cases for referral to psychiatric assessment. It seems that externally bizarre cases are readily taken up by the police in this way but that less obvious cases may continue to go to prosecution and trial. For instance, it appears easier for the police to identify possible cases of schizophrenia than of clinical depression (Gudjonsson, *et al.* (1994)). It also seems that more serious offences, especially if they are perceived to indicate a threat to public safety, will still be sent forward for prosecution (Robertson, Pearson and Gibb (1995)). As regards the view of police officers themselves, research carried out in the 1980s revealed a feeling on the part of most police officers that they had received insufficient training to deal with this kind of case (Dunn and Fahey (1987)). But more recent research does not suggest so much of a lack of confidence (Robertson, Pearson and Gibb (1995)).

The general conclusion to be drawn about police diversion of the mentally disordered would seem to be that it still accounts for a relatively small proportion of the total number of people dealt with by the police and that there remain difficulties in effectively identifying many who might be appropriate cases for referral. Nonetheless, it is potentially a very useful procedure; as Burney and Pearson comment: "a police power which enables a mentally disordered person to be taken directly to hospital or another 'place of safety' for assessment without being charged would seem to offer the most sensible and readily accessible diversion route in many situations." (Burney and Pearson (1995)).

"Court-based assessments"

Apart from the power to remove to a place of safety, there is no other precise statutory power for those involved in prosecutorial decision-making to refer mentally disordered persons to other agencies. However, Circular 66/90 urges that, if place of safety powers have not been used, the police should consider a number of options: charging the offender, administering a caution, or thirdly whether it would be in the public interest to use compulsory "civil" admission to psychiatric treatment under the Mental Health legislation. This last option requires a court order and pre-supposes effective co-operation between a number of agencies—the police, the Crown Prosecution Service, the courts and health authorities. A number of statutory provisions (in particular, Mental Health Act 1983, ss. 2, 3, 35 and 36) could be used for purposes of a psychiatric order, but for such an outcome to be achieved as soon as possible, what is required is, in Peay's words:

> "an innovative and pro-active approach of getting psychiatrist, Crown Prosecution Service, mentally disordered alleged offender and sentencer together at court. They aim to prevent offenders having to be remanded in custody for reports merely because they do not enjoy stable community ties or because of the absence of bail hostels; ultimately disposal into a custodial setting should be avoided where a therapeutic one would be more appropriate." (Peay (1994), at p. 1134.)

One of the advantages of a court-based assessment leading to diversion at a relatively early stage is the opportunity to avoid lengthy remands in prison, the beginning of a trial or even the whole process of trial and conviction, when during any of those later stages it may be decided to make an order for psychiatric treatment under section 37 of the Mental Health Act or under the Criminal Procedure Act of 1991. If it is thought appropriate to divert an alleged offender for purposes of assessment and/or treatment, it is clearly preferable to do so as early as possible and to avoid both the cost and the trauma of further criminal proceedings. At the same time a court-based assessment allows the wider public interest—including issues of public protection, the interests of victims and the seriousness of alleged offences—to be taken into account.

Any such court-based assessment needs to be as fully-informed as possible and therefore requires inter-agency co-operation. Such liaison as a pre-requisite for a system of court assessments is outlined by James and Hamilton on the basis of operating a liaison service to Clerkenwell Magistrates' Court in London:

> "The pre-requisites . . . are the availability of psychiatrists to take on the work and agreement of the court in question to host such a service. The agency best placed to negotiate the setting-up of liaison schemes is the probation service, who has regular contact with both psychiatrists and the court. The key figure at the court is the Senior Chief Clerk who . . . is able to facilitate the practical aspects of a liaison scheme." (James and Hamilton (1992), p. 168.)

The Clerkenwell scheme, established in 1990, deals with referrals by magistrates, prosecuting or defence lawyers, probation officers or prison authorities, but in relation to persons already remanded in custody. Assessment and liaison may be a complicated process, involving discussion at one end with the Crown Prosecution Service about discontinuing proceedings in order to make a "civil" hospital admission possible and with the hospital authorities at the other end for a place to be made available (receiving hospitals usually prefer to admit under the civil rather than the criminal sections of the Mental Health Act). The development of and future prospects for such liaison schemes would appear to depend largely on the availability of resources, or more precisely to be a matter of bringing about some re-allocation of resources to support this kind of liaison (James and Hamilton (1992), pp. 175–6).

The ideal route for this kind of diversion would appear to be quite simply: decision not to prosecute—court-based psychiatric assessment—order for appropriate treatment under the civil provisions of the mental health legislation. The main problem is that the legislation itself does not specifically provide for such a process. Present practice is therefore essentially the outcome of local initiatives with a consequent regional variation and is very much at the mercy of local policy and resourcing priorities. Nor is there any clear institutional responsibility for activating this kind of procedure, although it seems to be generally agreed that the probation service is best placed to play the co-ordinating role. Existing practice appears to have very much a metropolitan base. A report published in 1993, for instance, showed that 15 out of 18 inner London courts had their own psychiatric assessment programme or access to one nearby, but that this was so in the case of only eight of 18 outer London courts. Nor is it clear what precise form the diversionary mechanism should take in terms of personnel or details of procedure. The Islington Mentally Disordered Offenders Project (IMDOP), set up in 1992 at Highbury Corner Magistrates' Court, for example, employed a psychiatric nurse as a full-time Mental Health Court Worker, with a base in the Court Probation Office (Burney and Pearson (1995), p. 297). But more generally there is enthusiasm for the use of inter-agency panels modelled on those which have been established in the context of juvenile justice. Burney and Pearson point out that such an approach may:

> "provide a multi-disciplinary assessment team which considers the options and makes a recommendation to the court . . . multi-agency panels involve from the start representatives of those agencies and interest groups who will implement the plan to be recommended for the individual concerned." (Burney and Pearson (1995), p. 294.)

Inter-agency co-operation, although taking a variety of forms, has become more widespread during the 1990s and the Home Office and Department of Health have made more funds available to cover the costs of assessments being carried out in magistrates' courts (Gordon and Heddermann (1993), pp. 9–12).

There are thus ongoing questions about both the form and resourcing of diversion via court-based psychiatric assessment. But in addition there are equally important questions relating to the purposes and destination of such diversion. In particular, is the ultimate destination some kind of institutional (*i.e.* hospital) treatment or some kind of community care? In recent years hospital places have been reduced and hospitals themselves may question their ability to provide effective treatment in some cases (Fennell (1991), pp. 336–7; Peay (1994), p. 1135). In 1992 the Reed Committee (Department of Health and Home Office (1992), p. 40) argued that mentally disordered offenders be dealt with in the community rather than in an institutional setting. But the actual provision of appropriate community care to "diverted" mentally disordered offenders may be problematical. A report from the NACRO Mental Health Advisory Committee in 1993 noted that many mentally disturbed offenders will simply need access to those community care services which exist to meet the needs of mentally disturbed people in general but that involvement in the criminal justice system was often a reason why these services are denied to them (NACRO (1993)). Clearly it would be helpful in the first place to have a clearer profile of the range of needs of mentally disordered persons who may be diverted from the criminal process into a community care situation in this way. Research into the Islington Project, referred to above, sought to identify significant areas of need among the Project's clientele. Four main areas of need emerged from this enquiry, each presenting a considerable challenge for the relevant agencies which may seek to address these needs: a precarious accommodation situation; a significant incidence of substance misuse; an over-representation of black people among those diagnosed as psychotic; and the role of violence in the pattern of offending of mentally disordered persons (Burney and Pearson (1995), pp. 299, *et seq.*). If diversion in this context is to be at all meaningful it would thus seem evident that a number of areas of social policy need to be coordinated, so reinforcing the imperatives of inter-agency liaison and a more focussed resourcing for such a solution to dealing with this area of mentally disordered offending. Burney and Pearson's conclusion may serve to make this argument:

> "... psychiatric assessment alone does little if unaccompanied by effective follow-up to community resources. That is where panel assessment schemes, or court schemes employing psychiatric nurses ... offer more chance of active liaison." (Burney and Pearson (1995), p. 308.)

Underlying questions

In the case of mentally disordered offenders the possibility of diversion from criminal proceedings continue into the later stages of the process (the period of remand before trial, the trial itself, at the point of deciding sentence, and during a prison sentence), although of course the later a diversion takes place, the less of a diversion it consititutes, and it is no longer in any real sense a diversion from prosecution. There is already a body of commentary and research on aspects of this later diversion (summarised in Fennell (1991); Peay (1994)) and many of the problems and arguments already considered above in relation to the earlier diversion of mentally disordered persons reappear once more: the identification of both disorder and needs, the appropriate destination of diversion and the resources to support this process. But there are also common philosophical questions underlying any instance of diversion of the mentally disordered, and most fundamentally the question of responsibility for dealing with problematic mentally disordered behaviour. Most delinquency which is related in some way to mental disorder gives rise to a basket of moral, psychiatric and social welfare questions which cannot easily be disentangled from each other. In other words, it may be too simplistic and often morally questionable to re-define the problem as being purely of a psychiatric nature. While it may well be true in many cases that psychiatric treatment, whether compulsory or voluntary, is an appropriate response, that does not mean that the whole response can be made in psychiatric terms alone. Inevitably, there will be legal and ethical issues to consider (for instance, the need for any public protection, treatment without consent, the extent of detention or other loss of liberty), even if the "offender" is wholly removed (as a "patient") to the psychiatric and medical sphere. The very concept of diversion in this context assumes that criminal proceedings and penal sanctions are not appropriate; yet in many cases, issues of moral responsibility, individual autonomy and distributive justice are not so clearly resolved and the mental health system's "ownership" of mentally disordered persons is at least open to question, even in some of the extreme cases of anti-social behaviour (this problem is perhaps most clearly typified by the problem of deciding how to deal with psychopathic conduct). Finally, in more practical terms, the resolution of the problem of what to do about mentally disordered delinquency is a matter of social policy as much as psychiatric treatment or legal sanctioning. There are often, for instance, interrelated problems of drug abuse, homelessness, social dislocation and dysfunctional families, and remedies depend upon an examination of social trends and structures as well as an analysis of individual pathologies. In short, while official policy and legal principle suggest that the mentally disordered person is the candidate par excellence for diversion, on closer examination the attempt to implement diversionary policy in this context begs very difficult questions about the allocation of responsibility for dealing with the disordered delinquent.

Mediation of disputes

The initiative of a prosecuting authority to steer an alleged offence away from formal criminal proceedings and towards mediation of the dispute giving rise to the offence has been developed significantly in the Scottish legal system during the last decade. This has contributed to a notable shift within the culture of prosecutorial decision-making in Scotland, which until the early 1980s had been very much based on a proprosecution policy (Tombs and Moody (1993)). Part of the impetus for this change of policy came from the Second Report of the Stewart Committee on Alternatives to Prosecution (Stewart Committee (1983)): in addition to the use of fixed penalties and fines by the Procurator Fiscal (see the discussion in Chap. Eight, below), the Committee was enthusiastic about the possibility of co-operation between the Fiscal's Office and local authority Social Work Departments to deal with some offending that appeared to be clearly related to marital or family problems or poverty (Stewart Committee (1983), para. 3.29). Diversion to social work support had been pioneered by a scheme in Ayr (Moody (1983)), and was then taken up by other Fiscals' Offices, and further followed by experiments in Edinburgh and Glasgow seeking to use mediation and reparation to victims in place of prosecution. Although in quantitative terms such procedures account for a very small proportion of cases (a major problem is funding the requisite social work resources (Stedward and Millar (1989)), in theoretical terms they represent an important alternative model. A significant initiative was taken by the Scottish Association for the Care and Resettlement of Offenders (SACRO), which undertook referrals for mediation from the Procurator Fiscal on a deferred prosecution basis—where the alleged offender and victim come to an agreement through mediation, the criminal proceedings will be dropped. This programme, based in Edinburgh and Glasgow, has been assessed positively (Warner (1992)), in that a majority of victims and accused persons were able to reach an agreement which was sustainable, at least for several months and without succumbing to further offending.

The objectives of the SACRO project were to promote both reparation and mediation as alternatives to criminal proceedings and, in so doing, address the rights and needs of victims and also give offenders the opportunity to experience a constructive and demanding response to the consequences of their behaviour, a kind of direct accountability without recourse to the court system (Warner (1992), pp. 7–8). The cases typically dealt with were less serious offences arising from neighbour and family disputes or broken relationships; but occasionally there were cases where the parties were strangers to each other (for instance, motoring encounters).

Mediation was performed either by trained volunteer mediators (Edinburgh) or by a full-time project worker (Glasgow) and the mediation was often carried out indirectly—victims were not pressurised to meet the accused party, and most preferred not to do so. The agreements reflected the requests of the victims and usually involved payment of compensation, undertaking work for the victim, apologising, promising to desist from further harassment, or making a donation to charity. Mediation of this kind is increasingly viewed as appropriate for dealing with neighbour disputes; Mackay and Moodie argue, for instance:

> "... that neighbourhood disputes are troublesome to prosecutors and that the court system does not deal effectively with them ... a considerable number of cases that are referred to prosecution authorities might be diverted to community mediation facilities, and ... there was support for this innovation amongst prosecutors." (Mackay and Moody (1996), p. 310.)

The significance of the SACRO project is that, compared with the use made of mediation in England and Wales, it has contemplated referral to mediation as a complete alternative to prosecution in a variety of cases. English initiatives in the field of mediation have for the most part used the process either as an adjunct to criminal proceedings (for instance, as something to be taken into account when sentencing) or as a component of cautioning practice in relation to juveniles (see the discussion in Chap. Seven; Wright and Galaway (eds) (1989); the one exception in England was the Kettering Adult Reparation Bureau, set up in 1987). In either situation, mediation remains a component of official penality, effectively an element of sentencing or cautioning. Although the Scottish mediation and social work initiatives still depend on filtering and monitoring by the Procurator Fiscal, if they are seen to work they do then represent a significant diversion from formal criminal justice. As such they approach more closely the model of non-punitive resolution of "offending" conduct supported by many "abolitionist" criminologists and social scientists (for instance, and notably, Christie (1982); Habermas (1984) and (1988); de Haan (1990)).

Warner has attempted a detailed evaluation of the SACRO initiatives and her conclusions represent an instructive assessment of an operational non-confrontational method of responding to offending conduct. The participants appeared to be clear in their own minds about the advantages of mediation in relation to minor crime:

> "The level of consensus was striking. Where the offence related to a dispute, fiscal, victims and accused regarded mediation as a better solution than court proceedings which could exacerbate the situation ..." (Warner (1992), p. 144.)

While prosecution could appear heavy-handed, taking no further action at all could damage the credibility of the system; mediation and reparation steered a middle course, while also involving victims more in the process. But, as with most instances of diversion, beneficial "resolution" outcomes need to be viewed in the context of resources and cost. Diversion to mediation could prove costly. If, for instance, it is reserved principally for minor offending, the saving of prosecution costs is likely to be small (particularly if it is diversion from guilty pleas), while at the same time an increasingly successful and popular mediation programme would generate its own costs. Not surprisingly, there are also net-widening fears, especially in relation to minor offending: the risk, for example, that a decision to take no action or a simple reprimand may be replaced by attempted mediation (itself, in a sense, an extension of social control) which, if it fails, may then bring the offender back fully into the net of formal criminal proceedings. Or, to put the matter another way, to what extent should "simple" but nonetheless penal responses, such as cautions, guilty pleas, or fines be replaced by a "constructive" but more invasive approach embodied in reparation and mediation?

Certain key questions therefore emerge from an examination of what has been done so far in practice as regards diversion to mediation. First, there is the issue of whether such an approach should embrace some more serious offending behaviour than is usually the case at present (whatever the categories of "minor" and "serious" offending are thought to include), or whether retributive concerns should restrain such a development. Secondly, there is the substantive question of what kind of case appears to benefit most from mediation. On the evidence to date, the answer might be relatively less serious but repetitive offending arising in the context of continuing disputes or bad relations, typically neighbour or domestic arguments. In other words, the offences in such cases are symptomatic of a wider dysfunction which itself (and so also the consequent offences) could be best addressed by mediation. Thirdly, there is the question of resources. Warner's study contains an interesting attempt to calculate the relative costs of prosecution and diversion to reparation and mediation (Warner (1992), Chap. 8). This is a far from straightforward exercise and as a matter of general public expenditure may in the end resolve itself into no more than shifting resources and costs from one government department to another. If mediation and prosecution were equally expensive, the answer might then depend upon a preference for one or another on other grounds. But Warner sounds a cautionary note: "The two SACRO mediation and reparation schemes were not *cheap* alternatives to prosecution. They supplemented the prosecution process which currently cost less . . ." (Warner (1992), p. 137).

This therefore suggests that, insofar as resources are being taken into account, care should be taken as to exactly how diversion to mediation is inserted into the system. In particular, this may mean that mediation as an adjunct to prosecution and sentence rather than as a total alternative, may be especially expensive, unless ways are found to reduce the costs through a combined use.

The allocation of responsibility

As a brief comparative and summarising comment, it may be noted that diversion both to psychiatric treatment and to mediation raises questions as to the "ownership" of the underlying problems and pathologies of conduct. If society as a whole, acting through appropriate state agencies, has the responsibility (which may itself be questioned by some "abolitionist" writers) for addressing the root causes of some "offending" behaviour, a primary question is then one of allocating such responsibility as between, typically, the criminal justice system, health services, welfare services and voluntary community organisations. The issue of diversion therefore tends to mask much more fundamental questions of this kind. Casting the matter in the language of diversion is useful in so far as it focuses on the interrelationship between issues of cost and fair treatment. But the fundamental relevance of criminal justice, as a species of social control, to some of these situations is also an essential component of the problem.

Chapter 7

The Police and Diversion

It is essential when discussing the criminal justice system to realise both the practical and the theoretical importance of police discretion at an early stage in the process. Contrary to popular belief, the police do not ordinarily come across criminal activity themselves but rather they respond to calls from the public (Bottomley and Pease (1986)). As has been mentioned earlier (see Chap. Three) many victims choose not to report offences to the police for a variety of reasons thereby diverting a considerable amount of offenders from the criminal justice system. However, the police in England and Wales have a discretion in responding to an incident once it is reported. This is not necessarily an undesirable outcome. It may often be expedient for the officer to merely "keep the peace" by diffusing a potentially hostile conflict rather than invoking the full powers at his or her disposal. Furthermore, the police do not have adequate resources to pursue every offence that comes to their attention and, therefore, it has to be recognised that in practice some degree of prioritisation is necessary. It should also be said that even in those jurisdictions, such as the German system, which theoretically require the police to instigate criminal proceedings on every occasion when there is sufficient evidence, officers will still divert many criminal disputes (Williams (1984); Herrmann (1992)).

Informal cautioning

Law enforcement officers have always had a variety of options available to them, and warning an offender at the scene of the incident has been one of those alternatives available to an officer (Steer (1970)). The first major British sociological study of this aspect of policing was undertaken by Banton in 1964. In his work Banton found that, by using their discretion not to continue with many incidents which could have resulted in prosecutions, there was a general tendency by the police to under-report offences (Banton (1964)). Again, the decision not to proceed further may be desirable public policy. In his report into the 1981 Brixton riots, for example, Lord Scarman highlighted the need for the police to use their discretion with sensitivity in order to avoid exacerbating volatile situations (Scarman (1982), p. 104):

> ". . . it is equally well recognised that successful policing depends on the exercise of discretion in how the law is enforced. The good reputation of the police as a force depends upon the skill and judgement which policemen display in the particular circumstances of the cases and incidents which they are required to handle. Discretion is the art of suiting action to particular circumstances. It is the policeman's daily task."

As such it was recognised that the individual officer had considerable power in deciding how to deal effectively with a case. Muir (1977) argued that in effect each officer was a "street level politician", balancing up the evidence quickly before determining an effective response. Not only would such a decision influence that particular case but it could also affect the subsequent classification of other similar incidents at a later date. If it appears to be the norm to respond informally to certain types of criminal behaviour, an officer is unlikely to want to bring such an incident to the attention of his superiors unless there are strong aggravating circumstances present, such as a particularly uncooperative offender.

An American commentator also stressed the inverted hierarchy of police officers in the extent of their discretion (Wilson (1968)); in contrast to many comparable organisations, most of the everyday decisions in policing are taken by the officers responding to an incident. It is probable that these officers will be of a relatively low rank as the more high ranking members of the force tend to remain in the station to co-ordinate their officers. In other words, not only do officers influence the criminal justice system on a daily basis by their decisions on how to deal with each particular case that comes to their attention, but the officers who are entrusted with these important decisions typically are those lower down the police hierarchy. There is a considerable body of research which has focused on the internal structure of the police force and the interrelationship between the everyday decisions of the "street" officers and the official policy as determined by their superiors (see especially McBarnet (1978, 1981)). McBarnet (1981) went as far as to suggest that policy makers deliberately did not specify the exact extent of an officer's discretion and gave them instead a very broad general power to interpret incidents and to act accordingly. This, she contended (at p. 156), allowed policy makers to blame specific officers for any perceived injustice that might occur rather than accept that they themselves were at fault for providing inadequate guidelines.

In making their decision as to how best to deal with the problem officers on the ground will be influenced not only by official policy, which will often be vague, but by common practice in their force. This common practice will emerge as the result of many value decisions taken by officers themselves as to the most appropriate method to deal with certain types of offence or offender. The practice then becomes reinforced through repetition. For example, many commentators have argued that the police often appeared reluctant to intervene in cases of alleged domestic violence (Pizzey (1974); Pahl (1985); Hanmer, Radford and Stanko (1989)). Even when there was clearly sufficient evidence to warrant a prosecution for assault, research indicated that the police preferred to pacify the situation rather than invoking the full powers at their disposal (Dobash and Dobash (1979)). When it became more evident in the 1970s and 1980s that domestic violence was a serious social problem the attitude of the police towards complainants received much criticism. Although the police have taken constructive measures towards rectifying public perception, it is questionable to what extent the dominant police attitude regarding domestic violence has altered (McCann (1985); Sheptycki (1991)). This clearly demonstrates the difficulty of changing not just official policy from senior officers but the ingrained perceptions, values and objectives of junior officers.

A further cause for concern is that informal diversion by police officers may operate in a discriminatory manner. Reiner comments ((1994), pp. 725–726):

> "The problem with this is that research on police practice has shown consistently that police discretion is not an equal opportunity phenomenon. Some groups are much more likely than others to be at the receiving end of the exercise of police powers. A general pattern of benign underenforcement of the law disguises the often oppresive use of police powers against unpopular or uninfluential and hence powerless minorities."

This discrimination may start with stop and search decisions (Willis (1983)) and continue through to the decision on whether or not to prosecute an offender (Landau and Nathan (1983)). These studies would suggest that white offenders are more likely to avoid prosecution for a number of reasons. First, the police stop and search comparatively fewer white people than black; secondly, it would appear that the police are more inclined to deal informally with white offenders; and, finally, of those offenders who are taken into the police station, a white offender is more likely to receive a caution than his black counterpart. The disproportionate number of black people who are prosecuted rather than dealt with informally by the police, quite apart from the obvious injustice, has a number of other undesirable effects. This targeting of a particular class of offender is liable to distort perceptions of the actual levels of criminality and may help foster misleading popular impressions about the extent of criminal activity in ethnic minority groups. In turn this can lead to calls for increased targeting of such groups by the police; a deviancy amplification spiral could then develop as increased resources further distort perceptions of criminality and appear on face value to vindicate the channeling of even more resources to deal with the "problem". Moreover, such discrimination in law enforcement can have the effect of alienating the police from the targeted community. Lord Scarman recognised that some of the black community in London held the view that the Metropolitan Police were racist and that this belief stemmed from the fact that certain officers used their powers in a discriminatory manner ((1982), pp. 105–106):

> "Such plausibility as this attack has achieved is due, sadly, to the ill-considered, immature and racially prejudiced actions of some officers in their dealings on the streets with young black people. Racial prejudice does manifest itself occasionally in the behaviour of a few officers on the streets. It may be only too easy for some officers, faced with what they see as the inexorably rising tide of street crime, to lapse into an unthinking assumption that all young black people are potential criminals ... The damage done by even the occasional display of racial prejudice is incalculable. It goes far towards the creation of a hostile police force, which was the myth which led the young people into these disorders."

It would also appear that the police often have to make what can be termed moral judgments about individuals before deciding how to deal with them. Research into police interactions with juveniles in the United States suggests that the perceived "moral character" of the juveniles in question was seen by officers to be of considerable importance in determining whether they should be arrested. Piliavin and Briar (1964) found that such decisions were based primarily on personal characteristics of the offender and the extent to which the offender complied with the officer's demands rather than on the severity of the actual offence. This research would appear to support Bittner's (1967) intuitive observation that a police officer is more likely to arrest an individual who threatens the officer's authority either by failing to cooperate or by demonstrating open hostility. Such resistance to authority may, in part, be triggered by perceived discriminatory treatment.

How an individual police officer perceives a situation is, therefore, a key consideration in understanding the method employed to deal with it. A high proportion of incidents are informally diverted from the criminal justice system by officers at the scene of an incident. However, criminologists are mainly concerned with such incidents that the police decide to deal with in a more formal context. That is particularly true of the relatively minor incidents that receive official cautions as opposed to informal warnings; as will be shown later in this chapter there is a considerable academic literature on formal cautioning, whereas comparatively little work has been done on the use of police discretion at an earlier stage in the process. Primarily this may be due to the methodological hurdles that would have to be overcome. To what extent, for example, would the police modify their ordinary behaviour due to the presence of the researcher? Moreover, some of the instances where police officers use an informal caution would be inclusionary rather than diversionary in nature. In some cases the officer may act in such a manner in the full knowledge that there would be insufficient evidence to warrant a full prosecution. When this happens it may be a question of "net-widening" as much as diversion. Yet such methodological difficulties, real as they are, should not detract from the significance of this exercise of police discretion and the need for further research into this area of police activity.

Formal cautioning

In combination with the use of informal warnings described above, a more formal system of diversion by the police has a considerable history in the United Kingdom. In his leading study into cautioning, Steer (1970) traced its usage back as far as 1833. However, the Commissioner of the Metropolitan Police at that time was concerned about its use in that he felt that there was an inherent danger that the police might employ it when there was insufficient evidence for a prosecution (quoted in Steer (1970), p. 54):

> "If the charge is in itself a proper one, it is to be received, and the person sent before a Magistrate. If the charge is such as to justify the Inspector in refusing to receive it, the particular reason for its being refused is to be stated, which will enable the Commissioner to judge of the propriety of the Inspector's conduct; if the Constable has exceeded his duty in apprehending the person, he is to be instructed in his duty, or dealt with by the Commissioner according to the circumstances."

In some respects this attitude may be explained by the unease expressed in certain quarters towards the newly emerging role of the police at this time, and the consequent desire on the part of the police to bolster their legitimacy. The manner in which the Metropolitan Commissioner stated his position suggests that there was a considerable onus on the individual officer to justify his position if the Inspector decided not to continue with the prosecution. Whilst this may have gone some way in deterring over zealous policing, which was a particular concern of the Commissioner, it may also have inadvertently given rise to an increased use of informal cautions by officers who did not wish all of their actions to be scrutinised.

There is little at present known about cautioning during the 19th century. This is primarily due to the fact that there are no published statistics relating to the employment of cautions. One has to remember that the official criminal statistics have only been published since 1876 (Maguire (1994)) and that it was not until 1977 that minor criminal damage offences were recorded, a category that has often resulted in a caution. It would appear that the caution gradually became more accepted by Police Commissioners as their own position became more secure and they realised that cautioning may actually increase public confidence in the police in relation to relatively minor breaches of the law. Steer (1970) refers to specific instructions to caution those involved in two particular activities in the 1850s: advertising lotteries for game, wine or spirits and children running beside omnibuses "turning somersaults" to encourage passengers to throw them coins. The wording of the instructions suggest that the cautions were to be of an informal, advisory manner and given by the officer at the incident rather than at the police station by a senior officer. Although the police were soon seen to be less of a threat, at least to the middle classes, their position remained precarious during this period (Radzinowicz (1968); Weinberger (1981)) and this resulted in a potential conflict of interests for the police between the advantages of informally settling disputes that could become volatile and the desire for legitimacy and due process to help allay fears that the police were operating in a sinister manner.

Just as little is known about cautions in this period, there is little information about informal warnings from police officers. Due to the onus on officers to explain to their superiors why they did not continue with a case, it would appear probable that a large number of incidents were kept hidden from senior officers and dealt with in an informal manner. Emsley (1983) refers to the memoirs of officers serving in the last century and notes the considerable discretion an officer had to give an informal warning, particularly in respect to breaches of by-laws and regulations concerning public order; in one case an officer reputedly carried a drunk, homeless woman onto another officer's beat so as to avoid the "bureaucratic rigmarole" associated with arresting her (Emsley (1983), p. 139). Even assuming that this was an unusual example, there appeared to be some incentive for a police officer to avoid arresting an offender and disposing of the incident by way of a warning.

It should be added that, quite apart from being understandable given the structure of policing during the last century, this policy may have accorded with parliamentary intent. The Metropolitan Police Act 1829 was remarkably general in its terms of reference. An officer's role was simply "the preservation of peace, the prevention of crimes, the detection and committal of offenders". It is interesting to note that the preservation of peace was listed before both the prevention of crime and the committal of offenders. Arguably a policy using both informal warnings and more formal cautions was the most effective way of realising these aims; a warning may both calm an incident and persuade an offender not to become involved in future criminal activities. However, this had to be balanced against the police wish to be seen as acting openly in accordance with the law and not in a covert manner. Indeed Radzinowicz (1968) argues that this need for legitimacy and hence scrutiny did much to dispell fears that the "new police" would be a repressive organisation.

The first "formal" cautioning schemes

Towards the end of the nineteenth century it had become apparent that, despite a number of ventures aimed at rehabilitation, there had been a rapid growth in the rates of juvenile offending, particularly in the rapidly expanding urban areas. It was against this background of rising juvenile crime that the Glasgow Police introduced a novel method of police cautioning in 1905—the Superintendent's Court. There was a deliberate force policy that minor cases should be kept out of the usual court structure (Ferguson, (1952)). The aim was to make the proceedings informal and to ensure that both the child's parents and representatives of the welfare services were in attendance. The scheme was basically an adaptation of the traditional system of police warnings and as such required no specific statutory basis. Although the police claimed that the scheme was a marked success (Glasgow Police (1945)) its use diminished consistently from 1910 when it was used in 33.8 per cent of cases of juvenile offending dealt with by the police to 1950 when it was used in only 17.6 per cent (Ferguson (1952)). Given the police belief that the system was effective it is difficult to account for its progressively more limited role. The first reason might be that the scheme was not as effective as the police themselves publicly maintained. In his study, Ferguson (1952) found that 57 per cent of his sample who had been admonished in the superintendent's court had subsequent convictions compared with 46 per cent of those given probation, 49 per cent who had been fined, 64 per cent detained in a remand home, 41 per cent sent to an approved school or 26 per cent whose parents had been fined. These crude figures, however, are not of much value in actually analysing the effectiveness of each type of disposition. Sentencers presumably selected harsher sentences for those whom they considered most likely to relapse into criminal activity and those dispositions which involved restricting the juvenile offender's liberty clearly afforded less opportunity for recidivism.

The fall in the use of admonitions appeared to be largely compensated for by the increased use of probation and detention in a remand home. Although probation was not a new concept, it was the subject of radical change in the early twentieth century north of the border. Until 1905 probation officers had been voluntary social workers but, in that year, the Corporation of Glasgow approved the establishment of a full probation system in the city comprised of probation officers who were serving police officers. This policy continued until the Probation of Offenders (Scotland) Act 1931 took the responsibility for probation work out of the hands of the police. It is possible that police involvement in probation was one of the reasons behind the declinine in use of the Superintendent's Court as a period of supervision by a police officer may have been seen as preferable to a mere warning given by a senior officer. It is also possible that the admonition was the victim of both the desire to punish some offenders whilst offering support to others. In comparison with the Superintendent's Court, there was more room for continued police involvement in the rehabilitative process with probation. On the other hand, when the police wished to adopt a more punitive stance, prosecution would also be favoured over the Superintendent's Court. Moreover, the inter-war years were a period of considerable state intervention (Garland (1985)) and this meant that this process of state encroachment and greater interference went largely unchallenged. Nonetheless, despite its decreased use, the Glasgow scheme both survived and also acted as a model for other forces in responding to their own particular needs.

Such schemes were assessed in two official reports in the early 1960s on juvenile offending and how the legal system responded to juvenile crime (Ingleby (1960); Kilbrandon (1964)). Although their ambits were considerably wider, both of the reports commented on the role of the police in diverting offenders from the traditional criminal justice system. The Ingleby Report, which was concerned with England and Wales, argued that a delicate balance had to be struck in deciding whether to caution a juvenile ((1960), p. 49):

> "On the one hand, it seems unnecessary and indeed undesirable to bring a child before a court if the shock of being found out and the effect of a caution from the police are enough to make it unlikely that he will offend again; on the other, it is important to ensure that one whose delinquency results from more deep-rooted causes and calls for more lasting treatment should receive the kind

of help and guidance he needs at the earliest possible stage, and often the right form of treatment can be provided only by the decision of a court."

It is of note that the Committee avoided any conclusion about the value of cautioning generally, other than to highlight the dilemma mentioned above. Instead the Report concentrated on the juvenile liaison schemes by then operating in some cities. However, many of the criticisms that were made of the latter would appear to be equally applicable to more traditional methods of cautioning.

The Ingleby Committee highlighted a number of problems with juvenile liaison schemes. First, there was concern that such schemes were being used for children who were either below the age of criminal responsibility or who had not actually broken the criminal law but "whose behaviour is such that it might lead to crime" (p. 50). Apparently parents were even seeking the help of the police to assist with their children, especially when parents believed that their daughter was behaving in an immoral way. This had a "net-widening" effect and meant that the police had become involved in supervising children who had not actually committed an offence but had merely behaved in a way considered to be "out of character". Although the long term involvement of the police in a juvenile liaison scheme contributed to this tendency, cautioning might have led to the same outcome, being administered where no offence had technically been committed but where the individual's behaviour, for whatever reason, was judged to be objectionable. Secondly, the Committee was concerned that the police did not have the necessary skills to perform what was in effect a social work function. Again this primarily relates to the role of a juvenile liaison officer, although the Committee's concern that "trivial offences were often only a symptom of an underlying condition, requiring early and specialised treatment, that was revealed only by the full enquiries made when the child came before a court" (p. 51) would again appear to be equally applicable to traditional cautioning. Finally, the Committee felt that the more general recommendations that they proposed would negate arguments that juvenile liaison schemes were beneficial in that they allowed juveniles to avoid the stigma of appearing in court. For these reasons they concluded that the juvenile liaison model should not be extended to other areas although, notably, they stopped short of arguing that the existing schemes should be abolished.

The Kilbrandon Report (1964), which concerned Scottish practice, considered many of the same arguments but came to a different conclusion on the role of cautioning. Again the Report acknowleged the fundamental importance of police discretion in diverting offenders from the traditional criminal justice system (p. 9):

"Given the tremendous range of acts recognised as offences under statute or

> common law, it is plain that in practice the police have always—and necessarily—exercised some measure of discretion, at a variety of levels, in the reporting of alleged offences, and that equally prosecutors for their part may, on considering reports made to them, decide not to institute proceedings, and sometimes to deal with the matter by warning. These factors are common to the consideration of proceedings in respect of offenders of all ages, but have for long been recognised as having particular application to children, and clearly any assessment of the volume of juvenile delinquency must take account of the effect of these preliminary sifting processes."

The Kilbrandon Committee took an essentially pragmatic view of cautioning; it was the Committee's understanding that about 90 per cent of juveniles cautioned did not come into contact with the police again (p. 62). It therefore appeared to the Committee that cautioning was an effective response to juvenile crime. Moreover, the urban liaison schemes that were in operation in Greenock, Stirlingshire and Clackmannon, Coatbridge, Kilmarnock, Paisley and Perth were seen as a practical way of cautioning young offenders in a non-rural environment, although, if this were the case, one wonders why such schemes were not to be found in any of Scotland's four major cities: Glasgow, Edinburgh, Aberdeen and Dundee. It was recognised that there were criticisms of such schemes which the Committee felt came under three main categories. First, that supervision measures should only be decided by a court, secondly, that the operation of such schemes went beyond the scope of police duties and that, finally, the police were not properly trained for such a function. Each of these arguments were rejected in turn. It was felt that it would be counterproductive to prosecute every juvenile offender who came to the police's attention; instead the operation of discretion at an earlier stage could ensure that the interests of the juvenile could be adequately taken into consideration. The problem with this response is that it did not address the point of the criticism; the police had, in effect, also become sentencers and had gone beyond their traditional discretion in determining whether to prosecute or issue a warning. There was a clear difference between deciding whether or not to prosecute and setting an appropriate period of supervision. The Committee's response to the second criticism, to say that "police duty can never be static" (p. 63), partly answers this concern but still begs questions about the constitutional role of the police and also raises the issue of accountability. It was also concluded in the Report that juvenile liaison officers in Scotland had adequate training through a series of courses held at Glasgow University which were designed to make officers aware of signs that the offender was in need of more specialist help.

The Kilbrandon Committee recommended the extension of juvenile liaison schemes to other parts of Scotland but felt that it would not be desirable for there to be a uniform statutory scheme for the whole country as this would not cater for the geographical differences between areas. Although the Committee's main proposal was to establish a system of children's panels to deal with juvenile offenders rather than a court, it was recognised that cautioning would still form an important integral part of the overall official response to juvenile crime (p. 62). The Kilbrandon Report succeeded in placing cautioning both in its historical context and recognising the effects that cautioning has on the criminal justice system as a whole. It is notable, however, that the Report did not give so much consideration to the potential dangers of extending police involvement in supervising juvenile offenders.

The expansion of cautioning

In their seminal study *Crime in England and Wales*, McClintock and Avison found that although there had been a marked increase in the number of cautions issued in the period from 1955 to 1965 the proportion of known offenders cautioned remained remarkably constant, leading them to comment that "the increase in police cautioning merely kept pace with the overall increase in the conviction rates" (1968), p. 157). In quantitative terms most cautions were given for minor property offences, however McClintock and Avison's analysis demonstrated that a comparatively high proportion of sexual offences were also dealt with by cautioning. To take the 1962 figures by way of example 31.7 per cent of offenders who had committed sexual offences received a caution.

The 1960s saw a number of radical proposals in relation to juvenile justice (Morris and Giller (1979); Pitts (1988); Gelsthorpe and Morris (1994); Dingwall and Davenport (1995)) which culminated in the far reaching Children and Young Persons Act 1969 in England and Wales and the Social Work (Scotland) Act 1968 north of the border. The 1969 Act provided both a radical reorientation of the juvenile justice system and the first statutory recognition of police cautioning. Although a subsequent change of government meant that the Act was not implemented in its entirety, its emphasis on the welfare model was pronounced. The juvenile court was very much left as a last resort and diversion at an earlier stage in the process encouraged in the majority of cases. This policy failed to attract universal support and it was reported in *The Times* (June 26, 72) that an experienced magistrate had resigned in protest at the fact that "the impartial judiciary has been devalued in favour of the executive". Bottoms, *et al.* (1970), however, in an early critique of the new law concluded that it was sensible for the police to act as a filter to ensure that, after investigation, only the most serious cases should be processed further although they questioned whether this mechanism was exactly what the 1969 Act had intended.

In the years following 1969 the use of cautioning expanded considerably, (see Figure 1 below).

It is important to realise though that in practice the use of cautioning has been largely determined by each individual police force and that there has been considerable variance between forces in this respect. Such discrepancy is still apparent today. After *The Sunday Mirror* (August 13, 72) claimed that the rate of cautioning for "juvenile law breakers" varied between 11 per cent in Teeside and 74 per cent in Devon and Cornwall, James (1972) was prompted to comment:

> "Now Teesiders may very likely be tougher than Devonshire kids, but are they really that much tougher? Is there such a very much smaller proportion of first offenders? One cannot help wondering whether such a comparatively high proportion of court appearances is really necessary."

Despite attempts at conformity through national Home Office guidelines (Home Office (1985), (1990a), (1994a)) cautioning policy is still largely determined by each individual police force. The most recent set of cautioning guidelines (Home Office (1994a)) recognised that this has led to considerable regional variance in cautioning rates across the country. In 1992 the percentage of indictable offences cautioned varied between police forces from 27 per cent to 57 per cent. The Home Office related this phenomenon to police practice (at para. 9):

> "This discrepancy may result from different perceptions of the boundary between informal warnings and formal cautions . . ., or of that between formal cautions and prosecutions. Either way, this degree of variation is undesirable. Accordingly, forces which caution a disproportionately high or low number of offenders should ensure that their force guidelines on cautioning are sound and are being interpreted sensibly."

Whilst the Government may not want to interfere directly in force policy, the solution given is disappointing in that it fails to take account of the inherent difficulties in interpreting excessively broad Home Office guidelines. This criticism has been made of earlier guidelines, Evans and Wilkinson ((1990), p. 174) commenting that it "advises forces what to do but not how to do it". They argue that uniformity could not be achieved without limiting individual discretion and providing an effective means to regulate cautioning decision making. For example, they state that the guidelines could perhaps define criteria based on notions of offence

Figure 1

Persons cautioned 1966–1975

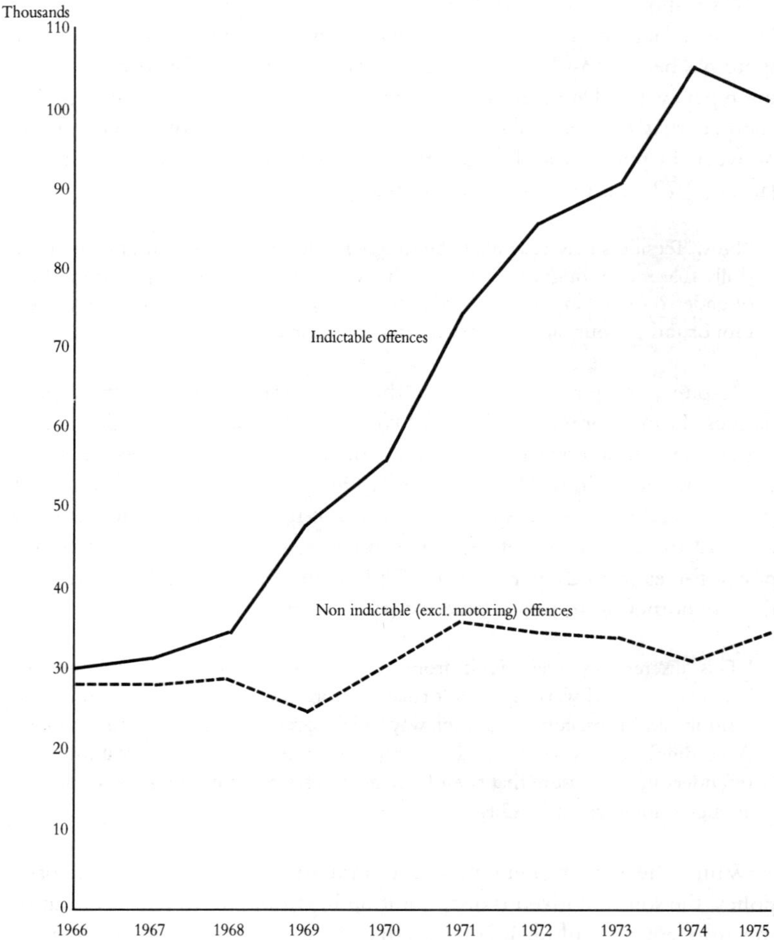

severity by specifying degrees of violence or monetary loss, thereby reducing the police's overall discretion. However, the latest circular of 1994, in keeping with earlier guidelines, offers only general principles to be applied by officers rather than the specific advice urged by Evans and Wilkinson (para. 4):

> "It is impossible to lay down hard and fast rules such as that first time offenders must be cautioned, or that certain minor offences should attract only a caution regardless of the offender's record. Nor does the presumption in favour of diverting juveniles from the courts mean that they should automatically be cautioned, as opposed to prosecuted, simply because they are juveniles. Ultimately the proper use of discretion is a matter of common sense: the questions to be asked in each case are—
>
> —whether the circumstances are such that the caution is likely to be effective, and
>
> —whether the caution is appropriate to the offence."

There has been a considerable body of recent research which has highlighted the continued variance in cautioning rates between police forces (Ditchfield (1976); Tutt and Giller (1983); Giller and Tutt (1987); Gelsthorpe and Giller (1990); Wilkinson and Evans (1990); Evans and Wilkinson (1990); Westwood (1991); Evans (1991)). Tutt and Giller (1983) argued that this variance was caused in part by different police forces adopting radically different policies in relation to juvenile offenders. Out of the 15 forces that they studied it was argued that there was a spectrum of approaches in operation which, at the extremes, could be termed "welfare" and "justice" based. This dichotomy between "justice" and "welfare" was reflected in many of the other strategies employed to respond to juvenile offending in the 1970s and 1980s (Tutt (1981); Morris and Giller (1987)). Under the "welfare" model the purpose of any formal state intervention was to help cater for the particular offender's rehabilitation whereas a "justice" based approach recognised the minor nature of most juvenile offending and was concerned that a rehabilitative approach may be used to justify an unacceptably high level of state intervention. In a "justice" model the primary concern was the offence committed by the juvenile. Forces in which such a model predominated would ordinarily have strict criteria for cautioning based on offence severity: often repeat cautioning would not be allowed, some more serious offences would not be included in the criteria and any particular offence causing popular concern, such as vandalism or soccer hooliganism, would also often result in prosecution. Such forces would tend to make cautioning decisions without undertaking lengthy social investigation into the offender's background.

Conversely, the focus of a "welfare" model was the offender rather than the offence. Forces who operated such a model were more likely to make extensive background enquiries, often involving other agencies, prior to deciding whether to issue a caution. Often the cautioning criteria would be defined more broadly than under a "justice" model to give the police greater discretion to determine the most effective manner in which to deal with a particular offender. "Welfare" based cautioning schemes were often seen to be more intrusive in that the offender may additionally have been required to join an intermediate treatment programme or to be supervised by a juvenile liaison officer as for instance in the scheme operated in Liverpool (Kilbrandon (1964)).

Tutt and Giller, however, argued that developments in policing tended to favour those forces operating a "justice" model and that, in time, financial constraints could undermine "welfare" based programmes ((1983), p. 593):

> "The cost efficiency and manpower arguments have raised a fundamental financial question mark over the appropriateness of elaborate decision-making structures for juvenile offenders. Whatever decision-making structure is adopted, a large proportion of first time offenders coming to the notice of the police will receive a caution. This questions the purpose of undertaking protracted and costly investigations by the police into the child's background when a first offence is committed. The impact of this argument can be seen in the last three years by the emergence of the instant caution procedure for juvenile offenders."

Similarly, the call by the public for more beat officers was seen as threatening the "welfare" model. This form of policing tended to result in the closing down of specialist juvenile liaison departments, as in parts of Lancashire (Tutt and Giller (1983)), and the subsequent devolution of such duties to beat officers. From the perspective of cautioning such officers would, for practical reasons, become increasingly reliant on less time-consuming "justice" criteria; consistency would be maintained through tighter offence-specific criteria and there would no longer be the same opportunity to undertake lengthy and expensive consultation with other agencies, nor would there be the opportunity to prepare exhaustive background reports on offenders.

Laycock and Tarling (1985) also found that different forces had different amounts of discretion built into their force guidelines. For example, both the Metropolitan and the Merseyside Police stressed that each case was viewed independently and that cautioning was not a routine response to certain offences. Both these urban forces had comparatively low cautioning rates. This can be contrasted with forces such as Devon and Cornwall which had a higher cautioning rate and a clear presumption in favour of cautioning juvenile offenders unless there were strong factors favouring a prosecution. Laycock and Tarling also attempted to explain the discrepancy between cautioning rates with regard to the proportion of first offenders that each force had to deal with. Their study showed that all nine forces in their sample cautioned more than two thirds of first offenders but that the proportion of all offenders who had no previous convictions or cautions varied between 47 per cent in the Metropolitan force and 76 per cent in Suffolk. Forces with a comparatively high rate of first offenders also tended to caution a comparatively high proportion of offenders; in their study Suffolk cautioned 62.5 per cent of juveniles and the Metropolitan Police cautioned only 37.3 per cent. Their research did not address the reasons why some forces had a far higher proportion of first offenders than others but they hypothesised that demographic factors, the level of crime and criminality, the proportion of crime that is minor and police practice would all have some bearing on this figure. Their overall conclusion was that more effective monitoring by the police was required (Laycock and Tarling (1985), p. 91):

> "It will always be unrealistic to expect all forces to have the same cautioning rates, but each force could be encouraged to evaluate its own practice to see whether force policy is being implemented effectively and whether it should be amended or more precisely defined. Such evaluation depends on the careful collation of statistics. In most forces at present policy is monitored only through internal meetings or conferences and the only information available is from routine statistics showing the number of offenders cautioned or prosecuted by age and offence."

It has been advanced by Ditchfield (1976) that about half of the variation in cautioning rates between forces could be attributed to different patterns of crime. However, a more sophisticated study (Wilkinson and Evans (1990)) has cast doubt on this assertion. In this study, Wilkinson and Evans concentrated solely on the offence of shoplifting, primarily as this is the offence for which juveniles are most frequently cautioned. No direct correlation was found between the crime pattern and the overall cautioning rate for that police force. The authors concluded that variance was more likely to be due to force cautioning practice than in differences in the pattern of crime or in the force's higher level policy.

During the 1980s two events might have led to a reduction in variance between police forces in their cautioning rates. First, a Home Office Circular (Home Office (1985)) was issued which sought to encourage the use of cautioning, particularly for juvenile offenders, in all police forces. Secondly, the establishment of the Crown Prosecution Service under the Prosecution of Offences Act 1985 was supposedly brought about in part by the desire to achieve greater national consistency in prosecution decision making. Giller and Tutt (1987), however, still found there to be a considerable variance in cautioning practice between forces after these reforms. After noting an increase across the board in the rate of cautioning, they extracted a number of points from the official statistics. First, with two exceptions, the higher average rate of cautioning occured in all police forces. Rather than levelling the playing field as had been hoped, the discrepencies remained intact. Secondly, it was observed that the forces which made the greatest comparative use of cautioning were all rural forces—the West Midlands force was the only predominantly urban force with a higher than average cautioning rate. Finally, those forces with a low recorded cautioning rate in 1981, that is to say before the introduction of the Crown Prosecution Service and before the issuing of the Home Office Guidelines, still had comparatively low rates in 1985. In summary, Giller and Tutt concluded that neither the Home Office Guidelines or the introduction of the Crown Prosecution Service had led to a levelling off in cautioning rates. Yet, despite a clear presumption in favour of diverting juveniles via cautioning in the Code for Crown Prosecutors (Crown Prosecution Service (1986)), it has to be remembered that it could take a period of time for transitions in the criminal justice system to be achieved. Giller and Tutt, however, saw cautioning as a challenge for the Crown Prosecution Service ((1987), p. 374): "Can the Crown Prosecutor as one of the few remaining means of levelling the diversity push for equality and justice where others have failed?"

The role of the Crown Prosecution Service in determining independent prosecution policy has been analysed by other commentators. Sanders (1987) argues that the police still "construct" the case for the prosecution prior to the file being sent to the Crown Prosecution Service. Sander's model is based on the police manufacturing a strong case by eliminating superflous or counter-productive evidence, failing to examine claims by the defendant and by diverting cases that the police do not want prosecuted at an early stage before Crown Prosecution Service involvement. In other words the police still effectively determine prosecution practice by either diverting the case or by presenting the case in such a manner that the Crown Prosecution Service are left with little alternative but to prosecute. Similarly, Gelsthorpe and Giller (1990) concluded, in relation to discontinuing the prosecution of juveniles, that the Crown Prosecution Service was primarily dependent upon the police for information about both the offence and the offender. Accordingly, their brief to act as a counterweight to the increased powers given to the police in the Police and Criminal Evidence Act 1984 was limited. The Service did not have adequate resources to independently investigate the majority of cases coming before it and, furthermore, Gelsthorpe and Giller argue ((1990),

p. 162) that the Crown Prosecution Service has an operational philosophy of maintaining a "smooth functioning of the prosecution process", presumably due in part to resource constraints. Wilkinson and Evans (1990) also concluded from their study that the Crown Prosecution Service has had very little impact on the use of cautioning by the police. They argued, however, that greater consultation and collaboration between police forces and the Crown Prosecution Service in determining cautioning policy could help reduce disparity.

On the other hand, whilst the concept of "justice by geography" appears inherently unjust there may be dangers in adopting too inflexible national guidelines in the interests of consistency. First, innovative schemes such as those in Liverpool and Glasgow would not be given the opportunity to experiment with alternative responses to dealing with offenders. It is also, of course, possible that guidelines determined nationally would fail to understand the different styles of policing and geographical constraints in certain areas. For instance, all too often national policy would appear to be based on a predominantly urban model which fails to appreciate the needs of more rural areas (Hirst (1994)). Finally specific national guidelines may prove resistent to change. It should also be noted in passing that similar problems are also apparent in sentencing (Hood (1962, 1972); Tarling (1979); Darbyshire (1984); Moxon (1988)). For example, in a sample of 30 magistrates' courts Tarling (1979) found that the use of probation varied between 1 per cent and 12 per cent, suspended sentences between 4 per cent and 16 per cent and fines between 46 per cent and 30 per cent. Just as force practice would appear to be a key factor in cautioning disparity, so the membership of a particular magistrates' bench would appear to influence a sentencer's guiding philosophy (Hood (1972)). Just as there is considerable debate about sentencing reforms, often driven by the perceived need for consistency, radical reform of the cautioning system would also raise important issues regarding accountability, discretion and the separation of powers.

Accountability

It is readily apparent that cautioning has developed in a spontaneous manner in different police forces at different times. Indeed this may largely explain its attraction; the police can modify existing practice to deal with what they perceive to be particular contemporary local concerns. The inherent flexibility is arguably derived in part from the fact that the police retain considerable discretion in the use of cautioning and are subject to few external constraints. Research by Evans and Wilkinson (1990) suggests that there is also variation between different divisions in the same force in their cautioning rates. This again suggests that cautioning may be perceived as being particularly appropriate to certain types of geographical area. Yet the obvious question then arises—to what extent are cautioning decisions taken by the police, either at force or divisional level, accountable?

The Home Office guidelines (1985), (1990a), (1994a)) would appear to offer some degree of accountability, arising from extensive dialogue between the Crown Prosecution Service and the Association of Chief Police Officers (Ashworth (1994)). However, the guidelines only offer general advice on whether or not to caution an individual and do not provide a detailed framework of either the types of offence or offender who are suitable for such a disposition. The 1990 guidelines, for example, state that the police should take account of the nature of the offence, the likely penalty if convicted in court, the offender's age and state of health, the offender's previous criminal history and the offender's attitude to the offence. It is not stated though which offences are to be treated as satisfying this first criterion, nor does it specifically restrict the use of a caution to offences which would ordinarily attract a minor penalty such as a discharge or a fine following conviction. Similarly, although there is a presumption that cautions will be used primarily with young offenders, there is no particular guidance on cautioning adult offenders. The 1994 guidelines have effectively limited the circumstances in which cautions can be used with offenders who have previous convictions or cautions (Evans (1994)), thereby removing one ambiguity in the earlier guidelines. Finally, gauging the offender's attitude to the offence is a highly subjective process. McConville, *et al.*, comment thus ((1991), p. 123):

> "The official guidelines contain several different criteria, set out in no order of priority. Many cases contain some elements which are favourable to caution, and others which are not. This makes it easy to justify any decision, and to dismiss any alternative. Thus whether drunks are prosecuted or not can depend on the individual's sexuality or demeanor, yet any decision can be justified by 'legitimate' criteria. The same is true of, for instance, 'seriousness' in theft and the wishes of the victim. Thus victim withdrawl is used to justify non-prosecution when that is the result desired by the police, but when they want to prosecute they ignore the views of the victim."

Moreover, even if the guidelines were blatantly ignored it is unlikely that the courts would intervene with what has traditionally been regarded as an executive function. In *R. v. Chief Constable of the Kent County Constabularly, ex p. L.* [1993] 1 All E.R. 756, the applicant applied for judicial review in order to quash a police decision to prosecute him and the subsequent decision taken by the Crown Prosecution Service not to discontinue the proceedings. It was the applicant's contention that he should only have received a caution as his case fulfilled the criteria contained in the Home Office guidelines. In such circumstances it was held by Watkins L.J. that any action would lie against the C.P.S. and not the police as it was ultimately the C.P.S. which decides whether or not to continue with a prosecution. Watkins L.J. stated that, in principle, the discretion of the C.P.S. to continue or discontinue criminal proceedings was susceptible to judicial review, but only where it could be shown that the decision was "made regardless of or clearly contrary to a settled policy of the Director of Public Prosecutions" (p. 770). It was envisaged by Watkins L.J. that such an action would only succeed rarely and would apply primarily to cases involving fraud or dishonesty or a "total disregard of the policy ... (or) a lack of inquiry into the circumstances and background" of the offence and offender (p. 770). On the facts both applications were dismissed. It is also notable that Watkins L.J. felt that juveniles were a "special case" (p. 771) and that it would be highly unlikely that an adult could ever successfully challenge a C.P.S. decision to continue a prosecution.

This case reinforces the role of the C.P.S. as an independent body with the primary responsibility for prosecution in England and Wales. Therefore, if the police decide not to caution an offender, the onus is on the C.P.S. to review the case to ensure that the matter could not be dealt with more appropriately by cautioning (Code for Crown Prosecutors (1986), para. 10). However, the latitude provided by the Home Office guidelines mean that in reality the police can usually justify their position to the C.P.S. (McConville, *et al.*, 1991). The conclusion has to be drawn that if the police and the C.P.S. decide to prosecute rather than caution, any action in judicial review will be unlikely to succeed given both the generality of the Home Office guidelines and the Code for Crown Prosecutors and the understandable reluctance of the courts to intervene in executive decision making.

It is also difficult to envisage a scenario where a decision to caution would be challenged in the courts, although in *R. v. Director of Public Prosecutions, ex p. C.* [1995] 1 Cr.App.R. 136 an alleged victim had the relevant locus standi to successfully challenge a C.P.S. decision not to prosecute (Dingwall (1995)). Ordinarily, of course, the offender would regard a caution as a far preferable option to prosecution. It has been suggested by a number of commentators that the threat of prosecution may be so great that innocent people are tempted into accepting a caution (Sanders (1988a); Ashworth (1994)). The police are theoretically susceptible to judicial review, but only under the severely circumscribed basis outlined by Denning M.R. in *R. v. Metropolitan Police Commissioner, ex p. Blackburn* [1968] 2 Q.B. 118 and *R. v. Metropolitan Police Commissioner, ex p. Blackburn (No. 3)* [1973] Q.B. 241. In the former case Denning M.R. stated that force policy is to be determined by the Chief Constable without governmental interference (at 136):

> "I hold it to be the duty of the Commissioner of Police of the Metropolis, as it is of every chief constable, to enforce the law of the land. He must take steps so to post his men that crimes may be detected; and that honest citizens may go about their affairs in peace. He must decide whether or no [*sic.*] suspected persons are to be prosecuted; and, if need be, bring the prosecution or see that it is brought. But in all these things he is not the servant of anyone, save of the law itself. No Minister of the Crown can tell him that he must, or must not, prosecute this man or that one. Nor can any police authority tell him so. The responsibility for law enforcement lies on him. He is answerable to the law and to the law alone."

The only circumstances in which Denning M.R. argued that the courts could intervene would be where the Chief Constable was "failing in his duty to enforce the law" (at 136); he gave the hypothetical example of a policy decision not to prosecute anyone stealing goods valued at less than £100. Salmon L.J. also stated that the courts would only intervene where there was a clear breach of duty rather than where the Chief Constable was lawfully exercising his "wide discretion as to whether or not they will prosecute in any particular case" (at 139).

The resultant position is intriguing; the Home Office feel sufficiently concerned to issue a series of guidelines on cautioning ((1985), (1990a), (1994a)) yet have not taken the step of giving the guidelines a statutory basis as recommended by the Royal Commission on Criminal Justice (1993), para. 5.57). Recently, however, the Government has advocated replacing the caution with a new police reprimand and warning scheme as part of its programme of reforming juvenile justice. The Crime and Disorder Bill currently before Parliament states in section 52 that a constable may warn or reprimand a child or young person if:

(a) the constable has evidence that the individual concerned has committed an offence;
(b) the evidence is such that, in the constables' opinion, there would be a realistic prospect of the individual being convicted if he was prosecuted;
(c) the individual admits to the constable that he committed the offence;
(d) the offender has not previously been charged with an offence (other than one of which he was acquitted or in which proceedings were discontinued); and

(e) the constable does not think that it would be in the public interest to prosecute the offender.

A reprimand may be given if the offender has not previously been reprimanded or warned (s. 52(2)) and a warning may be given if the offender has not previously been warned or if he has been warned more than two years ago and the constable does not consider the latest offence to merit prosecution (s. 52(3)). Further guidance on the circumstances in which it would be appropriate to warn or reprimand an offender and details surrounding the category of police officer who may administer these dispositions and the manner in which they should be given, shall be supplied at a later date by the Home Secretary (s. 52(6)). A reprimand would appear to equate to the current police caution in so far as the offender merely receives an, as yet unspecified, castigation from an, as yet unspecified, police officer. The warning, however, represents a novel diversionary mechanism in that it requires the offender to partake in a programme designed to facilitate his rehabilitation. This programme will be arranged by a youth offending team which will have assessed his particular needs. The Home Secretary will publish further details as to what such programmes should involve at a later date (s. 53(3)). It is proposed that reprimands (s. 53(5)(a)) and warnings (s. 53(5)(b)) may be cited in subsequent criminal proceedings in the same manner as a conviction. It is to be hoped that the guidance which the Home Secretary supplies will be sufficiently detailed to lead to greater consistency in the use of diversion by the police. A comparison can be drawn with the Criminal Justice Act 1991 which attempted to make sentencing decisions more consistent yet largely failed to have this effect because the guiding principles contained in the Act were framed too generally with the result that sentencers retained nearly all of their pre-Act discretion (Wasik and Taylor (1994); Ashworth (1995); Harding and Koffman (1995)). These issues of discretion, accountability and the separation of powers will be considered more fully in the final chapter of this work.

Chapter 8

Diversion by Public Prosecutors

It may appear somewhat paradoxical that the body charged with instigating criminal proceedings in England and Wales has an important diversionary role. After all, earlier chapters have shown that official agencies have the power to divert wrongdoers from the criminal process either unconditionally (for example, through the use of police cautioning) or conditionally (for example, upon payment of a "compound" in the case of tax evasion) after the investigative stage has been exhausted. It is clear from the statistics that these powers are frequently used; indeed there would often appear to be a presumption that diversion is the norm and that prosecution will be reserved for either particularly "heinous" cases or for recidivist offenders (Keith Committee (1983) and, more generally, Chap. 5 of this work). Given the earlier opportunities for diversion, one may well be tempted to conclude that the pool of cases reviewed by the Crown Prosecution Service is comprised of that select group of cases which not only merit but objectively require prosecution.

There is a further reason why one may foresee a limited diversionary role at the prosecutorial review stage. Although the Prosecution of Offences Act 1985 tried to separate the investigative role of the police from the decision of whether to prosecute an offender which would be taken by an independent Crown Prosecution Service, it is clear that the latter is heavily influenced by the former. Sanders (1987) argues that the Crown Prosecution Service can not function independently from the police. He maintains that the Crown Prosecution Service has a dual mandate which is inherently contradictory: it is supposedly investigatory, and hence independent, yet, at the same time, has an accusatory function in the adversarial system which necessitates working in partnership with the police in pursuance of the common aim of securing a conviction. This dual role that the Crown Prosecution Service has to maintain is further complicated by the fact that case vetting and prosecution policy are not easy to separate as the accumulation of evidence is an on going process and the strength of the case against the accused evolves accordingly. Finally, due to the limited resources vested in the Crown Prosecution Service, there is little practical opportunity for them to investigate the police evidence further and they are therefore highly reliant upon the way in which the police originally interpret the case and then present the evidence to the Crown Prosecution Service (Gelsthorpe and Giller (1990)). As Sanders ((1987), p. 234) comments:

> "Cases have to be built out of what people say or think about those facts. The content of cases is, therefore, fluid and uncertain. The police (and, of course, the defence) find that some cases change over time when crucial witnesses change their minds or disappear. Sometimes they make their cases change by eliciting thoughts and statements. Evidential strength is, therefore, determined by a complex and variable interaction between the events in question, witnesses to those events, and the police."

Not only could the cases which the Crown Prosecution Service have to review be those which objectively are not suitable for diversion, but the Crown Prosecution Service will have to make this decision on the basis of a case "constructed" by the very organisation which had previously decided not to divert the offender. However, as this chapter will demonstrate, the Crown Prosecution Service do have an important, and often ignored, diversionary function in the criminal process, despite the fact that they prosecute the majority of cases with which they come into contact (Home Office (1994b)). It will also be shown that the Crown Prosecution Service could be given a far greater diversionary role than at present, particularly with regard to conditional diversionary strategies akin to those available to prosecuting authorities in some comparable jurisdictions.

The current scope for diversion

The Crown Prosecution Service have to decide whether or not to prosecute an individual according to the criteria listed in the Code for Crown Prosecutors (*R. v. Director of Public Prosecutions, ex p. C.* [1995] 1 Cr.App.R.136) which is compiled by the Director of Public Prosecutions in accordance with section 10 of the Prosecution of Offences Act 1985. Unlike some other jurisdictions (see Herrmann (1974); Van Der Wyngaert (1993)), there is no rule of law requiring prosecution in England and Wales for all cases where there is a *prima facie* prosecution case (for a consideration of this see Ashworth (1984)). The Code cites with approval the classic position articulated by Lord Shawcross in parliament: "It has never been the rule in this country—I hope it never will be—that suspected criminal offences must automatically be the subject of prosecution" (House of Commons Debates, Vol. 483, Col. 681, quoted at para. 6.1 of the Code). In continental European parlance, England and Wales follows the "opportunity" rather than the "legality" principle.

The first paragraph (1.1) of the Code recognises that the decision to prosecute is an important one in that it is "essential to the maintenance of law and order" and has "serious implications for all involved—the victim, a witness and a defendant". Paragraph 4.1 states that there are two stages that have to be satisfied before a prosecution should be instigated. First, there is an evidential test to establish whether there is sufficient evidence for the prosecutor to be satisfied that there is a "realistic prospect of conviction". If this stage is not satisfied, the prosecution must not go ahead regardless of the seriousness of the offence or the public interest in a prosecution being brought.

Assuming that the evidential requirement is met, the second stage requires the prosecutor to determine whether or not prosecution is in the public interest (para. 4.1). Although the Code states that "in cases of any seriousness, a prosecution will usually take place unless there are public interest factors tending against prosecution which clearly outweigh those tending in favour (para. 6.2), the prosecutor in reality is granted considerable discretion in determining which factors are of relevance and what respective weight to attach to them. A non-exhaustive list of factors that the prosecutor should consider is provided (paras 6.4 and 6.5). These factors relate primarily to the gravity of the offending conduct and the culpability of the alleged offender and, therefore, largely replicate items that would ordinarily be considered by the court as aggravation or mitigation at the sentencing stage (see generally Walker and Padfield (1996)). To take but one example, a prosecution is "likely to be needed" if the defendant was in a position of authority or trust over his victim (para. 6.4.d). Not only would a defendant in such a position be more likely to be prosecuted but he would probably receive a harsher sentence following conviction (see *e.g. Dawson* (1987) 9 Cr.App.R.(S.) 248).

Implicit in the Code is a sense that prosecution can be a disproportionate response to minor offending. The first factor listed as making a prosecution "less likely" is that a court would be likely to impose only "a very small or nominal penalty" following conviction (para. 6.5.a). Special categories of offender are also mentioned: prosecution is less likely to be necessary if the defendant is elderly or was suffering from significant mental or physical ill health at the time of the offence (para. 6.5.f) and prosecutors must have consideration to the especially harmful effects of prosecution on young offenders (para. 6.8). It would be wrong to state that either of these provisions amount to a presumption against prosecution as the offender's age has to be off-set against the seriousness of the offence committed and, one presumes, a high proportion of offenders in these categories who commit less serious offences will already have been cautioned by the police if they admit guilt. Allied to the twin concepts that (a) a prosecution should not be brought in all cases where there is a *prima facie* case against the defendant; and (b) the decision about whether prosecution is in the public interest depends mainly on issues of proportionality, is the notion that the very process of prosecution is too punitive a response in certain cases.

Of the two distinct grounds for not bringing a prosecution, insufficient evidence and prosecution not being in the public interest, only the second is truly diversionary. In the first scenario there is insufficient evidence for the prosecution to successfully discharge the evidential and legal burdens of proof (at least in the prosecutor's subjective opinion) and there is therefore no case for the defendant to answer (see further McEwan (1992)). In the second scenario there is a "realistic prospect of conviction" and the prosecution is discontinued purely on policy grounds. Although there is always the danger that the distinct grounds could become blurred in practice, it would appear that a higher proportion of cases are terminated by the Crown Prosecution Service on evidential rather than public policy grounds. A recent empirical study into decision making by the service found that the reasons for termination were as follows (Home Office (1994b), p. 16):

Reason for Terminating Case	**Non-Motoring**	**Motoring**
	%	%
Dropped on evidential grounds	58	47
Dropped on public interest grounds	34	24
Defendant not traceable	03	25
Court refused CPS request for adjournment	03	02
Other reasons	02	02

The sample, however, demonstrated that the proportion of terminated cases that had been so designated on the grounds of public interest varied considerably depending upon the offence in question (*ibid*., p. 23): 50 per cent of shoplifting cases that had been terminated by the Crown Prosecution Service had been terminated on public interest grounds, compared with 43 per cent of terminated public order offences, 35 per cent of terminated criminal damage cases and 30 per cent of terminated burglary cases. This appears to support the view that the less serious the offence the greater the probability that, if it is terminated by the Crown Prosecution Service, it will be terminated on public policy as opposed to evidential grounds. However, according to the reasons given by the prosecutors in the sample for terminating cases on public interest grounds, the gravity of the offence seldom appeared to be a primary concern (*ibid.*, p. 20; as more than one reason could be given in each case the totals add up to more than 100 per cent):

Reason for terminating cases on public interest grounds	**Non-motoring** %	**Motoring** %
Accused being dealt with for other matters	42	46
Nominal penalty likely	40	29
Offence trivial	14	27
Complainant did not want to proceed	16	01
Offence stale	07	25
Defendant mentally ill/stressed	11	08
Youth of defendant	12	01
Defendant of good character/suffered enough	07	04
Recompense made to victim	07	—
Case suitable for caution	04	01
Defendant old/infirm	02	05
Defendant on periphery of offence	02	—

The Code for Crown Prosecutors: clarity and conflict

The Code, which was first introduced in 1986, has generally been welcomed as an improvement to the pre-existing situation in so far as it gives greater transparency to prosecutorial review and formally attempts to balance the need for discretion to reflect the diversity of each particular case and the need for decisions to be taken in a consistent, reasoned and fair manner (see, *e.g.* Ashworth (1987)). Of course there are inherent problems with the Code but that should not detract from what is in itself a worthwhile development in a key area of criminal procedure. One problem that does occur is the potential conflict between the need for the Crown Prosecution Service to enforce the law and, at the same time, manage resources in a responsible manner. As Ashworth comments ((1987), p. 597):

> "The law allows a person charged with theft of goods worth £10 to elect Crown Court trial; the cost of that trial, especially if there is a not guilty plea, will inevitably be high in relation to the value of the goods (and the preventive effect of a conviction); so the prosecutor may resolve to drop the case as being insufficiently in the public interest. Yet when defendants and their legal advisers get to know this, they may express their intention to elect Crown Court trial in order to secure impunity."

Also somewhat ambiguous is the extent to which prosecutors should have regard to the wishes of the victim(s) of an offence. The Code generally states that this should be taken into account by the prosecutor but should not become an overriding concern. In other words the public interest usually necessitates giving due attention to what the victim desires but means that, on occasion, these considerations will be overridden by more compelling factors. Of course victims can, and frequently do, decide never to report the incident to the authorities in the first place (a process described in more depth in Chap. 3). One may, therefore, presume that victims who do continue with formally reporting the incident want the matter to result in a prosecution. However, those victims may, at a later date, decide for a variety of reasons that they do not want a prosecution to be brought. There is, for example, the very real possibility that rape complainants are sometimes reluctant to participate in a trial process where they could be subjected to a lengthy, public and strident cross-examination of the most intimate aspects of their life despite initially reporting the incident to the police (Adler (1987), Edwards (1996), Tempkin (1987)). Prosecutions are thus often terminated on the ground that a key prosecution witness is unwilling to testify and, as a direct consequence, there is insufficient evidence to satisfy the evidential requirement in the Code (see Home Office (1994b)) despite the fact that in law most witnesses are compellable for the prosecution.

Conversely, if the victim does want a prosecution to be brought, the Crown Prosecution Service may still decide that prosecution is not in the public interest. This in itself is not problematic: there is little public interest in unwarranted prosecutions being brought due to the economic costs involved and the disproportionate effect conviction would have on the offender (see further Ashworth (1994)). What is problematic is that it appears that certain offences are being more routinely discontinued by the

Crown Prosecution Service despite the clear public interest in prosecutions being brought for what are objectively serious criminal offences (Sanders (1988b)). Cretney and Davis (1996) found, for example, that in cases of domestic violence 38 per cent of cases were discontinued when the suspect and complainant were no longer living together and an alarming 60 per cent of cases were discontinued where the suspect and the complainant were still cohabiting. It is not readily apparent how many of these discontinuances can be attributed to policy decisions taken by the Crown Prosecution Service notwithstanding the victim's wish to prosecute, although it is probable that a high proportion could be attributed to the withdrawing of complaints. These figures are even more concerning when one realises that the Crown Prosecution Service devised a statement of prosecution policy in respect of domestic violence (Crown Prosecution Service (1993)) which sought to encourage prosecutions even where the victim subsequently withdraws the complaint. As there is no requirement for the Crown Prosecution Service to give reasons for not prosecuting an offender (a point discussed by Ashworth (1987)) it is highly problematic for a victim to challenge such a decision successfully.

Challenging Crown Prosecution Service decisions

Increasingly the judiciary are showing a willingness to challenge discretionary decisions in many areas of public law (see generally De Smith, Woolf and Jowell (1995); McEldowney, (1994)) but it is clear that there is a marked reluctance on the part of the courts to intervene in the sphere of pre-trial decision making. According to Dotan ((1997), p. 514):

> "So far, the courts in England have shown considerable reluctance to apply the normal standards of judicial review to prosecutorial decisions. The opinions of the courts reflect either a tendency to view prosecutorial discretion as almost completely immune from judicial scrutiny or a tendency to apply a minimal standard of review. This restrictive view dominates the decisions of the courts in most aspects relating to the judicial review of prosecutorial discretion."

It is difficult though to see why this should be the case. After all, as Osborne ((1995), pp. 140–141) notes:

> "The rationale for the jurisdiction to review decisions of prosecutors is one rooted soundly in general principles of public law. Decisions of prosecutors are decisions made by public officials which potentially impact both directly and significantly upon the individual, be he or she the defendant in criminal proceedings or, alternatively, the victim of a crime the suspected perpetrator of

which the DPP does not intend to prosecute. Taken at this level and coupled with the large latitude of discretion which public prosecutors enjoy, their decisions were an obvious candidate for judicial review."

Early indications were that the courts would be reluctant to intervene, despite the fact that prosecuting authorities would appear to have been susceptible to judicial review (*Metropolitan Police Commissioner, ex p. Blackburn* [1968] 2 Q.B. 118; *General Council of the Bar, ex p. Percival* [1991] 1 Q.B. 212 and *Chief Constable of Kent Constabulary, ex p. L.* [1993] 1 All E.R. 756). An example of the reticence demonstrated by the judiciary to become involved in prosecutorial decisions is provided in the case of *R. v. Humphrys* [1977] A.C. 1 where the House of Lords expressed the view that a judge should not appear to have any responsibility for the institution of prosecutions nor should a judge refuse a prosecution to proceed on the grounds that it is not in the public interest, save in extreme cases where "the prosecution amounts to an abuse of the process of the court and is oppressive and vexatious" (*per* Lord Salmon at 46).

With the advent of the Crown Prosecution Service it has been held that, if a prosecutor patently fails to act in accordance with the overall policy as set out in the Code for Crown Prosecutors, the decision will be set aside by the Divisional Court and remitted back to the Director of Public Prosecutions for further consideration. A clear example of this occurred in *R. v. Director of Public Prosecutions, ex p. C.* [1995] 1 Cr.App.R. 136 (see further comment by Dingwall (1995)). In this case the Crown Prosecution Service decided not to prosecute the applicant's husband who had allegedly buggered his wife without her consent. Although the prosecutor felt that the evidential criterion had been met, he terminated the proceedings on the ground that it was not in the public interest, despite a general proviso in the Code that "there will seldom be any doubt that prosecution will be in the public interest" for sexual offences (para. 8.6). His reasoning was that there was no evidence to support the view that the acts in question had been non-consensual and, had both the parties been male and over the age of 21 and the act had been consensual, such conduct would not be criminal provided it had occurred in private (Sexual Offences Act 1967, s. 1(1), as amended by the Criminal Justice and Public Order Act 1994, s. 145(1)). Furthermore, the prosecutor argued that, unless there was clear evidence that the conduct was non-consensual, the matter would be more appropriately dealt with in civil rather than criminal proceedings.

Kennedy L.J. found in favour of the applicant on the narrow ground that the prosecutor had failed to consider all of the possible defences that the applicant's husband could have argued. By failing to consider the possibility that the defendant would argue that buggery had not occurred, the prosecutor had failed to consider all of the possible defences and had acted in breach of the Code. The case is of wider importance though as it considered the circumstances in which a prosecutor could terminate proceedings arguing that it was not in the public interest to prosecute a certain type of offence. Regrettably the Court failed to adequately answer this important question. Instead they relied upon the reasoning in *Metropolitan Police Commissioner, ex p. Blackburn* [1968] 2 Q.B. 118 where Lord Denning M.R. drew a distinction between a decision that a Police Commissioner could legitimately make, such as not prosecuting those who attempt to commit suicide, with "unlawful" decisions which the court could legitimately interfere with; Lord Denning's famous example being a decision not to prosecute those who steal goods valued at less than £100. Other than a question of degree, Lord Denning's distinction is problematic as, at the time, both attempted suicide and theft, were criminal offences. Would the Police Commissioner not technically be failing in his duty to uphold the law in both scenarios if he failed to prosecute? In *Director of Public Prosecutions, ex p. C.* the Divisional Court confirmed that a policy of not prosecuting those who steal goods valued at less than a £100 would amount to an "unlawful policy" and, therefore, one which the court could legitimately set aside whilst, intriguingly, not specifying whether a decision not to prosecute consensual buggery would be classified in a similar manner. The case, however, highlights the need for prosecutors "to apply the guidelines and not to reform them" (Dingwall (1995), p. 267). What is also clear, however, is that prosecutors in England and Wales do have considerable discretion in determining whether prosecution is in the public interest and that the courts will only intervene in the most extreme cases where the Code has been blatantly ignored. As such the Crown Prosecution Service does have an important diversionary role but this role is limited to the extent that the only form of diversion at their disposal is unconditional, as opposed to the conditional schemes available to their Scottish and Dutch counterparts.

Scotland the brave?

Although the Crown Prosecution Service has the option of not instigating proceedings, thereby unconditionally diverting the offender, the Procurator Fiscal in Scotland (see generally Moody and Tombs (1982); White and Willock (1993)) has a far greater range of diversionary options at his or her disposal. A fiscal can (Walker (1997), p. 547): formally warn the person that his behaviour is unacceptable and, if repeated, will result in prosecution; can direct an offender to receive help from a voluntary organisation such as Alcoholics Anonymous; in the case of minor motoring offences, a fixed penalty can be offered (Road Traffic Offenders Act 1988, ss 75–77) and, most notably, the alleged offender can be given the opportunity of paying a fine as a direct alternative to prosecution for offences triable by a district court. This last option, commonly termed a "fiscal fine" or a "prosecutor fine", is deserving of particular attention (for greater discussion of the other available options see Tombs and Moody (1993)) given the fact that both the Royal Commission on Criminal Justice (1993) and the Crown Prosecution Service (Home Affairs Committee (1990)) have recommended that such a scheme be introduced in England and Wales.

The fiscal fine was one of a number of strategies recommended by the Stewart Committee which was set up in 1977 with the aim of finding suitable diversionary mechanisms in a bid to reduce the pressure on the criminal court system in Scotland. The first report (1980) was limited in scope to road traffic offences and argued for the extension of the existing system of fixed penalties. This report was followed three years later (1983) by a wide ranging review of diversionary mechanisms which considered how these strategies could be gainfully employed as a response to a variety of both statutory and common law offences. The Committee considered evidence from comparable jurisdictions, including the Netherlands (see later), which suggested that a fine administered by the prosecuting agency in lieu of prosecution was deserving of particular attention, especially in light of Parliament's willingness to extend the use of fixed financial penalties instead of prosecution in the case of road traffic offenders.

The professional bodies which gave evidence to the Stewart Committee, including the Law Society of Scotland and the Sheriffs' Association, were not supportive of moves to introduce a fiscal fine to Scotland for a number of reasons including the inherent dangers of adopting diversionary mechanisms from inquisitorial as opposed to adversarial systems of criminal justice, the undesirability of extending a fixed penalty system to encompass not only regulatory road traffic offences but "real" crimes and, above all, the fact that an administrative body, namely the Procurator Fiscal Service, would be granted what was perceived to be a judicial function (Duff and Meechan (1992)). The fiscal fine was also opposed by the Scottish Council for Civil Liberties on the basis that it was wrong as a matter of principle for prosecutors to become involved in the sentencing realm (Stewart Committee (1983), para. 4.26). Although such bodies were correct to recognise the dangers of transferring a judicial function to the Procurator Fiscal, it should be noted that the Procurator Fiscal already had an important role in deciding the manner in which an offender would be dealt with: not only does the Procurator Fiscal decide whether to instigate proceedings against an individual but, unlike the position south of the border, the Procurator Fiscal also selects the venue and form of a trial.

Notwithstanding the abovementioned professional misgivings and the allied concerns of the Scottish Council for Civil Liberties, the majority of the Committee recommended that the fiscal fine be introduced as a new diversionary measure in Scotland. Although their justifications were largely pragmatic—delays in the system were adjudged to be more problematic than the "niceties of the philosophy of justice" (*ibid.*, para. 4.38)—they rejected the notion that the fiscal fine would give prosecutors a judicial function. As the offender would have to admit his guilt before accepting a fiscal fine, the prosecutor would not in any way have to determine the guilt or innocence of the suspected offender and would merely be responding to a pre-agreed group of offenders in a pre-agreed manner. The majority were also mindful that the individual (a) had the option of rejecting the offer of a fiscal fine and could therefore have his guilt or innocence determined by a court and (b) could receive legal advice prior to deciding whether to accept a fiscal fine. This line of reasoning ignores two factors discussed elsewhere in this work which are often cited as inherent dangers associated with diversionary mechanisms. First, the threat of prosecution and the possibility of a harsher post-conviction penalty may induce someone who is innocent into accepting the lesser of two evils, even though he may have been acquitted at trial. Secondly, legal advisors may take the view that accepting the diversionary option is preferable to risking the uncertainties of a trial, even in situations where the suspect is factually innocent.

The majority of the Committee were of the opinion that the amount of a fiscal fine should be determined by the prosecutor subject to an overall maximum of £50 (the then maximum that could be imposed in court for a Level 1 offence). This recommendation, however, would appear to partly negate the argument of principle that they employed: the prosecutor may not determine the guilt or innocence of an individual, but nor is the prosecutor merely applying a set penalty on a set class of offender if the prosecutor can effectively determine the fine's punitive effect. There are strong arguments of principle that a fine has to take into account the offender's ability to pay so that a proportionate penalty can be imposed; fixed penalty fines can have vastly different consequences for rich and poor offenders and, therefore, penalise the poor disproportionately. Similarly, prosecutors might be more willing to divert offenders from prosecution if they have a wider range of fines at their disposal. It is notable that the legislature rejected the idea of a sliding scale in Scotland and allowed prosecutors only to impose a fixed penalty set by the Secretary of State for Scotland (Criminal Justice (Scotland) Act 1987, s. 56) whereas the Royal Commission (1993) recommended that prosecutors in England and Wales be given "an appropriate range of fines". This may in part reflect the greater readiness to accept that the level of a fine has to reflect the offender's ability to pay that has become apparent in England and Wales in the 1990s. Despite the untimely failure of the "unit fine" system introduced by the Criminal Justice Act 1991 (Wasik (1993)), the general principle remains that a court has to have regard to an offender's ability to pay when setting a fine (Criminal Justice Act 1991, s. 18(5) as substituted by Criminal Justice Act 1993, s. 65(1) see comment by Dingwall (1994)).

The Criminal Justice (Scotland) Act 1987 set out the procedure for administering the fiscal fine, or to adopt the statute's terminology, the "conditional offer". If a procurator fiscal decides to offer a fiscal fine he sends a notice to that effect to the alleged offender and also notifies the clerk of the court specified in the notice that an offer has been made (s. 56(1)). The offer that is sent to the alleged offender specifies (a) the particulars of the circumstances alleged to constitute the offence; (b) the amount of the fixed penalty and whether this can be paid in instalments; (c) that, if the amount is paid in a specified period or a first instalment is received, any liability to conviction of the offence shall be discharged; (d) that proceedings shall not be instigated against the alleged offender until the period for accepting the conditional offer has expired; and, finally, (e) that the acceptance of the offer will not amount to a conviction (s. 56(3)). The onus for administering the scheme falls largely upon the clerk to the court to whom initial payment should be made. If no payment is made in the specified period, the clerk has a duty to notify the procurator fiscal (s. 56(4)) and no proceedings can be instigated until the prosecutor is informed to this effect (s. 56(5)). The Act stated that a procurator was at liberty to offer a fiscal fine in respect to any offence for which an alleged offender could competently be tried before a district court (s. 56(2)). Finally, the level of the fine that could be imposed was fixed by s. 56(7) of the Act to be a sum specified by the Secretary of State for Scotland not exceeding level 1 on the standard scale for fines. Initially the Secretary of State set this at a level of £25 (S.I. 1987 No. 2025).

Due to the level of the fixed penalty in its initial guise, it appeared that the fiscal fine was not being used to such an extent that it was having any discernible diversionary effect. The official criminal statistics demonstrate that, between 1988 and 1992 inclusive, the fiscal fine represented between 4 per cent and 5 per cent of all disposals. However, according to Duff *et al.* (1994) there was considerable variety in the extent to which it was being used by different procurator fiscal offices. They reported (*ibid.*, p. 152) that the ten largest offices had usage rates that varied between 2.2 per cent and 12.3 per cent in 1990. One medium sized office was only using the fiscal fine in 0.1 per cent of cases that they were called to deal with.

The type of offences which were being diverted in this manner appear to have been largely influenced by the level of the fine that could be imposed. The following offence profile emerged from a sample of 600 fiscal fines drawn from 10 different offices from across Scotland (*ibid.*, pp. 152–153):

Offence	**No. of cases**	**Percentage of sample**
Breaches of the peace	172	28.7
Urinating to public annoyance	134	22.3
Theft	76	12.7
Offences under the Railway Acts	54	9.0
Assaults	40	6.7
Drunkenness at sports grounds	35	5.8
Being drunk and incapable	29	4.8
Other	60	10.0

The author urged caution in the interpretation of these figures as the bulk of the assault cases came from one office as did the bulk of the cases involving drunkenness at sports grounds (*ibid.*, p. 153). Of those offered a fiscal fine, it was found that the acceptance rate in most offices was consistently around 70 per cent (*ibid.*, p. 153). As was anticipated by the Stewart Committee those who refused to accept a fiscal fine were ordinarily prosecuted: the four largest offices in the sample prosecuted between 73 and 87 per cent of those who refused an offer (*ibid.*, p. 154). Two tentative conclusions can be drawn at this stage. With a limited penalty at their disposal, procurators appeared to be using the fiscal fine for only the most minor of offences which, in England and Wales, may well have been diverted anyway through the use of police cautioning. The overall diversionary effect of the fiscal fine was, therefore, limited. However, the high acceptance rates associated with the fiscal fine documented in the study appear to suggest that many offenders were keen to avoid prosecution making diversionary strategies of this kind attractive to policy makers.

Yet there was cause for concern. The official statistics appeared to demonstrate no reduction in the proportion of cases being prosecuted in the district court following the introduction of the fiscal fine, but a sizeable reduction in the proportion of cases being dealt with by warning letters and decisions not to prosecute. Assuming a similar offence profile, the stark reality appeared to be that a new more invasive form of diversion had merely replaced older, less invasive diversionary responses to minor offending: the net had, once again, widened. Duff (1993) identified three main factors which help explain why net widening occurred in the case of the fiscal fine. There was considerable external pressure on procurator fiscal offices to standardise the rates of non prosecution or "no-pros" with the inevitable result that offices with high initial rates of no-pros may have used the fiscal fine to try and reduce their reliance on "no-pros". Prosecutors may also have taken the view that the fiscal fine may have been a proportionate response to offences that do not merit prosecution but require some penalty in addition to a warning. Prior to the availability of the fiscal fine, such cases would have to be diverted by other means rather than prosecuted. Finally, the pressure of resources meant that prosecutors were having to be selective in the cases that they prosecuted, even though some that resulted in "no-pros" would be deserving of prosecution. As Duff comments (*ibid.*, p. 494):

> "It may be that the fiscal fine is serving to bring back into the criminal justice process some cases which, in an ideal world, would never have left it, but the inescapable fact is that they have left the system. It is impossible to assess the influence of this factor. The difficulties are exacerbated by the fact that its impact is likely to vary from office to office depending upon workloads and court waiting-times. Thus, in some offices the majority of fiscal fines might represent cases which previously would have been marked 'no pro' purely as a result of excessive workloads; in other offices, however, most fiscal fines might represent cases which previously would have escaped prosecution as the result of an unfettered decision that the case was too trivial to prosecute—albeit with a hint of prosecutorial regret that the offender was escaping rather lightly."

Due to the limited impact of the diversionary fine, the Government proposed two major changes (Scottish Office (1994)) to the fiscal fine. It was proposed both to extend the range of offences which could attract a fiscal fine and to increase the discretion given to procurators by allowing them to choose whether to fine offenders £25, £50, £75 or £100 rather than the fixed amount previously available. These changes were implemented in the Criminal Justice (Scotland) Act 1995: the divisional court became competent to try any statutory offence which was triable summarily (s. 60(1)) thereby extending the range of offences which could be diverted by a fiscal fine and a scale of fixed penalties was introduced which would be set by the Secretary of State for Scotland (s. 61(6)). The procurator would have to determine which fixed penalty was appropriate "having regard to the circumstances of the case" (s. 61(2)). The law relating to fiscal fines was consolidated, along with many other aspects of Scottish criminal procedure, in the Criminal Procedure (Scotland) Act 1995 and the Secretary of State delimited the scale of fixed penalties in the Criminal Justice (Scotland) Act 1987 Fixed Penalty Order 1996. One will have to see whether the extension of the circumstances in which a fiscal fine can be offered will result in a notable reduction in the proportion of cases which are prosecuted in Scotland.

The Dutch *transactie*

The apparent failure of the fiscal fine in Scotland to have any meaningful diversionary effect, and the extent to which it would appear to have been used as an alternative to other diversionary options (Duff (1993)) contrasts with the *transactie*, a diversionary mechanism available to Dutch prosecutors. There are obvious dangers in drawing parallels between Dutch and Scottish penal policy (for an introduction to the former see Chorus and Jeroen (1993); Downes (1982), (1988); Leigh and Hall-Williams (1981) and Steenhuis (1988)), however it is noticeable that the Dutch *transactie* is used in a far greater proportion of cases than the fiscal fine and that the *transactie* offers greater flexibility to the prosecuting agency than the fiscal fine. At the outset, the *transactie* was only available to prosecutors as an alternative to prosecution if the alleged offender had committed an *overtredingen*, or "infraction", as opposed to a *misdrijven*, or "crime", and the infraction was punishable by a fine alone, however the circumstances when a *transactie* could be offered were extended firstly, in 1921, to include infractions punishable by imprisonment and then, in 1983, to encompass crimes where the maximum penalty did not exceed six years" imprisonment (Duff (1994); for the difference between infractions and crimes see Brants and Field (1995)).

The other key difference between the *transactie* and the fiscal fine is that *transacties* can be set at any amount by the prosecutor rather than being limited to a number of comparatively small fixed amounts. The amounts imposed can be considerable; Fionda (1995) refers to a company which had committed a number of offences being offered a series of *transacties* worth a total of £17 million. This flexibility means that the *transactie* is suited not only to minor offending but to more serious offences which would ordinarily be prosecuted in other jurisdictions (although Chap. 8 of this work comments that, in exceptional cases, comparatively serious offences may be dealt with by police cautioning in England and Wales). Brants and Field ((1995), p. 138) report that in 1989 prosecutors dealt with some 211, 807 *misdrijven* (the most serious category of offence) of which only 36 per cent resulted in a prosecution. Of the cases which were diverted at this stage, the *transactie* was used in 33 per cent, 36 per cent were "policy waivers" and 31 per cent were "technical waivers". This shows that, as in Scotland, the Dutch prosecutor has the option to divert either conditionally or unconditionally and it is notable that unconditional diversion is used to a greater extent than conditional diversion even for this most serious category of offence notwithstanding the flexibility offered by the *transactie*. The average sum imposed by a *transactie* in 1989 was f. 389 (*ibid.*, p. 138. It is not clear whether this includes *transacties* imposed for *overtredingen* as well as *misdrijven*).

This level of prosecutorial discretion in the setting of *transactie* may appear alarming to a British observer, however the Dutch strategy has to be seen in the context of a jurisdiction which has a far more rigid sentencing framework than England and Wales (Kelk, Koffman and Silvis (1995)) where sentencers have traditionally enjoyed considerable latitude in determining an appropriate sentence for any given case. In keeping with detailed sentencing guidelines, the Public Prosecution Department has drafted detailed guidelines on setting appropriate levels for *transactie* (Duff (1994)). Moreover, Dutch prosecutors are used to advising judges on sentencing matters, unlike their British counterparts, and share elements of common training with the judiciary (Brants and Field, 1995) giving them a different status and function in the criminal justice system. It is more difficult to criticise the *transactie* on the basis that it supplants a judicial function onto an administrative body if that body already possesses a judicial function. This concern would, however, remain valid if such an option was made available to British prosecutors due to their traditional administrative function.

Concluding comments

One can detect a number of alternative strategies in operation across the jurisdictions considered in this chapter, ranging from a compulsory prosecution policy in all *prima facie* cases through a selective prosecution policy to a system where the prosecutor has a range of options at his or her disposal to a system where the prosecutor can impose a variable penalty. The diagram below (Figure 1) summarises these four positions.

The further along this continuum one moves, the greater the potential diversionary impact and hence the greater the attraction to policy makers. Yet, simultaneously, the further along the continuum one moves the greater the conflict between the administrative and judicial function. In a system where all *prima facie* cases are prosecuted the role of the prosecutor is limited to the extent that he or she assesses the evidence before determining whether there is sufficient evidence for the case to proceed. Although cases may be removed from the process at this stage, this is diversionary in a limited sense as the offender (at least in the prosecutor's opinion) would not have been found guilty at trial: it is a process designed to remove a

Figure 1

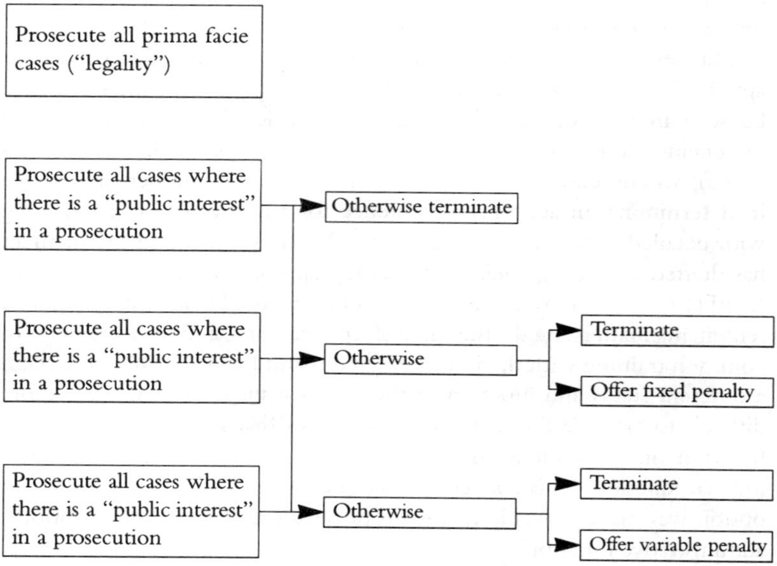

weak case and not an offender from the system. At the next stage, which approximates to the current situation in England and Wales, the prosecutor has to determine whether the "public interest" requires prosecution. This clearly extends the prosecutor's discretion in that he or she is no longer solely concerned with evidential factors but has to consider policy concerns which may or may not favour diversion. When one moves to the third stance, based on the Scottish position, the prosecutor not only has to consider evidential and policy factors in determining whether to prosecute but also has to decide whether it would be appropriate to impose a fixed penalty *in lieu* of prosecution. Finally, a Dutch prosecutor has to determine not only whether to prosecute or issue a *transactie* but the exact terms of the *transactie* if that option is deemed appropriate. At this stage it is clear that the prosecutor is in effect sentencing the offender.

It is noticeable that in all three jurisdictions considered in this chapter there have been moves to increase the diversionary strategies available to the prosecuting agencies. In England and Wales, both the Royal Commission for Criminal Justice (1993) and the Crown Prosecution Service (1990) have advocated the introduction of a prosecutorial fine. In Scotland, disappointment with the initial diversionary effect of the fiscal fine has led to the introduction of a sliding scale of penalties following the enactment of the Criminal Justice (Scotland) Act 1995. Even the Netherlands, which has a considerable history of allowing prosecutors discretion to conditionally divert infractions, has extended the scope of the *transactie* to cover crimes punishable with imprisonment of up to six years.

In all three jurisdictions the primary motivation behind extending the prosecutor's potential for diversion would appear to be bureaucratic, in that scarce resources can be allocated more effectively if fewer offenders are prosecuted (and, of course, monetary penalties such as the fiscal fine and the *transactie* also raise revenue). The changing role of the prosecutor in adversarial jurisdictions may be symptomatic of a broader trend towards the "Europeanisation" of criminal justice exemplified by the adoption of measures employed in other jurisdictions and the potential confluence of adversarial and inquisitorial systems of criminal justice (see Harding, *et al.*, 1995) which may partly be explained by the common desire for an efficient, yet economical, method of dealing effectively with offenders.

Chapter 9

Diverting Trials Through Guilty Pleas

Despite the popular perception that the criminal court is a venue for flowing rhetoric and tense adversarial justice, where defendants have their guilt or innocence decided upon by a magistrate or a jury comprised of peers who listen meticulously to the available evidence before deciding whether or not the prosecution have successfully established the defendant's guilt beyond reasonable doubt, the reality is rather different and rather less glamorous. In the majority of cases, criminal courts do nothing more than process people who have pleaded guilty (McConville, *et al.* (1994)). Recent figures show that, in 1995, 64 per cent of Crown Court cases were disposed of by a guilty plea (Lord Chancellor's Department (1996), p. 65). In the magistrates" courts, which deal with the vast majority of criminal cases, the guilty plea rate was even higher at 81 per cent (Home Office (1996a), p. 135). This trend is mirrored in other jurisdictions which have adversarial systems of criminal justice (McConville and Mirsky (1986); Chatterton (1991)). Despite the availability of several opportunities for earlier diversion from the formal criminal justice system (see earlier chapters), the majority of defendants who are eventually prosecuted admit their guilt, bypass the trial process and are thereby diverted directly to the sentencing stage in most adversarial systems of criminal justice. Furthermore, it would once again appear to be the case that certain types of offender are more likely to be diverted at this stage of the process. Offenders who come from ethnic minority groups are less likely to plead guilty (Hood (1992)), possibly due to a greater reluctance to participate in a system which research suggests discriminates against them at every stage in the process (Smith (1994)).

Why do such a high proportion of offenders forfeit the right to a trial and the chance of a possible acquittal? The first rationale is that a proportion, and possibly a high proportion, of the defendants who plead guilty are factually guilty and have no realistic possibility of mounting a plausible defence. Research by McConville, *et al.* (1994) into the work of defence solicitors found many instances where defendants openly admitted their involvement in the crime, which was in keeping with the findings of earlier studies (Heumann (1978), Mather (1979)). Whilst the adversarial model of criminal justice may be dependent upon due process ideals which insist upon the duty of the state to prove the case against the defendant beyond reasonable doubt in the belief that this will reduce the likelihood of convicting the innocent (Packer (1968)), there is clearly little social justification for insisting upon a full criminal trial when the defendant is willing to voluntarily waive his right to such a trial. However, as will be seen later, there may be reasons other than factual guilt that could lead an individual into pleading guilty. Commentators have argued that the criminal justice system has increasingly moved more towards a crime control model which has sought to facilitate guilty pleas through the inducement of offering a substantial sentence discount (Young and Sanders (1994); Davies and Dingwall (1996)). It is this "advantage" to pleading guilty that has led to a substantial body of critical literature which has argued, with varying degrees of sophistication, that the official encouragement of rewarding guilty pleas in this manner has led to both a practical reorientation of the aims and values of the criminal justice system and to the increased likelihood of miscarriages of justice. This chapter will start by considering the advantages to the defendant in pleading guilty and the possible justifications for rewarding a guilty plea with a reduced sentence, before analysing the dangers inherent in such an approach and the effects that this form of diversion has on our traditional criminal justice system.

Rewarding those who plead guilty

The courts in England and Wales have traditionally treated a guilty plea as a mitigating factor and have accordingly dealt with those who plead guilty more leniently than those who are convicted following trial (Stockdale and Devlin (1987)). In a detailed study of the process of mitigation, Shapland (1981) found that barristers routinely made specific reference to a guilty plea notwithstanding the fact that this information would be readily available to the sentencer. Baldwin and McConville (1978) state that pleading guilty can be advantageous at two levels: firstly, courts appeared to be more willing to use alternatives to custody with those who plead guilty and, secondly, the terms of imprisonment imposed were shorter for guilty pleaders than for those who were convicted following trial. The difference in terms of sentence can be marked. For example, in *Hollington* (1985) 7 Cr.App.R.(S). 281 the Court of Appeal did not allow an appeal on the basis that a defendant who was convicted after trial was sentenced to three months' imprisonment whilst his co-defendant, who pleaded guilty, received a suspended sentence. Wasik (1993) suggests that the appellate authorities show that a guilty plea in the Crown Court will ordinarily attract a discount in the region of between one quarter and one third of the length of a custodial sentence. Guilty pleas are also rewarded, although possibly to a lesser extent (see Bing (1996)), in the magistrates courts. The latest guidelines on sentencing compiled by the Magistrates' Association recommend that a timely guilty plea should result in a sentence discount of about one third.

Although there may well be the expectation that pleading guilty will result in a reduced sentence, the court still retains discretion in this area. Robertshaw and Milne (1992) found considerable variance in the way in which Crown Courts rewarded guilty pleas. There are also some recognised limits to the courts' benevolence. When the offender has little option but to plead guilty, for example where he is caught in the act of committing the offence, the courts often either reduce the discount or make no reduction to the sentence whatsoever (see, *e.g. Stabler* (1984) 6 Cr.App.R.(S.) 129 and *Morris* (1988) 10 Cr.App.R.(S.) 216). In a similar vein, the court in *Hollington and Emmens* (1986) 82 Cr.App.R. 281 refused to give full credit for a guilty plea where the offender only entered the plea at the very last minute, and for largely pragmatic reasons in that he wished to remain on remand prior to trial as he would enjoy greater privileges than a convicted prisoner. Lawton L.J. commented (at 285):

> "This court has long said that discounts on sentences are appropriate but everything depends on the circumstances of each case. If a man is arrested and at once tells the police that he is guilty and co-operates with them in the recovery of property and the identification of others concerned in the offence, he can expect to get a substantial discount. But if the man is arrested in circumstances in which he cannot hope to put forward a defence of not guilty, he cannot expect much by way of discount. In between comes this kind of case, where the court has been put to considerable trouble as a result of a tactical plea. The sooner it is appreciated that defendants are not going to get full discount for pleas of guilty in these sort of circumstances the better."

A final area where the courts have sometimes been reluctant to fully award a guilty plea concerns offenders who are adjudged to present a danger to the public (see, *e.g. McLoughlin and Simpson* (1979) 1 Cr.App.R.(S.) 298). This, however, is far from a general principle, indeed it is often the case that the courts are especially willing to compensate sexual offenders who plead guilty on the basis that the offender has spared the complainant the additional anxiety of having to testify in court (*e.g. North* (1989) 11 Cr.App.R.(S.) 437). As Walker and Padfield (1996) note, mitigation is usually justified on retributive reasoning either on the basis that the offender's culpability is reduced, that the offender will suffer more than usual from the penalty imposed or, more rarely, that the offender has behaved in a manner which although it does not actually affect his culpability should be taken into account in his favour. However, in cases such as *McLoughlin and Simpson* the primary justification for the sentence is not retribution but the utilitarian principle of selective incapacitation (see generally von Hirsch and Ashworth (1992); Walker (1996)). This problem of attempting to reconcile a utilitarian justification for punishment with a form of mitigation based on retributive notions has become particularly marked due to the statutory sentencing principles contained in the Criminal Justice Act 1991. Although the choice of disposition was largely based on retribution, allowance was specifically made in section 1(2)(a) of the Act to imprison certain types of offender from whom the public needed protection. The Act provided that the length of sentence such individuals would receive would be "for such longer term (not exceeding that maximum) as in the opinion of the court is necessary to protect the public from serious harm from the offender" (CJA 1991, s. 2(2)(a)). It would appear on face value that a plea of guilty should make no difference to the length of sentence as the term should be that necessary to protect the public (Dingwall (1998)) yet the Court of Appeal has paradoxically said that credit should be given for a guilty plea even where harm to the public should be the sole determinant of sentence (*Crow and Pennington* (1995) 16 Cr.App.R.(S.) 409).

Even where the sentence is based on retribution under the 1991 Act, the theoretical justification for reducing the sentence for a guilty plea demands greater consideration. On face value the Act states that the sentencer "shall take into account all such information about the circumstances of the offence ... (including any aggravating or mitigating factors) as is available to it" (CJA 1991, s. 3(3)(a)) in determining the gravity of the offending conduct and, in turn, the proportionate punishment. To a desert theorist this is comparatively unproblematic (at least at a theoretical level): the offender's blameworthiness at the time of the offence and the resulting harm caused are the widely accepted determinants of overall seriousness (von Hirsch (1985)). It is therefore logical that anything that reduces the offender's culpability *at the time that the offence was committed*, such as provocation, entrapment or where the offender was under severe financial stress, should be treated as mitigation and should result in a lesser sentence being imposed. However, with a guilty plea one is concerned with the offender's moral status *after the offence* and not at the time that it was committed. It would appear that the courts are prepared to give credit to what can generally be termed redemptionary actions by the offender after the event. The courts have, for example, greatly reduced the sentence of offenders who have provided valuable information to law enforcement agencies (*e.g. King* (1986) 82 Cr.App.R. 210) or who have voluntarily made some form of recompense to their victims (but see *Crosby* (1974) 60 Cr.App.R. 234), neither of which would appear to have any bearing on the offender's blameworthiness at the time that the offence was committed. Rather the courts would appear to be engaged in a process which has been described vividly by Wasik (1993) as "moral accounting". The Criminal Justice Act 1991 allows these more general considerations about the offender's character to be taken into account by virtue of section 28(1) which states that nothing shall prevent a court from reducing an offender's sentence in consequence of "any such matters as, in the opinion of the court, are relevant in mitigation of sentence". As Ashworth (1993) notes, though, this section owes little to any principled theoretical justification and a great deal to the insistence by the judiciary that considerable discretion was needed in determining what was relevant as mitigation.

This chain of reasoning still assumes that a plea of guilty is morally creditable, yet one must be extremely wary of automatically equating a guilty plea with a genuine feeling of remorse on the part of the offender (Baldwin and McConville (1977); Shapland (1981)). The plea may well be motivated by a rational acceptance that there is no realistic chance of an acquittal and that a guilty plea is simply the lesser of two evils. This would explain why Shapland (1981) found that barristers frequently claimed that their clients demonstrated remorse as a distinct ground of mitigation from a guilty plea. If a defendant pleads guilty for purely tactical reasons and not out of a genuine feeling of remorse, it is exceptionally difficult to see how his moral credit is in anyway reduced either at the time of the offence or thereafter.

For the purposes of reconciling a reduction in sentence for a guilty plea with retributive penal philosophy, it may be more instructive to consider the effect of a guilty plea in the context of the harm caused. Gauging the harm caused by an offender is often problematic both in practice and in theory (Walker (1995)). Clearly, as well as the direct monetary or physical harm caused to the victim, there are a variety of other unpleasant consequences experienced by victims of crime (Maguire (1980); Walklate (1989)) which need to be included in any assessment of the aggregate harm caused. One of the consequences of the offence that often causes particular anguish to victims is the thought of having to testify in court (McBarnett (1983)). By relieving the victim of this trauma, the harm caused by the offender is thereby diminished and, according to desert theory, the resultant punishment should in turn be proportionately reduced.

There is, of course, another far more pragmatic reason for rewarding a reduction in sentence for a guilty plea. Like any other area of state responsibility, the criminal justice system has to function in an economically responsible manner and, in keeping with every other department of government, has to manage its budget effectively. The fact that the majority of offenders do not waste court time, and hence resources, obviously makes it tempting for the Home Office to encourage offenders to plead guilty. In the late 1980s and early 1990s the Government sought to facilitate early pleas of guilty (Davies and Dingwall (1996)), primarily on the basis that too many offenders, in the Government's opinion, were delaying pleading guilty until the last minute leading to a worringly high proportion of "cracked trials" and a considerable waste of resources (Bredar (1992)). The Government received the support of a number of prominent criminal justice practitioners, including the Bar Council, the director of the Serious Fraud Office, the Director of Public Prosecutions, the former Metropolitan Police Commissioner and the chair of Justice, in moving towards an officially-sanctioned plea-bargaining system (McConville and Mirsky (1993)).

A working party of the Bar Council (1992) under the chairmanship of Robert Seabrook Q.C. recommended the establishment of a formal system for rewarding guilty pleas based upon the stage in the proceedings where such a plea is entered: notification of an intention to plead guilty at the committal stage would attract a minimum discount of 30 per cent, for example, whilst notification between first Crown Court listing and arraignment would result in a minimum discount of 10 per cent. The Seabrook report proposed that the judge should indicate to the defendant the sentence that would be imposed on a plea of guilty, supposedly on the basis that this would allow the defendant to objectively consider his options before deciding how to plead. Allied to this, the report also advocated that the defence should routinely agree to make "extensive admissions" in advance of trial and that formal pre-trial conferences should be instigated either where the defendant intends to plead not guilty or where the Court, prosecution or defence think that it would be useful. This combination of, on the one hand, offering structured minimum sentencing discounts and, on the other, reducing the due process elements inherent in the traditional contested trial led to a considerable amount of academic criticism.

McConville and Mirsky (1993) attacked the proposals on a variety of grounds. First, they argued that (at p. 6):

> "The plea bargaining system advocated forgoes an open testing of the state's evidence for reasons wholly unrelated to a defendant's willingness to assume responsibility for the acts alleged and related solely to the existence of the judicially ordained discount, designed to save the state the time and money—and the risk of failure—in having to prove the defendant's guilt in open court."

They also expressed concern about the Bar Council's desire to obtain guilty pleas at the committal stage on the basis of the prosecution papers which may not be wholly complete as a number of high profile miscarriage of justice cases have demonstrated. The authors also criticised the proposals requiring the defendant to disclose information to the prosecution at a pre-trial stage and argued that these recommendations undermine further the central tenet of an adversarial model of criminal justice, namely that the prosecution have to prove every element of the offence against the defendant. Finally, McConville and Mirsky noted that the proposals undermined the centrality of the jury in the criminal justice system.

After a series of miscarriages of justice in the late 1980s, the Government announced the establishment of a Royal Commission on Criminal Justice under the chairmanship of Lord Runciman (for background see Field and Thomas (1994)). The terms of reference for the Commission were to "examine the effectiveness of the criminal justice system ... in securing the conviction of those guilty of criminal offences and the acquittal of those who are innocent, having regard to the efficient use of resources". One of the areas where the Commission seemed particularly concerned with effective resource allocation was in their endorsement of a clear system of sentence discount dependent, like the Seabrook proposals, on the stage in the proceedings where the plea is first entered, in the hope of encouraging "defendants who know themselves to be guilty to plead accordingly and so enable the resources that would be expended in a contested case to be saved" (p. 110).

Although the Commission expressly recognised the potential for miscarriages of justice to occur by rewarding defendants who plead guilty (p. 110), the report suggested that this was not a problem of great practical importance as the defendant should be advised not to plead guilty unless he actually committed the offence and, secondly, relying upon an empirical study made for the Commission, it was suggested that false guilty pleas were not a serious problem. Both of these assumptions have been widely challenged. As will be seen later, commentators have argued that, contrary to the defendant being warned not to plead guilty unless he is factually guilty, legal advisors often exert considerable pressure on clients to plead guilty even where there may be a valid defence (Baldwin and McConville (1977); McConville, *et al.* (1994)). Secondly, the research study commissioned by the RCCJ has been criticised (Bridges (1993)) on the basis that it was methodologically unsound, a point that has been partly accepted by the author of the study (Zander (1993)). The Commission also recommended (with the notable dissent of Michael Zander) the implementation of a system of pre-trial review.

The RCCJ's recommendations, of which the proposals for a formal system of plea bargaining represents but part, were subject to considerable criticism (Ashworth (1993); Carman (1993); Grosskurth (1993); Mansfield

(1993); McConville (1993); Owers (1993); Smith (1993); Bridges and McConville (1994) and Young and Sanders (1994)). The essence of much of the criticism was that the Commission failed to address fundamental problems in the criminal justice system at a satisfactory level, failed to recognise the conflicting (and sometimes contradictory) aims of any system of criminal justice and, most alarmingly, recommended a series of proposals which would appear to further undermine the protection of defendants from miscarriages of justice. By facilitating, or attempting to facilitate, the efficient conviction of the factually guilty the RCCJ failed to appreciate that they had also facilitated the conviction of the innocent. Young and Sanders conclude that ((1994), p. 448):

> "The first step to successful reform is accurate identification of the problem to be addressed. Reforms are doomed to failure if the system they are applied to is not understood in the first place. The Royal Commission on Criminal Justice's complacency, as we see it, means that an opportunity has been lost. It had the chance to raise the level of debate from the rhetorical to the factual and moral, and to identify real—not idealised—choices. That chance was wasted."

Despite the trenchant criticisms of the report outlined above, the government acted upon some of the Commission's recommendations in the Criminal Justice and Public Order Act 1994. As Field and Thomas (1994) note, the Act originated in a political landscape where the Conservative Government were losing ground in popular opinion polls and consequently ministers were "jockeying for position" to succeed John Major as Prime Minister. The Home Secretary, Michael Howard, clearly sought to establish himself as a right-wing hardliner through a series of populist law and order measures, many of which, such as the curtailment of the right to silence, directly opposed the conclusions drawn by the Runciman Commission. Given the extreme political sensitivity of certain sections of the Act (see generally Card and Ward (1994); Wasik and Taylor (1995)), such as the new "right to silence" provisions, the introduction of secure training orders for 12–14 year olds, the increased police powers to evict trespassers, the contracting out of aspects of the prison service and a free vote on the age of consent for homosexuals, the statutory plea-bargaining provisions were introduced with little debate; during the lengthy and heated exchanges in the House of Commons on the second reading of the bill, which lasted nearly seven and a half hours, no mention was made by either the Government or the Opposition to the proposals to put plea-bargaining on a statutory footing (*Hansard*, H.C., Vol. 235, cols. 20–132).

The Act did stop far short of following the proposals contained in the Seabrook Report and the recommendations of the RCCJ on sentence canvassing. Instead section 48 of the Act basically codified the existing case law outlined above (Davies and Dingwall (1996)). The section states that:

> "48(1) In determining what sentence to pass on an offender who has pleaded guilty to an offence in proceedings before that or another court a court shall take into account—
> (a) the stage in the proceedings for the offence at which the offender indicated his intention to plead guilty, and
> (b) the circumstances in which this indication was given.
> (2) If, as a result of taking into account any matter referred to in subsection (1) above, the court imposes a punishment on the offender which is less severe than the punishment it would otherwise have imposed, it shall state in open court that it has done so."

Although the practical effects of s. 48 might be limited, the granting of statutory recognition, and hence parliamentary approval, to a sentence discount for a guilty plea is notable. It represents open recognition by the government of a system of criminal justice where the priorities are economic efficiency and an increase in the number of convictions through the reduction of procedural safeguards notwithstanding a compelling body of research literature which exposes how rewarding a plea of guilty in the manner outlined above exarcerbates the possibility of miscarriages of justice. As Young and Sanders (1994) highlight, the quid pro quo of reforms designed to convict more criminals is that one will also convict an increased number of innocent individuals due to the relaxation of due process requirements. This policy in turn represents a clear view of the objectives of criminal justice policy, a view spelt out by Michael Howard in the House of Commons during a debate on the Criminal Justice and Public Order Bill (*Hansard*, Vol. 235, col. 22):

> "(the) measures that we are putting in place will achieve the most comprehensive and effective framework that it is possible to devise to prevent crime, to enable the police more effectively to catch criminals and to enable the courts more effectively to convict them and to deal with them when they have been convicted. That is the responsibility of Government and it is a responsibility that we are determined to discharge."

One of the presumptions that both the RCCJ and the Government made was that defendants are afforded protection in the criminal justice process by their legal representatives and that one can therefore reduce legal and procedural impediments which might reduce the possibility of a conviction without jeopardising the protection necessary to safeguard the innocent from wrongful conviction. In turn, this assumes a model of adversarial justice where defence lawyers always act in the best interests of their clients and are sufficiently apprised of both the law and the facts surrounding the offence to offer effective legal service. It would appear that this is not always the case and, due primarily to the stressful nature of criminal defence work (McConville, *et al.* (1994)) and the low rates of legal aid renumeration (Young and Wall (1996)), there is a potential benefit for defence solicitors if their clients plead guilty. This is not to suggest that defence solicitors routinely coerce innocent individuals into pleading guilty, rather it is an admission that not all defendants receive model advice from their representatives and that this in turn can lead to miscarriages of justice. Furthermore, it is not always easy for defence solicitors to ascertain what is in their clients' best interests.

The role of the defence lawyer in relation to advising on plea

The defendant is often in a particularly vulnerable position prior to trial. Not unnaturally, when one considers the strain of the trial and the ever present threat of conviction and sentence, the defendant is highly reliant on the advice that he receives from his legal advisor, if he elects to have one. This can pose a difficulty in relation to the decision on how to plead; to what extent, if at all, can the defence lawyer advise his or her client to plead guilty on the evidence available before them? On the one hand, there are clear policy reasons why it is desirable that the accused has to decide on the plea himself without undue influence from his legal advisor. In an adversarial model of criminal justice it is for the magistrate or the jury to determine the guilt of the accused not the defendant's lawyer. It is also clear that the traditional justification for rewarding a plea of guilty with a lesser sentence, namely that the offender admits that he has acted in a criminal manner and hence has reduced culpability under a desert model, cannot be invoked when the offender was coerced into pleading guilty. Conversely, it is clearly central to the defence lawyer's function to advise his or her client as to the most expedient course to take (Bar Council (1990)). In many cases, given the strength of the prosecution case, the best advice that could be given would be to plead guilty and, it could be argued, defence counsel would be failing in his or her professional duty if this advice was not given in strident terms in appropriate cases.

The Court of Appeal has established that a plea of guilty must be entered by the accused personally and not by his or her legal advisor (*Heyes*

(1950) 34 Cr.App.R. 161; *Boyle* (1954) 38 Cr.App.R. 111; *Ellis* (1973) 57 Cr.App.R. 571; and *Williams* [1978] Q.B. 373; a similar rule would appear to cover cases where the accused changes plea in the course of a trial: *Tasamulug* (April 29, 1971, unrep. CA). In *Ellis*, Edmund Davies L.J. outlined the justification for such a position (at 574–575):

> "... great mischief could ensue if a legal representative was generally regarded as entitled to plead on an accused's behalf. It would open the door to dispute as to whether, for example, counsel had correctly understood and acted upon the instructions which the accused had given him, and, if a dispute of that kind arose, the consequential embarrassment and difficulty could be difficult in the extreme."

The appellant in *Ellis* had sought to appeal against a sentence of 18 months' imprisonment that had been imposed in respect to a burglary and theft. Given the seriousness of the theft, the application for leave to appeal on the sentence was refused but "the vigilance of the staff of the Criminal Appeal Registry" disclosed an important irregularity regarding Ellis' plea. The Clerk of the Court had informed Ellis that he was charged with burglary contrary to section 9(1)(b) of the Theft Act 1968 and stated the particulars of the offence which alleged that he had stolen a number of cheques and cash totalling £1,687. Ellis was then asked whether he intended to plead guilty or not guilty. At this juncture, his defence counsel interjected and informed the Clerk that his client wished to plead guilty to the theft of £380 but not to the offence as charged. After some questioning of defence counsel by the recorder it was established that Ellis intended to plead guilty to burglary but that he was only willing to admit to stealing £380. The recorder sentenced Ellis on this basis, notwithstanding the fact that Ellis had given no personal indication on how he intended to plead. The Court of Appeal concluded that this failure to follow proper procedure meant that the conviction could not stand and ordered a retrial with the proviso that, if Ellis was subsequently convicted, the court should have regard to the period of imprisonment that Ellis had already served when determining sentence.

Although the court will not allow defence counsel to submit a guilty plea on behalf of his or her client, the position appears to be somewhat more relaxed if a plea of not guilty is proferred. In *Williams* [1978] Q.B. 373, counsel for the prosecution sought an adjournment, prior to Williams stating how he intended to plead, on the grounds that the defence wished to cross-examine a prosecution witness who was unable to testify due to illness. The trial was prosponed for this reason and the court record stated that the case had been "adjourned to date to be fixed. Plea N.G.". Although this clearly conformed with the defendant's intention, at no point in the proceedings had he personally stated that he pleaded not guilty to the charge. Two months later, and before a different judge, clerk and counsel, Williams entered the dock again and confirmed his identity. The clerk, assuming that Williams had entered a not guilty plea on the previous occasion, empannelled the jury and read out the indictment. Williams offered no protest when the clerk told the jury that the defendant pleaded not guilty. The jury convicted Williams and he was sentenced to a period of imprisonment. Williams appealed on a number of grounds, all but one of which were dismissed as being without substance or significance. The only matter that concerned the Court of Appeal was whether the failure to call upon the defendant to plead personally had resulted in a mistrial. Shaw L.J. considered the reasoning of the court in *Ellis* and came to the conclusion that (at 378–379):

> "There the critical issue was whether a plea of guilty tendered by counsel and not by the accused himself could be regarded as an effective and binding plea. It is of course plain to see why it cannot and should not be so regarded. It is a plea which is self-incriminatory and self-incrimination cannot be vicariously accomplished. Any contrary view would be fraught with manifest dangers. Injustice rather than justice would be the likely products of a principle which permitted indirect delegated confessions of guilt ... It does not seem to this court, at any rate at the present day, that the same fundamental objection exists where a plea of not guilty is vicariously offered or tacitly conveyed. It is difficult to conceive what possible prejudice to an accused person could derive from such a procedure."

Although no direct injustice appeared to have occured in that particular case, particularly in light of Williams' tacit acceptance of the not guilty plea in the subsequent proceedings, Shaw L.J. would appear to have overstated the case when he said that it would be difficult to see what prejudice could be caused to the accused by a vicarious plea of not guilty. If the defendant's legal advisor indicates that his or her client wishes to plead not guilty and this does not represent the defendant's personal desire or intention, prejudice could arise if, following conviction, the defendant received a harsher sentence that that he would have received following a guilty plea. As the plea can have a significant effect upon the sentence imposed by the court (see, *e.g. Hollington* discussed earlier), it would be desirable if, in all circumstances, the court required the defendant to plead personally and, it is respectfully submitted, that the reasoning employed in *Williams* is both flawed and potentially dangerous.

These cases are, however, of an exceptional nature. In practice the defendant is given the opportunity to plead in person. It is, of course, probable that, at least to some extent, the defendant is advised on plea by his legal advisor and that this advice has some direct bearing on his decision as to how to plead. Given his or her supposedly superior knowledge of the operation of the criminal justice system, the legal advisor may well be better placed to judge objectively the realistic probability of a conviction following a plea of not guilty. The defendant's judgment may well be clouded by factors such as confusion, embarrassment, vulnerability and fear and the defendant may not even be aware of the practice of the courts to reward a guilty plea with a reduced sentence. Family or friends may also exert pressure on the defendant to either plead guilty or to contest the charge. The supposed objectivity and experience of defence counsel may be highly advantageous to the defendant in deciding how to plead. Yet, at the same time, and, paradoxically, for largely the same reasons, it is important to ensure that the advice is not couched in such a way as to effectively remove the defendant's personal choice on the matter. Two excerpts from the Code of Conduct of the Bar of England and Wales (1990) demonstrate the potential difficulties for those advising defendants prior to trial: "[A] barrister acting for a defendant should advise his lay client generally about his plea. In doing so he may, if necessary, express his advice in strong terms. He must, however, make it clear that the client has complete freedom of choice and that the responsibility for the plea is the clients" (para. 12.3). A practising barrister also has to "promote and protect fearlessly and by all proper and lawful means his lay clients best interests" (para. 2.03(a)). Whilst there is no inherent contradiction in these two paragraphs, it remains problematic to state with any definitiveness exactly how much pressure it is legitimate for a barrister to put on a client to plead guilty. If a barrister oversteps the mark he or she would appear to breach paragraph 12.3. Conversely, if a barrister doesn't give strident enough advice in appropriate cases then there is a danger that he or she would be failing to comply with the more general duty contained in paragraph 2.03(a).

The formula adopted in the Code of Practice largely paraphrases the advice given by the Court of Appeal in *Turner* [1970] 2 Q.B. 321, the leading case on the "vexed question of so-called plea bargaining" (at 326). The facts of the case were somewhat bizarre in so far as Turner had been charged with the theft of his own car after refusing to pay a garage for repair work to the vehicle. When the police first spoke to Turner, he denied that he had taken the car to the garage but he later admitted to a Detective Sergeant Thompson that this had been a lie. It was the prosecution's contention that the garage had obtained a propriety interest in the vehicle and that the defendant's lies to the police demonstrated that the subsequent appropriation of the car from outside the garage had been dishonest.

At the outset the appellant pleaded not guilty to the indictment, however, his counsel became alarmed because Turner was proposing to argue that a key prosecution witness, Detective Sergeant Thompson, had not merely been mistaken about their conversation but that the police had deliberately fabricated the evidence against Turner in conjunction with the garage owner. This strategy was clearly not in Turner's best interests as a blatant attack on the character of a prosecution witness will ordinarily result in the jury being made aware of the defendant's own bad character (Criminal Evidence Act 1898, s. 1(f)(ii), see, *e.g. Tanner* (1977) 66 Cr.App.R. 56 and *McGee* (1979) 70 Cr.App.R. 247) and Turner had a number of previous convictions for dishonesty offences. During a lengthy adjournment, and in the presence of Turner's solicitor and his clerk, counsel advised Turner that the conduct alleged could amount to theft if it was established that there was a lien in existence in relation to the car and he asked Turner to seriously consider changing his plea to guilty. He informed Turner that his previous record was such that, were he to be convicted, he would risk facing a custodial sentence whereas, were a plea of guilty to be entered, his sentence may well be of a non-custodial nature. It was accepted that counsel had given this advice in strident terms.

During the course of the adjournment, the defence counsel had a meeting with the deputy chairman regarding sentence which he then reported to the appellant. Shortly after this, Turner changed his plea to guilty and was sentenced to a fine of £50, had his licence endorsed and was ordered to pay costs of £75. The appellant based his appeal on two grounds: first, it was submitted that counsel had exerted undue pressure on Turner to plead guilty and, therefore, the defendant had not been given sufficient freedom to decide on his plea; secondly, it was alleged that Turner had mistaken the advice of his counsel with the views of the judge and this had also pressurised him into changing his plea.

Lord Parker C.J. regarded the first submission as "a very extravagant proposition" and one which would succeed only "in a very extreme case" (at 325). Although the evidence was given in strong terms, the court found no evidence to suggest that undue influence was exerted on Turner by defence counsel during the adjournment. Indeed a number of individuals, including his solicitor and barrister, had emphasised that only Turner himself could decide how to plead. On the facts, the first submission failed and it was held that the advice given by counsel, although undoubtedly trenchant in nature, was appropriate in the circumstances and did not remove Turner's free choice on plea. The appeal succeeded on the second ground, though not without some reluctance on the part of Lord Parker C.J. It was accepted that, after counsel had spoken with the deputy chairman, Turner may have confused counsel's subjective response to this meeting with the personal views of the judge and, in the court's opinion, once Turner felt that the advice he had received emanated directly from the judge, it was wrong to think that the defendant had a free choice in the matter. Finally, and of particular importance to the current discussion, the Court of Appeal made the following more general "observations" (at 326–327) on plea bargaining and the respective roles of counsel and the judge.

Parker C.J. started with the general principle that defence counsel must not be hindered in his or her duty to provide the client with the best legal advice and this will often involve advising the client that a plea of guilty usually results in a lighter sentence than may otherwise be expected. Counsel, however, should state that the defendant should only plead guilty if he actually committed the offence or offences in question. Thereafter, the defendant must have "a complete freedom of choice" (at 326) regarding plea.

It was recognised that, whenever possible, justice should be administered in open court, but that, on occassions where it is strictly necessary, the judge should be available to meet counsel in private. In such cases both counsel for the prosecution and counsel for the defence should be present and, if he or she so desires, the defendant's solicitor should also be given the opportunity to attend. One matter which might legitimately be discussed in such a setting would be whether it would be proper for the prosecution to accept a plea of guilty to a lesser offence.

The Court of Appeal stated that, in general, the judge should not give counsel any indication of the sentence that he or she was likely to impose. This would forbid not just statements along the lines of "if your client pleads guilty he will receive a fine whereas if he is convicted following a plea of not guilty I will impose a custodial sentence", which would clearly place direct pressure on the accused to plead guilty, but also statements such as "if your client pleads guilty I will be minded to make a probation order" as this may lead the defendant to the conclusion that a not guilty plea would result in a harsher sentence and therefore indirectly pressurise the defendant into pleading guilty. The only circumstances where it was felt to be appropriate for the judge to comment on sentencing intentions was where the same type of sentence was going to be imposed regardless of plea. In such cases, the Court of Appeal presumably felt that the judge would not be exerting any pressure on the accused, whether directly or indirectly.

A more vivid example of how judicial pressure could remove a defendant's choice on plea is provided by *Inns* (1975) 60 Cr.App.R. 231. Defence counsel was so disturbed about two conversations that had been held in private with the trial judge that he made a note of what had been said shortly afterwards. All of the other counsel present confirmed that the note was an accurate representation of what had been discussed, although the judge felt that he had been misunderstood and that the conversation had been of a more general nature. According to the note, the judge stated, on more than one occasion, that if the defendants were convicted they would be sent to a detention centre whereas, if they pleaded guilty, a more lenient sentence may be imposed. The judge also made it clear that he regarded the theft of railway property to be a serious matter and did not believe the defendants' claim that they had not acted dishonestly as they had thought that the property had been abandoned. In light of what had been said, Inn's counsel asked for trial before another judge at the second meeting but this request was refused. It should come as no surprise, particularly as Inns was only 17 years of age, that he changed his plea to guilty after hearing of this conversation. Lawton L.J. was highly critical of the judge's actions (at 233):

> "It is to be hoped that this kind of conversation between judge and counsel will not again take place. It may be that on occasions the judge can send for counsel and tell them what the sentence is likely to be in any event—and I stress the words *in any event*—but it is clear in this case that, when Mr Murphy went back for the second time and told this appellant (who was only 17 years of age) what was likely to happen if he persisted in a plea of not guilty and was found guilty, he crumpled and took the view that contesting the case was not worth the risk. If a young man of 17, or indeed someone of any age, is faced with this sort of choice, he does not have a free choice as to his plea. The whole basis of a plea on arraignment is that in open court an accused freely says what he is going to do; and the law attaches so much importance to a plea of guilty in open court that no further proof is required of the accused's guilt. When the accused is making a plea of guilty under pressure and threats, he does not make a free plea and the trial starts without there being a proper plea at all. All that follows thereafter is, in our judgment, a nullity." [Italics in original.]

A further problem can arise if the prosecution offer some inducement to the defendant in exchange for a guilty plea. For example, prosecuting counsel may accept a plea to a lesser charge, such as accepting a plea of guilty to assault occasioning actual bodily harm (Offences Against the Person Act 1861, s. 47) on a charge of inflicting grievous bodily harm contrary to s. 20 of the 1861 Act (for the differences between these offences see Smith and Hogan ((1996) at pp. 436–444). From the defendant's perspective this would, in all probability, result in the imposition of a lesser sentence, yet there are obvious problems with such an approach which require further consideration. There would, of course, be the omnipresent danger that the likelihood of a lighter penalty could induce an individual to plead guilty to an offence that he did not actually commit, especially when one appreciates fully the anxiety that many defendants feel prior to trial. There is also the problem of reconciling this practice, often termed "charge bargaining", with a sentencing framework based, at least in theory, on principles of proportionality. Under the Criminal Justice

Act 1991 sentences were to be determined primarily on the basis of desert: custodial sentences, for example, were to be imposed where the severity of the offence was such that no other sentence would adequately reflect the gravity of the offending conduct (CJA 1991, s. 1(2)(a)). Allied to this, the Government have recently argued that there is a need for greater honesty in the sentencing process so that "all those involved—offenders, judges and the public—will know exactly where they stand" (Home Office (1996b) at p. 45). Both of these policies are undermined when someone is punished for a less serious offence than the one he or she actually committed. To some extent at least, desert theory can accommodate the principle of rewarding a guilty plea with a reduction in sentence, at a theoretical level it can not entertain the possibility of someone being sentenced for an offence that does not accurately reflect the gravity of the offending conduct, not withstanding the fact that the practical effect, a reduction in the sentence for a guilty plea, may be identical.

However, recent research by McConville, Sanders and Leng (1991) has demonstrated how prosecution agencies "construct" a case against a suspect from the available evidence by determining what facts are of relevance, omitting those which do not conform to the model that the prosecution agencies are trying to construct and presenting the "relevant" facts in such a way that a strong *prima facie* case against the suspect is made at an early stage in the process. Charge bargaining may appear less morally objectionable if one accepts that there is a high degree of arbitrariness in the way in which a prosecution case is originally framed; indeed one of the primary criticisms levelled against an adversarial model of criminal justice is that the objective truth may never emerge from two competing, and often contradictory, versions of the event.

Empirical studies have also suggested that, despite the protection supposedly given to the accused in the *Turner* guidelines, suspects are often put under considerable pressure by their legal representatives to enter a plea of guilty. In 1977 John Baldwin and Mike McConville published a study entitled *Negotiated Justice: Pressures to Plead Guilty* which was based upon material gathered as part of a large scale Home Office funded project to analyse the outcome of Crown Court cases. Prior to publication both the President of the Law Society and the Chairman of the Bar wrote to the press complaining that the study was "directly contrary to the public interest" and that "it cannot possibly be described as research" (Baldwin and McConville (1977)). In a written answer (*Hansard*, Vol. 932, col. 169) the Home Secretary, Merlyn Rees, reported that he had received representations from the Senate of the Inns of Court and the Bar about the study but that the Home Office had neither the desire nor the power to stop publication of the work. However, the Home Secretary argued (col. 170) that the methodology employed by the authors, and in particular their failure to discuss individual cases with the judges and barristers concerned, meant that the strident criticisms made of the police and the legal profession could not be substantiated (this conclusion was shared by at least one academic reviewer: Adams (1978)).

Notwithstanding these pre-publication concerns, the central thesis of the work was both alarming, in that it suggested the genuine possibility of miscarriages of justice occuring, and embarrasing to the legal profession in that the authors argued that "the high ethical standards of the profession are a by-word in legal writings, but they do not always seem to be matched by reality" (Baldwin and McConville (1977), p. 56). The authors cited a number of examples where the defendant believed that he had no option but to plead guilty due to the advice given by his legal advisors. One of the sample, for example, commented that (p. 53):

> "My barrister pleaded guilty for me. I told him that I was innocent but he said I was a bloody nuisance and that nobody would believe me. He said, 'The judge and the others will never believe what you say in court; they will always believe the police.' I said, 'How can this be so? What I am saying is true.' He said I must plead guilty . . . I was forced to plead guilty by my barrister; it was wrong of him."

Baldwin and McConville acknowledged the criticism that had been levelled by professional groups that convicted defendants may well present a distorted view of what had actually occured but they argued that there were a number of factors which suggested the defendants' concerns may have been valid. The researchers noted that the dissatisfaction demonstrated by those who had pleaded guilty was generally far greater than that expressed by a large sample of defendants in contested cases, a large proportion of which had been convicted. The defendants who were interviewed were given little prior indication of the purpose of the interview and were not asked primarily about the facts surrounding the particular offence (where it might be expected that defendants would lie about their involvement) but about their experiences of the legal system prior to trial. There were also opportunities for the authors to cross refer some of the accounts given with statements made by co-defendants and/or police officers and solicitors. In these cases the additional evidence never reduced the veracity of the defendant's story and "in important respects often strengthened it" (p. 11). Moreover, few of the defendants came across as the stereotypical "victim of the system" that the professional bodies had predicted. In truth many of the defendants regarded the system favourably in that they had received a tangible benefit from it in the way of a reduced sentence.

However, the most important reason advanced by the authors for listening to the defendants' accounts was that the subjective interpretation of the advice offered by counsel is of paramount importance: "where defendants say they have been 'forced' to plead guilty by their barrister, this interpretation of the encounter is more significant than whether the conduct of the barrister in question was in fact outside the strict ethical rules governing the advice that can be given" (p. 11). Notwithstanding the cases identified where the barrister appeared not to act in accordance with either the letter or the spirit of the law in this area, the work was of importance in that it highlighted how the available protection did not stop many defendants believing that they had no option but to plead guilty and that legal advisors routinely placed defendants under considerable pressure to do so (p. 56):

> "Advice is not infrequently taken by defendants as an order; protestations of innocence may be ignored or summarily dismissed; sentencing differentials of a grossly inflated nature threatened; and the sentencing propensities of the judge used as a stick to beat the unwilling."

Conclusion

In sum, the diversionary effect of guilty pleas is of enormous practical benefit to the criminal process and compensating a guilty plea with a concrete reward to the defendant in the guise of a reduced sentence greatly facilitates the operation of criminal justice in England and Wales. Its pragmatic appeals are obvious not just to an economist but to anyone concerned with the need to manage the criminal process in an efficient manner. As has been recognised earlier it is more problematic (though not wholly impossible) to justify a reduction in sentence for a guilty plea from a principled theoretical position and, more particularly, under the retributivist principle of "just deserts" currently in penological vogue. The traditional theoretical justification, namely that a guilty pleader deserves credit due to his recognition and acknowledgement of the wrong that he committed, is unduly deterministic: many defendants plead guilty not out of altruism but because they face no realistic chance of an acquittal. A guilty plea is often little more than a pragmatic response to a pragmatic offer.

Yet a desert theorist can legitimately claim that a sentence reduction is warranted if, by pleading guilty, the resultant harm caused by the offence is reduced in that victims and/or witnesses are spared the anxiety, inconvenience and expense of testifying at trial (a justification which is obviously more difficult to maintain in the case of so-called victimless offences). Given these attractions, it is easy to see why policy makers in most adversarial jurisdictions have sought to encourage this form of diversion. What is the benefit of a criminal trial if the majority of defendants don't appear to want one, it costs the state a considerable amount of money and it is traumatic to most of the lay participants?

There clearly is little benefit to a trial if the defendant, assuming he has been fully and fairly apprised of the situation, elects to forfeit his right to have one. However, as has been documented in this chapter, defendants are highly reliant upon the advice that they receive from their legal advisors and empirical research suggests that this advice may be, for a variety of reasons, slanted towards obtaining a guilty plea. It has been suggested (McConville, *et al.* (1994)) that defence lawyers "play a key, pivotal role in the process, serving more to transmit to the client the system's imperatives" (p. 281) one of which is to secure a timely guilty plea. It would also appear to be the case that, on occasion, the advice is given in such a manner that the defendant feels that he has no free choice in the matter, even though the barrister may have acted in full compliance with the relevant case law.

However, even if no pressure was placed on a defendant by his legal representative, might the defendant not be tempted to accept a reduction in sentence rather than face the stress of a trial and a potentially harsher sentence regardless of whether or not he was factually guilty? Many commentators have argued (*e.g.* McConville and Mirsky (1993); Young and Sanders (1994); Davies and Dingwall (1996)) that, by increasing the reward gained for a guilty plea, the Government have *re ipso facto* raised the potential for the factually innocent to plead guilty. The crime control model that has been adopted in the jurisprudence of the Court of Appeal and in the Criminal Justice and Public Order Act 1994 either assumes that only the factually guilty plead guilty or, more alarmingly, encourages guilty pleas by removing due process safeguards whilst being fully aware that this may lead to an increase in miscarriages of justice. This inherent presumption of guilt also directly contradicts a central principle espoused by most adversarial criminal justice systems, namely that the defendant is presumed to be innocent until the state proves otherwise (McEwan (1992)). By exercising his right to a trial and therefore his right to a presumption of innocence, the defendant is being penalised directly in so far as a subsequent conviction will almost automatically result in a harsher sentence. This theme will be addressed more fully in the concluding chapter as many diversionary mechanisms in the criminal process reward an admission of guilt, thereby calling into question notions about the presumption of innocence in the practical operation of the criminal justice system. Plea bargaining epitomises the inherent strain between the bureaucratic concerns of those charged with managing the criminal justice system (and some would argue of those charged with representing defendants in that system), the crime control polices that have been adopted by central government and the due process ideals supposedly enshrined in British criminal procedure.

Chapter 10

Conclusion: Diversion, Penal Theory and Penal Policy

Diversion is not new and nor is it unusual in the criminal process: it is, and to some extent always has been, both a practical reality and a deliberate policy choice in the way in which society responds to the majority of offending behaviour. Rather than being the exception to the rule, diversion at some stage from the traditional criminal justice process would appear to be the norm whereas the popular perception of adversarial justice, namely the trial process, would appear to be reserved for a comparatively small proportion of both actual and recorded offences. As Ashworth ((1994), p. 289) has commented the criminal justice system "tends strongly towards trial-avoidance". To this end, a complex phenomenon of diversion has evolved, some of it informal, in so far as it does not involve state agencies, and some of it formal, in that the diversionary mechanism forms an important part of the official state response to criminal activity. This work highlights a continuum of diversionary activity that operates alongside the traditional criminal process, ranging from the informal responses of victims, whether individuals, employers, institutions or interest groups through to more formal diversionary measures employed by investigators, prosecutors or lawyers representing the parties in criminal proceedings. This continuum, however, may give the false impression of a co-ordinated diversionary response to criminal activity. A study of the historical background (Chap. One) demonstrates that different measures have evolved at different times for very different reasons: diversion is not a system with an all encompassing rationale; different types of offender are dealt with in different ways because of a variety of political, economic and social factors, and the subject does not have a clear philosophical foundation. It is therefore of crucial importance that diversion is subjected to rigorous theoretical analysis in any study of the criminal justice process.

Given the fact that most offenders are diverted, why is the trial perceived to be the paradigmatic response to criminal activity in England and Wales and elsewhere? Contemporary popular perceptions regarding the administration of criminal justice are based, at least in part, on media representations of the process (Smith (1984); Home Office (1989); Sparks (1992)) which often centre on the trial. In addition, sociological analyses of punishment (Foucault (1977); Garland (1990)) have emphasised the symbolic importance of the trial. Garland commenting ((1990), p. 67):

> "Rituals do not just 'express' emotions—they arouse them and organise their content; they provide a kind of didactic theatre through which the onlooker is taught what to feel, how to react, which sentiments are called for in that situation. Rituals—including the rituals of criminal justice—are ceremonies which, through the manipulation of emotion, prompt particular value commitments on the part of the participants and the audience and thus act as a kind of sentimental education, generating and regenerating a particular mentality and a particular sensibility. Not every criminal case does this, of course, though ritualistic elements are involved in even the most mundane, 'conveyor-belt' procedures. But there are what one might describe as 'show-case' trials and punishments—solemn, emotionally charged affairs of high drama and real import—which tend to be the ones which are relayed by the media to the public to represent the meaning of justice."

It is Garland's contention that the public itself is not "immediately involved today in the direction or administration of punishment" (*ibid.*, p. 68) but rather forms the audience to which the criminal justice process is meant to appeal, in that its operation symbolises order and security in an environment which can appear unjust and disordered. The educative value and denunciatory aspects of the criminal trial have appealed to many penologists writing from both utilitarian and retributive stances (Walker (1991)). Feinberg's *Doing and Deserving* (1970) has been widely attributed (*e.g.* Duff and Garland (1994)) with re-emphasising the importance of the expressive function of punishment and led to a considerable body of subsequent work which refined, developed and criticised Feinberg's central observations (Morris (1981); von Hirsch (1993)). Primoratz (1989) outlines how the expressive elements of the criminal justice system can be both of utilitarian value, in that these elements could result in future benefit to society, and retributively justifiable in so far as it is intrinsically right that offenders should suffer public condemnation as a consequence of their offending behaviour. It is apparent though that prosecution is reserved for only a small proportion of cases (Chap. Five; Chap. Nine) and, of those cases which are prosecuted, the majority do not go to trial as the offender elects to plead guilty (Chap. Ten). Is it the case that society or the state wish to express particular revulsion to certain types of offending behaviour by prosecuting a disproportionate amount of such activity and diverting less heinous offenders from the system at an earlier stage in the process? By ensuring that not all cases result in prosecution, diversion may, paradoxically, heighten the expressive effect of those cases that are prosecuted successfully. This is unproblematic if the cases which are prosecuted are those which society most wishes to express collective abhorrence towards, but it is clear that prosecution is not dependant solely on grounds of seriousness and that, in practice, objectively serious offences which, one presumes, society would wish to express revulsion towards are frequently diverted. Domestic violence, for example, may be prosecuted but it may well not be reported by a victim, may well not be proceeded against by the police and may well not result in a prosecution.

The expressive function of punishment may be theoretically important but it is important in practice only in relation to a small proportion of cases. In many other instances there would appear to be a preference for personally motivated cost-effective solutions to illegal activity rather than invoking a process of formal, ritualised, public condemnation designed in part to reaffirm community values. This preference is discernible with respect to victims, who may elect not to report an offence and seek a more satisfactory form of redress through alternative channels (Chap. Three), professional organisations and other unofficial systems of discipline (Chap. Four) and official agencies such as Customs and Excise (Chap. Five). On one level it would be attractive to distinguish between the *communitarian* value of state punishment (see Lacey (1988)) and the *discrete* benefits that diversionary measures can afford to participants in the process, yet this is unduly simplistic. Diversion can afford an element of settlement which is attractive to all of those directly involved in the dispute whilst still retaining elements of penality which satisfy the public interest in punishing offenders. Indeed the attraction of what can be termed a strategy of "negotiated penalty" is obvious, even if it is accepted that the expressive function of such punishment may be limited. However, it is also clear that the public interest can be served by ensuring that the direct participants in the dispute receive some personal benefit not traditionally associated with the full trial process; until comparatively recently, for example, punishment often took priority over compensating the victim of the offence (see now Criminal Justice Act 1988, s. 104) if the offender was convicted, whereas a diversionary approach may have afforded a more tangible benefit to the victim. Whilst there has been a belated move to recognise the plight of victims in the court (Williams (1994)), the perception that victims have been marginalised and dealt with in an insensitive manner in court may, in part, explain their reluctance to report offences to the police (Chap. Three).

Similarly, it would appear that society's interests may often be better served by a strategy based on compliance and advice than on a strategy based on prosecution and punishment in the area of regulating certain types of activity, such as tax evasion, consumer transactions and the protection of the environment (Chap. Five). In the United Kingdom such an approach is characteristically reserved for agencies concerned with regulating social, economic, financial and environmental activity where the primary objective is to encourage compliance without recourse to the criminal law where possible. Given the limited resources available to the agencies charged with regulating such activity, prosecution is not an attractive option in that it is resource intensive and, even if a conviction follows, may not actually achieve compliance. The Keith Committee (1983) stated that it was difficult to recover tax arrears after prosecution as the offender usually made no provision to pay what was owed due to the belief that he would evade detection and that action short of prosecution, such as warnings, compounding or seizing assets, would often lead to a higher recovery rate. Although the Keith Committee recognised that criminal proceedings were necessary to deal with the most persistent and/or serious offenders, they argued that the civil law was a more effective response in many cases and that certain regulatory breaches should therefore be decriminalised. This suggestion was adopted by the government in the Finance Act 1985 and reports suggest that decriminalisation has led to a higher rate of successful recovery (Customs and Excise (1988); Rowan-Robinson, *et al.* (1990)). If one adopts the recovery of arrears as the sole criterion for evaluating policy in this area it is clear that a policy of diversion, decriminalisation and selective prosecution has been remarkably profitable, yet it is submitted that an analysis of this area should also consider broader aspects of policy. First, how can one justify a compliance strategy as a response to breaches of the law in one area, such as tax evasion, while a prosecutorial response is adopted to other forms of illegal activity? Is it any less morally repugnant to deliberately evade one's fiscal responsibilities than to defraud the DHSS? It was indicated in Chapter Five that official ideology differentiates between *failing* to surrender part of one's income to the state and *taking* the taxpayers' money in terms of criminal culpability; the latter being seen as active rather than passive and hence more reprehensible. This official view, which to some extent would appear to inform policy in respect of these areas (Cook (1989)), is highly questionable as both tax evasion and defrauding the DHSS usually involve deliberate criminal conduct for personal gain. Indeed, it could be argued that tax evasion involves a greater degree of criminal culpability than social security fraud as those that defraud the DHSS often are struggling to maintain even the most basic standard of living whereas tax evaders are often motivated by greed not need.

The Criminal Justice Act 1991 provided a framework for sentencing and a rationale for punishment based on retributive notions of proportionality (Cavadino and Dignan (1992); Harding and Koffman (1995); Wasik (1993)). Yet here we have an example where an arguably more culpable form of activity is being dealt with in a less punitive manner, or indeed often in a manner that no longer involves a punitive response, than another, objectively less serious, form of criminal activity (NACRO (1986)). Is this desirable, or even justifiable, on the basis of public policy? The first response may be one of economic expediency. If tax evasion is a problem in society, priority should be given to recovering the arrears and reducing the problem rather than invoking a financially ineffective prosecution. However, in making this policy decision, it is apparent that a considerable number of individuals involved in culpable and harmful activity are escaping both the direct and indirect consequences of prosecution and punishment. This naturally offends notions of distributive justice, particularly as those escaping prosecution, punishment and public denunciation in this manner tend to come from comparatively advantageous socioeconomic groups. As Norrie comments in the case of regulating the working environment ((1993), p. 89):

> "It is as difficult to imagine a *general* system of law enforcement of the lower social classes based upon advice, consultation and warning as it is to imagine an orthodox label of guilt being imposed on factory owners by a system of vigorous policing. The difficulty emerges from the different social functions of the legal forms, not from an *a priori* system of legal classification."

Although it has been argued in this work (Chap. Five) and elsewhere (Cook (1989); NACRO (1986)) that the differences of approach involved in combating welfare fraud and tax evasion are unsustainable in terms of offence seriousness under a retributive penological framework, one has to acknowledge one of the orthodox critiques of desert theory: namely the difficulty of establishing the relative seriousness of different types of offence and hence their respective punishments (Walker (1991)). Nonetheless, given the obvious and potentially serious harm that can be caused by breaching regulations in areas such as pollution control, consumer safety and health and safety at work, it is difficult to justify diverting such activity as any kind of proportionate penal response.

Whilst more formal diversionary strategies, such as police cautioning and discontinuance by the Crown Prosecution Service, may involve consideration of the gravity of the offence committed by the offender, more informal diversionary mechanisms such as victim waiver have no such requirement. Although research suggests that the most common reason for victims electing not to report a matter is that the offence is "not serious enough" (Skogan (1984); Hough and Mayhew (1985)), the victim may decide against reporting an offence for a variety of reasons unconnected with the relative seriousness of the matter (see Chap. Three). In an analysis of the patterns of nonreporting, Pease (1988) found instances of what he usefully termed "strange reports" and "curious silences", the former being comprised of surprisingly trivial matters that were brought to the police's attention and the latter relating to serious matters that were not disclosed to the authorities. The, often complex, reasons why victims choose not to report serious offences whilst reporting those of a more minor character raise serious policy issues because they can substantially undermine the integrity of a supposedly retributive penal system if decisions which enable state involvement are not taken on grounds of offence seriousness. As Ashworth ((1994), p. 290) comments:

> "There is no aspiration to treat like cases alike, that most elementary proposition of justice, and different agencies continue to operate in different ways. The police and the CPS have their different powers and their different spheres, although the National Standards for cautioning are closely parallel to the Code for Crown Prosecutors. The regulatory agencies follow their different paths and priorities. These variations, not to mention the discretionary power within each of them, leave open the possibility of practices that discriminate on irrelevant grounds such as class, social position, race, and gender. There is no common starting-point, no conception that people who commit offences of similar seriousness should receive similar responses (unless there are strong grounds for doing otherwise), and no real attempt to provide guidance on the relative seriousness of the various types of offence."

There are other dangers in the use of less formal diversionary processes. In particular, the paradigmatic trial process affords some degree of procedural protection to the accused. The prosecution have to prove the case against him beyond reasonable doubt and there are formal rules of evidence designed to ensure that unreliable evidence is not admitted before the bench or the jury. Although case law has ensured that elements of natural justice are followed (*per* Denning L.J. in *Abbott v. Sullivan* [1952] 1 Q.B. 189) it is questionable to what extent such safeguards exist in the everyday dealings of employers and employees and professional bodies and their members. Similarly recourse to self-help strategies on the part of victims often involve arbitrary decisions with potentially far reaching consequences. The vulnerability of individuals suspected of committing offences is exacerbated by the attraction of avoiding a criminal trial and the associated anxiety, notwithstanding the fact that there may not have been sufficient evidence to obtain a conviction (Moore (1981)) or that the penalty imposed following conviction might have been less severe than the negotiated settlement (Marshall (1985)). Furthermore, research suggests that individuals may well be put under considerable pressure by representatives of the state authority (for example with respect to the DHSS see Moore (1981), and with respect to the police see Steer (1970)) and by defence advisors (Baldwin and McConville (1977)) to accept a diversionary course of action despite the supposed protection contained in codes of practice and the case law (see, *e.g.* *Turner* [1970] 2 Q.B. 321 regarding pleas of guilty). It is against the very real possibility that innocent people will be coerced or induced into accepting some form of diversionary settlement, that many legal commentators have called for greater transparency, procedural safeguards and, in some cases, the abandonment of inducements in diversionary mechanisms designed to ensure compliance (McConville and Mirsky (1993); Young and Sanders (1994); Davies and Dingwall (1996)).

The latitude given to enforcement agencies often results in considerable inconsistency in diversionary practice between different geographical areas, a phenomenon often termed "justice by geography". For example, in his study into how local authorities dealt with housing benefit fraud Loveland (1989) found considerable variance in approach between a Conservative controlled authority in the South Midlands and a Labour controlled authority in North London. Whereas the Conservative authority adopted a policy of intrusive enquiries and threatened prosecution, their Labour counterparts used a far less invasive approach. Similarly research has shown that, not only do different police forces use cautioning to a different extent (Ditchfield (1976); Tutt and Giller (1983)), but different divisions within the same force also vary in their rates of cautioning (Evans and Wilkinson (1990)). Whilst there remains geographical disparity in the sentencing of convicted offenders (Tarling (1979); Moxon (1988)), greater potential for disparity arises due to the inherent amount of discretion and the lower level of visibility associated with diversionary approaches.

A further problem commonly associated with diversionary processes is the need to guard against abuse of power by the agency involved and the fact that the agency is often acting in the dual role of investigator and sentencer. To take the example of police cautioning, the police have to both investigate the offence and then determine whether it is appropriate to caution the offender, albeit with reference to Home Office guidelines. The decision to caution is usually taken by a senior officer but it is not unreasonable to assume that the senior officer concerned will be highly reliant upon the impression of the officer(s) who initially investigated the matter and apprehended the offender. If a decision to caution is reached, no agency other than the police will have been involved. What protection is there for the individual against arbitrary police decision making? First, the individual has the option of refusing to admit guilt and therefore refusing to accept the caution but this is a risky option due to the potentially worse outcome following trial. Indeed researchers have documented (McConville, *et al.*, 1991) how the police use the fear of prosecution to encourage individuals to accept a caution. Secondly there is the protection supposedly offered by the custody sergeant at the police station, but again these officers are highly dependent upon the information that they receive from their colleagues and therefore can not successfully fulfil an effective monitoring function (*ibid.*; Evans (1993); Sanders and Young (1994)). Thirdly, defence solicitors may challenge a caution if it is felt inappropriate but this is dependent upon the individual electing to have legal representation at the police station and there is additional evidence that defence solicitors may not adequately challenge police cautioning decisions (McConville, *et al.* (1991)). Finally there is the possibility of reviewing the decision in the divisional court (*R. v. Chief Constable of the Kent County Constabulary, ex p. L.* [1993] 1 All E.R. 756). Whilst this potentially affords some protection and supervision over the process it is likely to remain of little practical benefit due to the considerable discretion retained in the process by the police.

One clearly discernible trend in this work has been an increased willingness by the civil courts to judicially review diversionary decision making in areas such as disciplinary proceedings at a university (*Glynn v. Keele University* [1971] 1 W.L.R. 487); police cautioning (*R. v. Chief Constable of the Kent Constabulary, ex p. L.* [1993] 1 All E.R. 756); and decisions by the Crown Prosecution Service not to prosecute in the public interest (*R. v. Director of Public Prosecutions, ex p. C.* [1995] 1 Cr.App.R. 136). In part this is symptomatic of a greater willingness by the courts to review discretionary decision making in many areas of public law (De Smith, Woolf and Jowell (1995); McEldowney (1994)) but it also gives rise to a process that could usefully be termed "reverse diversion': areas which hitherto had little or no legal regulation are increasingly being diverted back *into* the formal legal system so that the individual concerned receives increased procedural safeguards. Two observations are worth making about this process. First, the process of "reverse diversion" does not, and is not intended to, supplant the existing diversionary process. Rather the aim is to improve the process generally by providing broadly applicable procedural safeguards to the system and, in specific cases, to act as an appellate body. Whilst "reverse diversion" may increase the procedural safeguards in the diversionary process in question, it may to some extent reduce the perceived benefits of diversionary strategies (see below) in that it may prolong the process by insisting upon greater transparency and legality. Secondly, it is notable that the legal process concerned is civil as opposed to criminal in character. Therefore, an offence which could be dealt with competently in a criminal court is diverted to another body which is controlled by a civil court.

The increasing reliance on judicial review procedures to control diversionary processes demonstrates an inherent tension between the bureaucratic attractions of diversion as a speedy, economic and potentially expedient response to certain types of criminal activity and the due process ideals underpinning, at least at a theoretical level, an adversarial system of criminal justice. It is important to note that diversion does not always favour the alleged offender (though often it will be presented to him in a way that suggests diversion would lead to a more favourable outcome than prosecution) and, in many instances, diversion results in the imposition of a considerable penalty without the procedural safeguards present in a criminal trial. For example, expelling a student from an educational establishment may well have a far greater punitive effect than a punishment imposed by a court on the same individual for the same offence. Although this increase in legal scrutiny may reduce the bureaucratic attractions of diversion, it is submitted that such intervention is an important development due to the need to protect individuals from potentially arbitrary decisions, which often have far reaching effects on the individuals concerned.

One other method of controlling discretionary decision making that has received prominence is the use of guidelines drawn by government departments which outline factors that should influence decision makers when it comes to determining whether or not to prosecute an alleged offender. However these guidelines are framed in such a manner that considerable discretion remains with the agency concerned. For example, the Crown Prosecution Service have to decide whether to prosecute an individual in accordance with the policy contained in the Code for Crown Prosecutors formulated by the Director of Public Prosecutions (*R. v. Director of Public Prosecutions, ex p. C.* [1995] 1 Cr.App.R. 136). Central to this decision is the requirement that any prosecution has to be "in the public interest" (Crown Prosecution Service (1994)) and that cases which do not fulfil this test should not be continued. It is clear that the prosecutor reviewing the file has a great deal of scope to divert the case if he or she decides this to be appropriate and that this power is used on a fairly frequent basis (Home Office (1994a)). The pattern emerges of decision makers having to act in accordance with a given set of broad criteria provided by the agency themselves with the divisional court considering only decisions which patently fail to have regard to these criteria (Dingwall (1995)). The latitude of the guidelines (Ashworth (1987); McConville, *et al.* (1991)) in combination with the reluctance of the divisional court to review prosecutorial decisions (Osborne (1995); Dotan (1997)) means that only in extreme cases will there be an effective remedy in respect of arbitrary decision making by those who determine whether to divert an offender from the criminal process. It is not only with respect to diversion that one finds broad guidelines, considerable discretion and a reluctance to review decisions in the criminal justice sphere. A useful parallel can be drawn with contemporary sentencing practice, where sentencers are constrained only by broad statutory provisions (Criminal Justice Act 1991; Harding and Koffman (1995); Walker and Padfield (1996); Wasik (1993)) and guidance from the Court of Appeal which often lacks specificity (Dingwall (1997)) with the result that there is widespread disparity in sentencing practice (Harding and Koffman (1995)). It is clearly difficult in both spheres to balance the need to ensure fairness and reduce disparity whilst, at the same time, avoiding an unduly prescriptive system that would restrict justice in individual cases.

However, on balance, the increasing legal control over diversionary decision making that has been identified above does not detract from the intrinsic benefits associated with diversion. The criminal trial may be appropriate in certain cases but it is undoubtedly expensive to the tax payer (in 1993/94 the average cost of a prosecution *excluding* the cost of implementing the sentence was estimated to be £2,000–£3,000 for an indictable offence and £200–£300 for a summary offence: Home Office (1995), p. 71), can result in justice being delayed (in 1994 the average time taken from offence to completion of indictable cases at magistrates' courts was 128 days: *ibid.*, p. 29) and at least one survey suggests that reconviction rates may be lower for those who are cautioned rather than prosecuted for certain offences (Home Office (1992)). Admittedly one has to exercise a degree of caution in interpreting the reoffending rates in the Home Office (1992) survey in so far as the sample is comparatively small and it is probable that the police tended to caution those whom they adjudged to present a lesser risk of reoffending than those who were eventually prosecuted. In their role as the initial interpreter of the incident, the police effectively construct the case against the individual (Sanders (1987)) which in turn determines the way in which it will subsequently be processed by the Crown Prosecution Service. This would help ensure that those cases which the police did not feel warranted a caution would result in prosecution. Nonetheless it may be argued generally that, unless the matter is sufficiently serious so as to merit prosecution, it is justifiable public policy to divert offenders in so far as it appears to be a cost effective, proportionate response to minor offending that would also seem to enjoy a measure of success that is not evident with regard to prosecution in terms of reoffending rates.

Although some utilitarian penologists argue that a public process of trial and punishment can have both an individual and a general deterrent value (Walker (1980); Wilson (1983)), this has been questioned on the grounds of empirical evidence (Beyleveld (1980)). The state of current knowledge into the deterrent effects of the paradigmatic criminal process is illustrated well by Walker and Padfield ((1996), p. 101) who state that:

> "Naive claims that deterrent policies are highly effective—or totally ineffective—have been replaced by the less exciting realisation that *some* people can be deterred in *some* situations from *some* types of conduct by *some* degree of

likelihood that they will be penalised in *some* ways; but we do not yet know enough to enable us to be very specific about the people, the situations, the conduct, or the likelihood or nature of the penalties." (Italics in original.)

Few commentators would reject outright the fact that the traditional process of trial and punishment will act as a deterrent in some cases. However, there may be a negative consequence of this process which could offset this deterrent effect and hence affect the rates of reoffending. Some of the earliest criminological research recognised that penal institutions could have an adverse effect on offenders. Lombroso, for example, believed that the process of being imprisoned could increase the chances of an individual offending again at a later date (Lombroso-Ferrero (1972)). This process was not fully developed until American writers such as Lemert ((1951), (1972)) and Becker (1963) developed the concept of "labelling". Lemert distinguished between "primary deviance" and "secondary deviance" and argued that criminologists had become unduly concerned with establishing why offenders first broke the community norms and had not addressed the more important question of why some offenders continually reoffended ((1951), p. 75–76):

"From a narrower sociological viewpoint the deviations are not significant until they are organized subjectively and transformed into active roles and become social criteria for assigning status. The deviant individuals must react symbolically to their own behavior aberrations and fix them in their socio-psychological patterns. The deviations remain primary deviations or symptomatic and situational as long as they are rationalized or otherwise dealt with as functions of a socially acceptable role ... Reorganization may be the adoption of another normal role in which the tendencies previously defined as 'pathological' are given a more acceptable social expression. The other general possibility is the assumption of a deviant role, if such exists; or, more rarely, the person may organize an aberrant sect or group in which he creates a special role of his own. *When a person begins to employ his deviant behavior or a role based upon it as a means of defense, attack, or adjustment to the overt and covert problems created by the consequent societal reaction to him, his deviation is secondary.*" (Italics in original.)

Lemert (1951) argued that the main task facing criminologists was to explain the factors which may lead to this secondary deviance. Becker (1963) was of the opinion that society's reaction to criminals could effectuate a self-fulfilling prophecy in that the original response to the offender could lead to the individual adopting behaviour in keeping with this label. It was argued that the public do not merely have distaste for an offender's criminal acts but that they also shun the individual as a consequence of his actions believing that he is inherently untrustworthy and liable to offend again; the offender is perceived as someone (*ibid.*, p. 34) "who is different from the rest of us, who cannot or will not act as a moral human being and therefore might break other important rules". As a result of this reaction, the offender will find it problematic to integrate with the rest of society again: legitimate employment prospects will suffer, personal relationships are destroyed and the offender will be drawn towards those in a similar position for friendship and crime may be seen to be the most attractive, or even the only, form of employment given the reticence of employers to hire those who have been convicted of a criminal offence. Therefore, in labelling an individual as a criminal, the state may actually increase his propensity to commit further criminal acts by reducing his opportunities to adopt a law abiding lifestyle (see also Sagarin (1975); Gove (1980)). If the offender does subsequently reoffend this serves to justify society's label of the individual and makes his isolation even more acute thereby reducing even further his opportunity to reintegrate into society and making crime even more attractive a way of life. This process, termed "deviancy amplification" (Wilkins (1964)), raises serious doubts about the paradigmatic responses to controlling crime. The work of those adopting the concept of labelling suggested that the standard approaches to dealing with criminals were counterproductive as they alienated individuals leading to "secondary deviance". The effects of the concept of labelling on criminal justice policy in the United States, where most of the commentators were based, has been significant and led directly to a substantial increase in the use of diversionary mechanisms in place of the traditional trial process (Schur (1973)).

Another contention made by these writers was that the concept of criminality is dependent upon certain types of behaviour being so labelled by the state (Becker (1963)). Previously criminologists had not been so concerned with the role of the state in determining what conduct should be defined as criminal, rather they had taken crime to be a fixed concept, defined simply as a breach of the criminal law, and had then sought to rationalise why certain individuals committed such acts. This recognition that crime was socially constructed, largely for what could be termed policy grounds, was of paramount importance to researchers in this area and they sought to analyse the reasons why the state had criminalised certain types of behaviour and why the state concentrated on criminalising certain activities at certain times (*e.g.* Pfohl (1977)). What emerged from their research was a pattern of selective enforcement by official agencies, often based on factors other than evidential sufficiency or offence severity (Hussanstamm (1975); Chambliss (1984)).

What these writers did not recognise so much was the crucial importance of victim reporting to the process. As emphasised above (Chaps Two–Four), by determining which offences require official action, non-state agencies are engaged in a process which effectively determines to a significant degree the frontiers of criminality. Lacey ((1995), p. 5) identified that:

> "... a wide number of groups which are not clearly 'state' or even directly 'state-sponsored' agencies have an important influence on decisions about, and practices of, criminalisation. For example, pressure groups of various kinds affect the legislative process and enforcement practices; the mass media affect legislative, judicial and enforcement processes and have enormous influence in constructing and legitimating particular conceptions of 'real' crime and shaping moral panics about particular forms of offending behaviour; lawyers play a part in preparing cases for court and, particularly, in advising clients whether to plead guilty and to what charge. Victims of, and witnesses to (what might be officially defined as) crime, play an important role in shaping officially recorded crime; if they do not recognise what has happened as 'criminal', or have reasons for avoiding contact with formal criminal justice agencies, particular areas or instances of potentially criminal behaviour will go unrecorded."

Diversion, therefore, is not only the usual way of responding to criminal behaviour when it is reported but diversion helps determine: (i) the practical boundaries of the criminal law; (ii) the parameters between state and private ownership of disputes; (iii) public perceptions regarding the seriousness of different types of conduct; (iv) official perceptions of the crime problem; and (v) priorities in policing and crime prevention strategies. In Chapter Three it was argued that, as most crime was brought to the attention of enforcement agencies by victims (Hough and Mayhew (1985)), decisions regarding reporting have a direct bearing on official policy-making, due to a reliance on criminal statistics for raw data. However, it was also argued that victims effectively determine whether or not an event which may technically be adjudged criminal is treated as such in practice, thereby leading to a dichotomy between substantive criminal law and criminal law in practice (see further Lacey (1995)). This process also raises important theoretical questions about the ownership of criminal disputes. State involvement in responding to crime is a comparatively modern concept (Sharpe (1990)) and commentators have recently questioned the extent to which the reliance upon victims to decide to report an offence undermines the traditional notion of crime as being an offence against society (Clarkson, *et al.* (1994)). In turn some penologists have argued that criminal justice should be concerned primarily with righting the wrong or compensating for the harm caused to the victim(s) by the offender (Watson, *et al.* (1981); Wright (1991), (1995); Walgrave (1994); Zedner (1994)) rather than allowing the state to usurp the process for its own ends. The extent to which victims and other interest groups divert offences from the official process suggests that to some extent the state's role is, despite its paradigmatic status, more limited than most orthodox accounts of criminal justice would suggest.

What is at stake is who should bear responsibility for dealing with the root problems and phenomena underlying and giving rise to delinquent and criminal behaviour; whether it should rest with the state or civil society; whether, within the sphere of state activity, it should be vested with criminal justice agencies or with agencies concerned with welfare, medical or educational functions. Rather than posing the question in such stark terms it may, in practice, be more feasible to search for a sensible system of joint responsibility. This would require more explicit consideration of the objectives in each particular area, allied to a holistic appreciation of the options for social control. It is, in short, not just necessary for criminologists to assess the traditional criminal process but to critically evaluate what are currently described as diversionary practices if one wishes to understand contemporary social control.

Bibliography

Abel, R.L. (1988), *The Legal Profession in England and Wales* (Oxford: Blackwell).

Adler, Z. (1987), *Rape on Trial* (London: Routledge).

Adams, J.E. (1978), "Review of *Negotiated Justice*" [1978] 41 M.L.R. 358.

Alford, V. (1959), "Rough Music or Charivari" 70 *Folklore* 505.

Ashworth, A. (1983), "Plea, Venue and Discontinuance" [1983] C.L.R. 830.

Ashworth, A. (1984) "Prosecution, Police and Public—A Guide to Good Gatekeeping" (1984) 23 *Howard Journal of Criminal Justice* 65.

Ashworth, A. (1987), "The Public Interest Element in Prosecutions" [1983] C.L.R. 595.

Ashworth, A. (1994). *The Criminal Process: An Evaluative Study* (Oxford: Clarendon Press).

Ashworth, A. (1995), *Sentencing and Criminal Justice* (2nd ed., London: Butterworths).

Baldick, R. (1965), *The Duel: A History of Duelling* (London: Chapman & Hall).

Baldwin, J. and McConville, M. (1977), *Negotiated Justice: Pressures to Plead Guilty* (Oxford: Martin Robertson).

Baldwin, J. and McConville, M. (1978), "The Influence of the Sentencing Discount in Inducing Guilty Pleas", in Baldwin, J. and Bottomley, A.K. (eds.), *Criminal Justice: Selected Readings* (Oxford: Martin Robertson).

Baldwin, R. (1990), "Why Rules Don't Work" [1990] 53 M.L.R. 321.

Ball, S. and Bell, S. (1995), *Environmental Law* (3rd ed., London: Blackstone Press).

Banton, M. (1964), *The Policeman in the Community* (London: Tavistock).

Bar Council (1990), *Code of Conduct* (London: Bar Council).

Bar Council (1992), *The Efficient Disposal of Business in the Crown Court: Report of a Working Party* (London: Bar Council).

Bean, P. (1986), *Mental Disorder and Legal Control* (Cambridge: Cambridge University Press).

Beattie, J.M. (1986), *Crime and the Courts in England: 1660–1800* (Oxford: Clarendon Press).

Becker, H.S. (1963), *Outsiders: Studies in the Sociology of Deviance* (New York: Free Press).

Beyleveld, D. (1980), *A Bibliography on General Deterrence Research* (Farnborough: Saxon House).

Bianchi, H. and van Swaaningen, R. (eds.) (1986), *Abolitionism: Towards a Non–Repressive Approach to Crime* (Amsterdam: Free University Press).

Bing, I. (1996), *Criminal Procedure and Sentencing in the Magistrates' Court* (London: Sweet and Maxwell).

Bittner, E. (1967), "The Police on Skid Row: a Study in Peacekeeping" 32 *American Sociological Review* 699.

Black, D. (1983), "Crime as Social Control" 48 *American Sociological Review* 34.

Black, D. (1989), *Sociological Justice* (New York: Oxford University Press).

Bottomley, K. and Pease, K. (1986), *Crime and Punishment: Interpreting the Data* (Milton Keynes: Open University Press).

Bottoms, A.E., McClean, J.D. and Patchett, K.W. (1970), "Children, Young Persons and the Courts: a Survey of the New Law" [1970] Crim.L.R. 368.

Brants, C. and Field, S. (1995), "Discretion and Accountability in Prosecution: a Comparative Perspective on Keeping Crime out of Court", Chap. 7 in Fennel, P. *et al.*, *Criminal Justice in Europe.*

Bredar, J.K. (1992), "Moving Up the Day of Reckoning: Strategies for Attacking the 'Cracked Trials' Problem" [1992] Crim.L.R. 153.

Bridges, L. (1993), "Guilty Pleas and the Politics of Research", *Legal Action,* April 9.

Bridges, L. and McConville, M. (1994), "Keeping Faith with their Own Convictions: the Royal Commission on Criminal Justice" [1994] 57 *M.L.R.* 75.

British Psychological Society (1980), *Report of a Working Party on Corporal Punishment in Schools* (London: BPS).

Buckett, A. (1986), *VAT Enforcement and Appeals Manual* (London: Butterworths).

Burney, E. and Pearson, G. (1995), "Mentally Disordered Offenders: Finding a Focus for Diversion" [1995] 34 *Howard Journal of Criminal Justice* 291.

Cane, P. (1996), *An Introduction to Administrative Law* (3rd ed., Oxford: Clarendon Press).

Card, R. and Ward, R. (1994), *The Criminal Justice and Public Order Act 1994* (Bristol: Jordans).

Carman, G. (1993), "The Royal Commission on Criminal Justice", *Counsel,* July 8.

Carson, W.G. (1970), "White-Collar Crime and the Enforcement of Factory Legislation", 10 Brit. J. Criminol. 383.

Chambliss, W.J. (1984), "The Saints and the Roughnecks", in Chambliss, W.J. (ed.), *Criminal Law in Action* (New York: John Wiley).

Chatterton, C.E.M. (1991), "Should There Be a Discount for a Guilty Plea?" [1991] 155 J.P. 135.

Chorus, J.M.J. and Jeroen, H.T. (1993), *Introduction to Dutch Law for Foreigners* (The Hague: Kluwer).

Christie, N. (1977), "Conflicts as Property" [1977] 17 Brit.J.Criminol. 1.

Christie, N. (1982), *Limits to Pain* (Oxford: Martin Robertson).

Clarkson, C., Cretney, A., Davis, G. and Shepherd, J. (1994), "Assaults: the Relationship between Seriousness, Criminalisation and Punishment" [1984]. *Crim.L.R.* 4.

Clegg, A. and Megson, B. (1973), *Children in Distress* (Harmondsworth: Penguin).

Cockburn, J.S. (ed.) (1977), *Crime in England 1550–1800* (London: Methuen)

Cook, D. (1989), *Rich Law, Poor Law* (Milton Keynes: Open University Press).

Cox, E.W. (1877), *The Principles of Punishment* (London: Law Times Office).

Cretney, A. and Davis, G. (1996), "Prosecuting Domestic Assault" [1996] *Crim.L.R.* 162.

Crown Prosecution Service (1986), *Code for Crown Prosecutors* (London: HMSO).

Crown Prosecution Service (1993), *A Statement of Prosecution Policy: Domestic Violence* (London: HMSO).

Customs and Excise (1987), *78th Report of the Commissioners of H.M. Customs and Excise,* Cm. 234 (London: HMSO).

Customs and Excise (1988), *79th Report of the Commissioners of H.M. Customs and Excise,* Cm. 453 (London: HMSO).

Danzig, R. (1973), "Towards the Creation of a Complementary, Decentralized System of Criminal Justice", 26(1) *Stanford Law Review* 1.

Darbyshire, P. (1984), *The Justices' Clerk* (Chichester: Barry Rose).
Davies, B. and Dingwall, G. (1996), "Defendants' Guilty Pleas and Section 48", *Legal Action*, February 8.
Davis, J.S. (1984), "A Poor Man's System of Justice: the London Police Courts in the Second Half of the Nineteenth Century", 27 *The Historical Journal* 309.
Davis, J.S. (1989), "Prosecutions and their Context", Chap. 9 in Hay, D. and Snyder, S. (eds), *Policing and Prosecution in Britain.*
De Haan, W. (1990), *The Politics of Redress: Crime, Punishment and Penal Abolition* (London: Unwin Hyman).
Department of Employment (1988), *Press Notice*, 112/88.
Department of Health and Home Office (1992), *Review of Health and Social Services for Mentally Disordered Offenders Requiring Similar Services*, Cm. 2085 (London: HMSO).
De Smith, S.A., Woolf, Lord and Jowell, J. (1995), *Judicial Review of Administrative Action* (London: Sweet and Maxwell).
Dickens, B.M. (1970), "Discretion in Local Authority Prosecutions" [1970] Crim.L.R. 618.
Dingwall, G. (1994), "The Dangers of Discretion in Determining a Just Fine After the Abolition of the Unit Fine in the Criminal Justice Act 1993", [1994] 158 J.P. 545.
Dingwall, G. (1995), "Judicial Review and the Director of Public Prosecutions" [1995] 54 C.L.J. 265.
Dingwall, G. (1997), "The Court of Appeal and Guideline Judgments" [1997] 48 N.I.L.Q. 143.
Dingwall, G. (1998), "Selective Incapitation After the Criminal Justice Act 1991: a Proportional Response to Protecting the Public?" [1998] 37 *Howard Journal of Criminal Justice* 177.
Dingwall, G. and Davenport, A. (1995), "The Evolution of Criminal Justice Policy in the U.K.", Chap. 2 in Fennell, P., *et al.*, *Criminal Justice in Europe.*
Ditchfield, J.A. (1976), *Police Cautioning in England and Wales* (HORS No. 37), (London: HMSO).
Ditchfield, J. and Duncan, D. (1987), "The Prison Disciplinary System: Perceptions [1987] of its Fairness and Adequacy by Inmates, Staff and Members of Boards of Visitors", 26 *Howard Journal of Criminal Justice* 122.
Ditton, J. (1977), *Part-Time Crime: an Ethnography of Fiddling and Pilfering* (London: Macmillan).
Ditton, J. (1977a), "A Note on Commercial Social Control" (Outer Circle Policy Unit).
Dobash, R.P. and Dobash, R.E. (1979), *Violence Against Wives: A Case Against the Patriarchy* (Shepton Mallet: Open Books).
Dobash, R.P. and Dobash, R.E. (1981), "Community Response to Violence Against Wives: Charivari, Abstract Justice and Patriarchy", [1981] 28 *Social Problems* 563.
Doggett, M.E. (1992), *Marriage, Wife-Beating and the Law in Victorian England* (London: Wiedenfeld and Nicolson).
Dotan, Y. (1997), "Should Prosecutorial Discretion Enjoy Special Treatment in Judicial Review?" [1997] *Public Law* 513.
Downes, D. (1982), "The Origins and Consequences of Dutch Penal Policy" [1982] 22 Brit.J.Criminol. 344.
Downes, D. (1988), *Contrasts in Tolerance* (Oxford: Clarendon Press).

Duff, A. and Garland, D. (1994), *A Reader on Punishment* (Oxford: Oxford University Press).

Duff, P. (1993), "The Prosecutor Fine and Social Control" [1993] 33 Brit.J.Criminol. 481.

Duff, P. (1994), "The Prosecutor Fine" [1994] 14 O.J.L.S. 565.

Duff, P. and Meechan, K. (1992), "The Prosecutor Fine" [1997] Crim.L.R. 22.

Duff, P., Meechan, K., Christie, M. and Lessels, D. (1994), "The Fiscal Fine" [1994] S.L.T. 151.

Dunn, J. and Fahey, T.A. (1987), "Section 136 and the Police" [1989] *Bulletin of the Royal College of Psychiatrists* 224.

Edwards, S.S.M. (1996), *Sex and Gender in the Legal Process* (London: Blackstone Press).

Emsley, C. (1983), *Policing and its Context 1750–1870* (London: Macmillan).

Emsley, C. (1985), "The Thump of Wood on a Swede Turnip: Police Violence in Nineteenth Century England" [1985] 6 *Criminal Justice History* 125.

Evans, R. (1991), "Police Cautioning and the Young Offender" [1991] Crim.L.R. 598.

Evans, R. (1993), "Comparing Young Adult and Juvenile Cautioning in the Metropolitan Police District" [1993] Crim.L.R. 572.

Evans, R. (1994), "Cautioning: Counting the Cost of Retrenchment" [1994] Crim.L.R. 566.

Evans, R. and Wilkinson, C. (1990), "Variations in Police Cautioning Policy and Practice in England and Wales" [1990] 29 *Howard Journal of Criminal Justice* 155.

Fahey, T.A., *et al.*, (1987), "Police Admissions to Psychiatric Hospitals: a Challenge to Community Psychiatry" [1987] 27 *Medicine, Science and the Law* 263.

Fahey, T.A., (1989), "The Police as a Referral Agency for Psychiatric Emergencies—a Review" [1989] 29 *Medicine, Science and the Law* 315.

Farrington, D. and Mattison, F. (eds) (1990), *Universities and the Law* (Reading: CUA).

Farrington, D.P. and Burrows, J.N. (1993), "Did Shoplifting Really Decrease?" [1993] 33 Brit.J.Criminol. 57.

Fennell, P. (1991), "Diversion of Mentally Disordered Offenders from Custody" [1991] Crim.L.R. 333.

Fennell, P., *et al.*, (eds.) (1995), *Criminal Justice in Europe: a Comparative Study* (Oxford: Clarendon Press).

Ferguson, T. (1952), *The Young Delinquent in his Social Setting—a Glasgow Study (Oxford: Oxford University Press).*

Field, S. and Thomas, P.A. (eds) (1994), Justice and Efficiency ? The Royal Commission on Criminal Justice (Oxford: Blackwell).

Fielding, H. (1751), *An Enquiry into the Causes of the Late Increase of Robbers with some Proposals for Remedying this Growing Evil* (ed. M.R. Zirker, Oxford: Clarendon Press, 1985, Wesleyan edition of the works of Henry Fielding).

Fionda, J. (1995), *Public Prosecutors and Discretion: a Comparative Study* (Oxford: Clarendon Press).

Fishman, G. (1984), "Differential Victimization Patterns", in Block, R. (ed.), *Victimization and Fear of Crime: World Perspectives* (Washington: Department of Justice).

Fitzgerald, E. (1985), "Prison Discipline and the Courts", Chap. 2 in Maguire, M., Vagg, J. and Morgan, R. (eds), *Accordingly and Prisons: Opening Up a Closed World* (London: Tavistock).

Foucault, M. (1977), *Discipline and Punish: the Birth of the Prison* (Harmondsworth: Penguin; translation of *Surveiller et Punir,* (Paris: Gallimard), 1975).
Freeman, M.D.A. (1979), *Violence in the Home* (Farnborough: Saxon House).
Garland, D. (1985), *Punishment and Welfare* (Aldershot: Gower).
Garland, D. (1990), *Punishment and Modern Society: a Study in Social Theory* (Oxford: Clarendon Press).
Gaskell, M. (1996), "The Displacement of Providence: Policing and Prosecution in Seventeenth Century and Eighteenth Century England", 11 *Continuity and Change* 341.
Gelsthorpe, L. and Giller, H. (1990), "More Justice for Juveniles: Does More Mean Better?" [1990] Crim.L.R. 153.
Gelsthorpe, L. and Morris, A. (1994), "Juvenile Justice, 1945–1992", Chap. 20 in Maguire, M., Morgan, R. and Reiner, R., *The Oxford Handbook of Criminology.*
Giller, H. and Tutt, N. (1987), "Police Cautioning of Juveniles: the Continuing Practice of Diversity" [1987] Crim.L.R. 367.
Glasgow Police (1945), *General Report.*
Golding, P. and Middleton, S. (1982), *Images of Welfare* (Oxford: Basil Blackwell and Martin Robertson).
Gordon, D. and Heddermann, C. (1993), "Panel Assessment Schemes and Other Responses to Mentally Disordered Offenders: a Survey of Probation Areas", Home Office Research and Statistics Department, *Research Bulletin* (34), 9 (London: HMSO).
Gove, W.R. (1980), *The Labelling of Deviance: Evaluating a Perspective* (2nd ed.) (London: Sage).
Graham, J. (1988), *Schools, Disruptive Behaviour and Delinquency: A Review of Research* (HORS No 96), (London: HMSO).
Grayson, E. (1994), *Sport and the Law* (2nd ed.) (London: Butterworths).
Gross, H. (1979), *A Theory of Criminal Justice* (Oxford: Clarendon Press).
Grosskurth, A. (1993), "From Anger to Action", *Legal Action,* December 6.
Gudjonsson, G., *et al.,* (1994), "Persons at Risk During Interviews in Police Custody: the Identification of Vulnerabilities", Home Office *Research Bulletin* (35) 31 (London: HMSO).
Habermas, J. (1984), *The Theory of Communicative Action, Vol. 1* (London: Heineman Education).
Habermas, J. (1988), *The Theory of Communicative Action, Vol. 2.* (Cambridge: Polity Press).
Hanmer, J. Radford, J. and Stanko, E.A. (1989), *Women, Policing and Male Violence* (London: Routledge).
Harding, C. and Ireland, R.W. (1989), *Punishment: Rhetoric, Rule and Practice* (London: Routledge).
Harding, C. and Koffman, L. (1995), *Sentencing and the Penal System: Text and Materials* (2nd ed., Sweet and Maxwell: London).
Harding, C., Swart, B., Jorg, N. and Fennell, P. (1995), "Europeanization and Convergence: the Lessons of Comparative Study", Chap. 19 in Fennell, P., et al., *Criminal Justice in Europe.*
Hart, H.L.A. (1968) *Punishment and Responsibility* (Oxford: Clarendon Press).
Hartung, F.E. (1950), "White Collar Offences in the Wholesale Meat Industry in Detroit", 56 *American Journal of Sociology* 25.
Hawkins, K. (1984), *Environment and Enforcement: Regulation and the Social Definition of Pollution* (Oxford: Clarendon Press).

Hawkins, K. (1990), "Compliance Strategy, Prosecution Policy and Aunt Sally: a Comment on Pearce and Tombs" [1990] 30 Brit.J.Criminol. 444.

Hay, D. (1975a), "Crime, Authority and Criminal Law" (unpublished thesis).

Hay, D., *et al.*, (1975b), *Albion's Fatal Tree: Crime and Society in Eighteenth Century England* (London: Allen Lane).

Hay, D. (1989), "Prosecution and Power: Malicious Prosecutions in the English Courts, 1750–1850", Chap. 8 in Hay, D. and Snyder, F. (eds), *Policing and Prosecution in Britain.*

Hay. D. and Snyder, F. (1989), "Using the Criminal Law, 1750–1850: Policing, Private Prosecution, and the State", Chap. 1 in Hay, D. and Snyder, F. (eds), *Policing and Prosecution in Britain 1750–1850* (Oxford: Clarendon Press).

Henry, S. (1978), *The Hidden Economy* (Oxford: Martin Robertson).

Henry, S. (1981), *Can I Have It in Cash: a Study of Informal Institutions and Unorthodox Ways of Doing Things* (London: Astragal Books).

Henry, S. (1982), "Factory Law: the Changing Disciplinary Technology of Industrial Social Control", 10 *International Journal of the Sociology of Law* 365.

Hermann, J. (1974), "The Role of Compulsory Prosecution and the Scope of Prosecutorial Discretion in Germany", 41 *University of Chicago Law Review* 466.

Hermann, J. (1992), "Bargaining Justice: a Bargain for German Criminal Justice?" 53 *University of Pittsburgh Law Review* 755.

Herrup, C. (1987), *The Common Peace: Participation and the Criminal Law in Seventeenth Century England* (Cambridge: Cambridge University Press).

Heumann, M. (1978), *Plea Bargaining* (Chicago: University of Chicago Press).

Hirst, P. (1994), "Problems Affecting Rural Policing", in Harding, C. and Williams, J. (eds), *Legal Provision in the Rural Environment* (Cardiff: University of Wales Press).

Home Affairs Committee (1990), *Fourth Report: Memorandum of Evidence Submitted by the Crown Prosecution Service*, H.C. Paper No 118.

Home Office (1985), *Circular 14/85: The Cautioning of Offenders* (London: HMSO).

Home Office (1986), *Report of the Working Group on Shop Theft* (London: HMSO).

Home Office (1989), *Report of the Working Group on the Fear of Crime* (London: HMSO).

Home Office (1990), *Circular 59/90: The Cautioning of Offenders* (London: HMSO).

Home Office (1990a), *Circular 66/90: Provision for Mentally Disordered Offenders* (London: HMSO).

Home Office (1992), *The Criminal Histories of those Cautioned in 1985 and 1988* (London: HMSO).

Home Office (1994), *Circular 18/94: The Cautioning of Offenders* (London: HMSO).

Home Office (1994a), *Case Screening by the Crown Prosecution Service: How and Why Cases are Terminated*, Research Study 137 (London: HMSO).

Home Office (1995), *Digest 3: Information on the Criminal Justice System* (London: HMSO).

Home Office (1996a), *Criminal Statistics, England and Wales*, Cm. 3421 (London: HMSO).

Home Office (1996b), *Protecting the Public*, Cm. 3190 (London: HMSO).

Hood, R. (1962), *Sentencing in Magistrates' Courts* (London: Tavistock).

Hood, R. (1974), *Sentencing the Motoring Offender* (London: Heinemann).

Hood, R. (1992), *Race and Sentencing* (Oxford: Clarendon Press).
Hough, M. and Mayhew, P. (1983), *British Crime Survey* (HORS No. 76), (London: HMSO).
Hough, M. and Mayhew, P. (1985), *Taking Account of Crime: Key Findings from the Second British Crime Survey* (HORS No. 85), (London: HMSO).
House of Commons Environmental Committee (1987), *Pollution of Rivers and Estuaries* (London: HMSO).
Howson, G. (1970), *The Thief-Taker General: the Rise and Fall of Jonathan Wild* (London: Hutchinson).
Hughes, D. (1992), *Environmental Law* (2nd ed.) (London: Butterworths).
Hussanstamm, F.K. (1975), "Bumper Stickers and the Cops", in Steffensmeier, D.J. and Terry, R.M. (eds.), *Examining Deviance Experimentally: Selected Readings* (Port Washington: Alfred Publishing Co).
Hutter, B.M. (1988), *The Reasonable Arm of the Law?* (Oxford: Clarendon Press).
Hutter, B.M. and Lloyd-Bostock, S. (1990), "The Power of Accidents" [1990] 30 Brit.J.Criminol. 409.
Ingleby Committee (1960), *Report of the Committee on Children and Young Persons*, Cmd. 1191 (London: HMSO).
Ingram, M. (1977), "Community and Courts: Law and Disorder in Early Seventeenth Century Wiltshire", in Cockburn, J.S. (ed.), *Crime in England 1550–1800* (London: Methuen).
Ingram, M. (1984), "Ridings, Rough Music and the 'Refrm of Popular Culture' in Early Modern England" [1984] 102 *Past and Present* 79.
Ingram, M. (1987), *Church Courts, Sex and Marriage in England 1570–1640* (Cambridge: Cambridge University Press).
Institute of Personnel Management (1979), *Disciplinary Procedures and Practices* (London: IPM).
James, C. (1972), "Children's Act in Trouble: Further Considerations" [1972] Crim.L.R. 688.
James, D. V. and Hamilton, L. W. (1992), "Settng Up Psychiatric Liaison Schemes to Magistrates' Courts: Problems and Practicalities" [1992] 32 *Medicine, Science and the Law* 167.
Jones, R.A.N. (1989), "Popular Culture, Policing and the 'Disappearance' of the Ceffyl Pren in Cardigan, c.1837–1850" (1989–90) *Ceredigion* 19.
Jones, D.J.V. (1992), *Crime in Nineteenth-Century Wales* (Cardiff: University of Wales Press).
Kagan, R.A. (1978), *Regulatory Justice* (New York: Russell Sage Foundation).
Keith Committee, (1983), *Report on Enforcement Powers of the Revenue Departments*, Cmnd. 8822 (London: HMSO).
Kelk, C., Koffman, L. and Silvis, J. (1995), "Sentencing Practice, Policy and Discretion", Chapter 16 in Fennell, P., et al., (eds.), *Criminal Justice in Europe.*
Kilbrandon Committee (1964), *Report of the Committee on Children and Young Persons, Scotland*, Cmnd. 2306 (Edinburgh: HMSO).
King, P. (1983), "Prosecution Associations, Courts and Community Concerns in Essex, 1740–1800" (unpublished paper, presented to the Conference on the History of Law, Labour and Crime, University of Warwick, September 1983).
Koffman, L. (1996), *Crime Surveys and Victims of Crime* (Cardiff: University of Wales Press).
Lacey, N. (1988), *State Punishment: Political Principles and Community Values* (London: Routledge).

Lacey, N. (1995), "Contingency and Criminalisation", in Loveland, I. (ed.), *The Frontiers of Criminality* (London: Sweet and Maxwell).

Landau, S. and Nathan, G. (1983), "Selecting Delinquents for Cautioning in the London Metropolitan Area", [1983] 23 Brit.J.Criminol. 128.

Laub, J. (1981), "Ecological Considerations in Victim Reporting to the Police" [1981] 19 *Journal of Criminal Justice* 419.

Laycock, G. and Tarling, R. (1985), "Police ForceCautioning: Policy and Practice", [1985] 24 *Howard Journal of Criminal Justice* 81.

Leigh, L.H. and Hall Williams, J.E. (1981), *The Management of the Prosecution Process in Denmark, Sweden and the Netherlands* (Leamington Spa: James Hall).

Lemert, E.M. (1951), *Social Pathology: a Systematic Approach to the Theory of Sociopathic Behaviour* (New York: McGraw-Hill).

Lemert, E.M. (1972), *Human Deviance, Social Problems and Social Control* (Englewood Cliffs, N.J.: Pentice-Hall).

Levi, M. (1993), *The Investigation, Prosecution and Trial of Serious Fraud* (Research Study No. 14 for the Royal Commission on Criminal Justice) (London: HMSO).

Levine, D. (1977), *Family Formation in an Age of Nascent Capitalism* (New York: Academic Press).

Littlewood, R. (1986), "Ethnic Minorities and the Mental Health Act" [1986] *Bulletin of the Royal College of Psychiatrists*, 1986: 10, 306.

Livingstone, S. and Owen, T. (1993), *Prison Law: Text and Materials* (Oxford: Clarendon Press).

Lombroso-Ferrero, G. (1972), *Criminal Man According to the Classification of Cesare Lombroso* (Montclair, N.J.: Patterson Smith).

Lord Chancellor's Department (1996), *Judicial Statistics, Annual Report*, Cm. 3290 (London: HMSO).

Loveland, I. (1989), "The Micro-Politics of Welfare Rights: the Interpretation and Application of the Cohabitation Rule in the Housing Benefit Scheme" [1989] *Journal of Social Welfare Law* 23.

Lundsgaarde, H.P. (1977), *Murder in Spce City: a Cultural Analysis of Houston Homicide Patterns* (New York: Oxford University Press).

Lyon, A. (1998), "After Findlay: a Consideration of Some Aspects of the Military Justice System" [1998] Crim.L.R. 109.

Mackay, R.E. and Moody, S. (1996), "Diversion of Neighbourhood Disputes to Community Mediation" [1996] 35 *Howard Journal of Criminal Justice* 299.

Maguire, M. (1980), "The Impact of Burglary Upon Victims" [1980] 20 Brit.J.Criminol. 261.

Maguire, M. (1994), "Crime Statistics, Patterns and Trends: Changing Perceptions and Their Implications", Chap. 6 in Maguire, M., *et al.*, (eds.), *Oxford Handbook of Criminology.*

Maguire, M., Morgan, R. and Reiner, R. (eds.) [1994], *The Oxford Handbook of Criminology* (1st ed., Oxford: Clarendon Press).

Mansfield, M. (1993), "Runciman Commission: Runciman Risks Rights" [1993] 20 *Socialist Lawyer* 17.

Marshall, T.F. (1985), *Alternatives to Criminal Courts: the Potential for Non-Judicial Dispute Settlement* (Aldershot: Gower).

Marshall, T.F. (1987), "Mediation: a New Model of Establishing Order in Schools" [1987] 26 *Howard Journal of Criminal Justice* 33.

Martin, J.P. (1962), *Offenders as Employees* (London: Macmillan).

Mather, L. (1979), *Plea Bargaining or Trial* (Lexington, Mass.: Heath).

Matthews, R. (ed.) (1988), *Informal Justice* (London: Sage)
Matza, D. (1964), *Delinquency and Drift* (New York: John Wiley).
Maughan, B. and Ouston, J., (1979), "Fifteen Thousand Hours: Findings and Implications" [1979] *Trends* 4.
Mayhew, P., Elliot, D. and Dowds, L. (1989), *The 1988 British Crime Survey* (HORS No. 111), (London: HMSO).
Mayhew, P. et al (1993), *The 1992 British Crime Survey* (HORS No. 132), (London: HMSO).
McBarnett, D. (1978), "The Police and the State", in Littlejohn G., *et al.*, (eds.), *Power and the State* (Beckenham: Croom Helm).
McBarnett, D. (1981), *Conviction* (London: Macmillan).
McBarnett, D. (1983), "Victim in the Witness Box—Confronting Victimology's Stereotype" [1983] 7 *Contemporary Crises* 279.
McCann, K. (1985), "Battered Women and the Law: the Limits of the Legislation", in Brophy, J. and Smart, C. (eds.), *Women in Law* (London: Routledge).
McConville, M. (1993), "A Comedy of Errors", *Legal Action*, November 8.
McConville, M., Hodgson, J., Bridges, L., and Pavlovic, A. (1994), *Standing Accused: The Organisation and Practices of Criminal Defence Lawyers in Britain* (Oxford: Clarendon Press).
McConville, M. and Mirsky, C. (1986), "Criminal Defence of the Poor in New York City" [1986] 15 *Review of Law and Social Change* 581.
McConville, M., Sanders, A. and Leng, R. (1991), *The Case for the Prosecution* (London: Routledge).
McEldowney, J. (1994), *Public Law* (London: Sweet and Maxwell).
McEwan, J. (1992), *Evidence and the Adversarial Process* (Oxford: Blackwell).
McLintock, F. and Avison, N.H. (1968), *Crime in England and Wales* (London: Heinemann).
McMahon, M. (1992), *The Persistent Prison: Rethinking Decarceration and Penal Reform* (Toronto: University of Toronto Press).
Merry, S.E. (1981), *Urban Danger: Life in a Neighbourhood of Strangers* (Philadelphia: Temple University Press).
Metzger-Preziger, G. (1978), "Summary and Consequences for Criminal Policy", in Felstiner, W. and Drew, A.B., *European Alternatives to Criminal Trials and their Applicability in the U.S.* (Washington: Department of Justice).
Moody, S. (1993), *Diversion from the Criminal Justice Process: Report on the Diversion Scheme at Ayr* (Edinburgh: Scottish Office, Central Research Unit).
Moody, S. and Tombs, J. (1982), *Prosecution in the Public Interest* (Edinburgh: Scottish Academic Press).
Moore, P. (1981), "Scroungermania at the DHSS", *New Society*, January 22.
Morris, A. and Giller, H. (1979), *What Justice for Children?* (London: Justice for Children).
Morris, A. and Giller, H. (1987), *Juvenile Justice* (London: Edward Arnold).
Morris, H. (1981), "A Paternalistic Theory of Punishment", 18 *American Philosophical Quarterly* 263.
Mowbray, A.R. (1988), "The Compounnding of Proceedings by the Customs and Excise: Calculating the Legal Implications" [1998] B.T.R. 290.
Moxon, D. (1988), *Sentencing Practice in the Crwn Court* (HORS No. 103) (London: HMSO).
Muir, W.K. (1977), *The Police: Street Corner Politicians* (Chicago: Chicago University Press).

Murray, K. and Hill, M. (1995), "The Recent History of Scottish Child Welfare", *Children and Society* 5/3, 266.

NACRO (1986), *Enforcement of the Law Relating to Social Security* (London: NACRO).

NACRO (1986a), *Working Party Report* (London: NACRO).

NACRO (1993), *Community Care and Mentally Disturbed Offenders*, Policy Paper No. 1 (London: NACRO).

National Audit Office (1992), *National Insurance Fund Accounts 1990–91*, 1991–92 H.C. 33.

Nergård, T.B. (1993), "Solving Conflicts Outside the Court System: Experience with the Conflict Resolution Boards in Norway" [1993] 33 Brit.J.Criminol. 1.

Norrie, A. (1993), *Crime, Reason and History: a Critical Introduction to Criminal Law* (London: Weidenfeld and Nicolson).

Osborne, P. (1995), "Judicial Review and the Criminal Process", in Hadfield, B. (ed.), *Judicial Review: a Thematic Approach* (Dublin: Gill and Macmillan).

Owers, A. (1993), "Speaking Up for Criminal Justice" [1993] 90 *Law Society Gazette* 43: 11.

Packer, H. (1968), *The Limits of the Criminal Sanction* (Stanford: Stanford University Press).

Pahl, J. (1985), *Private Violence and Public Policy* (London: Routledge and Kegan Paul).

Parnas, R. (1967), "Police Response to the Domestic Disturbance", *Wisconsin Law Review* 914.

Pease, K. (1988), *Judgements of Crime Seriousness: Evidence from the 1984 British Crime Survey* (Home Office Research and Planning Unit Paper 44), (London: HMSO).

Pease, K. (1994), "Crime Prevention", Chap. 14 in Maguire, M., *et al.*, (eds.), *Oxford Handbook of Criminology.*

Peay, J. (1994), "Mentally Disordered Offenders", Chap. 23 in Maguire, M. *et al.*, (eds.), *Oxford Handbook of Criminology.*

Pfohl, S.J. (1977), "The Discovery of Child Abuse" [1977] 24 *Social Problems* 310.

Philips, D. (1977), *Crime and Authority in Victorian England: the Black Country 1835–60* (Beckenham: Croom Helm).

Philips, D. (1983), "Good Men to Associate and Bad Men to Conspire: Associations for the Prosecution of Felons in England, 1770–1860" (unpublished paper, presented to the Conference on the History of Law, Labour and Crime, University of Warwick, September, 1983).

Piliavin, I. and Briar, S. (1964), "Police Encounters with Juveniles", 70 *American Journal of Sociology* 206.

Pitts, J. (1988), *The Politics of Juvenile Crime* (London: Sage).

Pizzey, E. (1974), *Scream Quietly or the Neighbours Will Hear* (Harmondsworth: Penguin).

Primoratz, I. (1989), "Punishment as Language" [1989] 64 *Philosophy* 187.

Prins, H. (1991), "Is Psychopathic Disorder a Useful Clinical Concept?" [1991] *International Journal of Offender Therapy and Comparative Criminology* 35/2, 119.

Public Accounts Committee (1986), *Vehicle Excise Duty Evason and Enforcement*, 50th Report, Session 1985–86, (H.C. 480).

Public Accounts Committee (1988), *HM Customs and Excise: Investigation of Fraud and Smuggling*, 33rd Report, Session 1987–88 (H.C. 452).

Radzinowicz, L. (1968), *A History of English Criminal Law, Volume 4, Grappling for Control* (London: Stevens).

Reiner, R. (1994), "Policing and the Police", Chap. 15 in Maguire, M., *et al.*, (eds.), *Oxford Handbook of Criminology.*

Richardson, G.M., Ogus, A.I. and Burrows, P. (1983), *Policing Pollution: a Study of Regulation and Enforcement* (Oxford: Clarendon Press).

Rider, B.A.K., Abrams, C. and Ferrar, E. (1989), *Guide to the Financial Services Act 1986* (2nd ed.) (Bicester: CCH Editions).

Robens Committee (1972), *Report of the Committee on Safety and Health at Work*, Cmnd. 5034 (London: HMSO).

Robertshaw, P. and Milne, A. (1992), "The Guilty Plea Discount: Rule of Law or Role of Chance?" [1992] 31 *Howard Journal of Criminal Justice* 53.

Robertson, G., Pearson, R. and Gibb, R. (1995), "The Mentally Disordered and the Police", Home Office Research and Statistics Department, *Research Findings* No. 21 (London: HMSO).

Robin, G.D. (1967), "The Corporate and Judicial Disposition of Employee Thieves", *Wisconsin Law Review* 685.

Rogers, A. and Faulkner, A. (1987), *A Place of Safety* (London: MIND).

Rollin, H.R. (1965), "Unprosecuted Mentally Abnormal Offenders" [1965] *B.M.J.* 831.

Rowan-Robinson, J., *et al.*, (1990), *Crime and Regulation: A Study of the Enforcement of Regulatory Codes* (Edinburgh: T. and T. Clark).

Rowan-Robinson, J. and Ross, A. (1994), "Enforcement of Environmental Regulation in Britain: Strengthening the Link [1994] J.P.E.L. 200.

Royal Commission on Criminal Justice (Runciman Commission) (1993), *Report* Cm. 2263 (London: HMSO).

Sagarin, E. (1975), *Deviants and Deviance* (New York: Praeger).

Samaha, J. (1974), *Law and Order in Historical Perspective: the Case of Elizabethan Essex* (New York: Academic Press).

Sanders, A. (1987), "Constructing the Case for the Prosecution", 14 *Journal of Law and Society* 229.

Sanders, A. (1988), "The Limits to Diversion from Prosecution", 28 Brit.J.Criminol. 513.

Sanders, A. (1988a), "Personal Violence and Public Order: the Prosecution of Domestic Violence in England and Wales" [1988] 16 *International Journal of the Sociology of Law* 359.

Sanders, A. and Young, R. (1994), *Criminal Justice* (London: Butterworths).

Scarman, Lord (1982), *The Scarman Report: the Brixton Disorders, 1981* (Harmondsworth: Penguin).

Scottish Office, (1994), *Firm and Fair*, Cm. 2600 (Edinburgh: HMSO).

Shapland, J. (1981), *Between Conviction and Sentence* (London: Routledge and Kegan Paul).

Sharpe, J.A. (1977), "Crime and Delinquency in an Essex Parish 1600–1640", in Cockburn, J.S. (ed.), *Crime in England 1550–1800* (London: Methuen).

Sharpe, J.A. (1980), "Enforcing the Law in the Seventeenth Century Village", Chap. 4 in Gatrell, V.A.C., *et al.*, (eds), *Crime and the Law: the Social History of Crime in Western Europe since 1500* (London: Europa Publications).

Sharpe, J.A. (1984), *Crime in Early Modern England 1550–1750* (London: Longman).

Sharpe, J.A. (1990), *Judicial Punishment in England* (London: Faber and Faber).

Scheptycki, J. (1991), "Innovations in the Policing of Domestic Violence in London, England" [1901] 2 *Policing and Society* 117.

Schneider, A., *et al.*, (1976), "The Role of Attitudes in Decisions to Report Crimes to the Police", in McDonald, W. (ed.), *Criminal Justice and the Victim* (London: Sage).

Schur, E.M. (1973), *Radical Non-Intervention: Rethinking the Delinquency Problem* (Englewood Cliffs, N.J.: Prentice Hall).

Shoemaker, R. (1991), *Prosecution and Punishment* (Cambridge: Cambridge University Press).

Shubert, A. (1981), "Private Initiative in Law Enforcement: Associations for the Prosecution of Felons, 1744–1856", in Bailey, V. (ed.), *Policing and Punishment in Nineteenth Century Britain* (Bekenham: Croom Helm).

Skogan, W.G. (1984), "Reporting Crimes to the Police: the Status of World Research" [1984] 21 *Journal of Research in Crime and Delinquency* 113.

Smith, D.J. (1994), "Race, Crime and Criminal Justice", Chap. 22 in Maguire, M., *et al.*, (eds.), *Oxford Handbook of Criminology.*

Smith, J. and Hogan, B. (1996), *Criminal Law* (8th ed.) (London: Butterworth).

Smith, R. (1993), "Integrity or Convictions?" [1993] 90 *Law Society Gazette* 38: 2.

Smith, R.G. (1994), *Medical Discipline: the Professional Conduct Jurisdiction of the General Medical Council 1858–1990* (Oxford: Clarendon Press).

Smith, S. (1984), "Crime in the News" [1984] 24 Brit.J.Criminol. 289.

Sparks, R. (1992), *Television and the Drama of Crime: Moral Tales and the Place of Crime in Public Life* (Milton Keynes: Open University Press).

Stedward, G. and Millar, A. (1989), *Diversion from Prosecution* (Edinburgh: Scottish Office Central Research Unit).

Steenhuis, D. (1988), "Criminal Prosecution in the Netherlands", in Williams, H. (ed.), *The Role of the Prosecutor* (Aldershot: Avebury).

Steer, D. (1970), *Police Cautions—A Study in the Use of Police Discretion* (Oxford Occasional Papers, No. 2), (Oxford: Blackwell, for the Penal Research Unit).

Stewart Committee (1980), *The Motorist and Fixed Penalties*, Cmnd. 8027 (Edinburgh: HMSO).

Stewart Committee (1983), *Keeping Offenders Out of Court: Further Alternatives to Prosecution*, Cmnd. 8958 (Edinburgh: HMSO).

Stockdale, E. and Devlin, K. (1987), *Sentencing* (London: Waterlow)

Tarling, R. (1979), *Sentencing Practice in Magistrates' Courts* (HORS, No. 98) (London: HMSO).

Taylor, I., Walton, P. and Young, J. (1975), *Critical Criminology* (London: Routledge and Kegan Paul).

Tempkin, J. (1987), *Rape and the Legal Process* (London: Sweet and Maxwell).

Thompson, E.P. (1991), *Customs in Common* (Harmondsworth: Penguin).

Tombs, J. and Moody, S. (1993), "Alternatives to Prosecution: the Public Interest Redefined" [1993] Crim.L.R. 357.

Topping, K.J. (1983), *Educational Systems for Disruptive Adolescents* (Beckenham: Croom Helm).

Tutt, N. (1981), "A Decade of Policy" 21 [1981] 21 Brit.J.Criminol. 246.

Tutt, N. and Giller, H. (1983), "Police Cautioning of Juveniles: the Practice of Diversity" [1983] Crim.L.R. 587.

Underdown, D. (1985), *Revel, Riot and Rebellion: Popular Culture and Politics in England 1603–1660* (Oxford: University Press).

U.S. Department of Justice (1981), *Criminal Victimization in the U.S. 1979 (Washington: U.S. Department of Justice, Bureau of Justice Statistics).*

Utting, D. (1996), Reducing Criminality Among Young People: A Sample of Relevant Programmes in the U.K. (HORS No. 161), (London: HMSO).

Van Den Wyngaert, C. (ed.) (1993), *Criminal Procedure Systems in the E.C.* (London: Butterworths).

Vera Institute of Justice (1977), *Felony Arrests: their Prosecution and Disposition in New York City's Courts* (New York: Vera Institute).

Von Hirsch, A. (1985), *Past or Future Crimes: Deservedness and Dangerousness in the Sentencing of Criminals* (Manchester: Manchester University Press).

Von Hirsch, A. (1993), *Censure and Sanctions* (Oxford: Clarendon Press).

Von Hirsch, A. and Ashworth, A. (eds) (1992), *Principled Sentencing* (Edinburgh: Edinburgh University Press).

Walgrave, L. (1994), "Beyond Rehabilitation: In Search of aConstructive Alternative in the Judicial Response to Crime" [1994] 2 *European Journal on Criminal Policy and Research* 57

Walker, D.M. (1997), *The Scottish Legal System* (Edinburgh: W. Green/Sweet and Maxwell).

Walker, N. (1980), *Punishment, Danger and Stigma* (Oxford: Blackwell).

Walker, N. (1991), *Why Punish?* (Oxford: Oxford University Press).

Walker, N. (ed) (1996), *Dangerous People* (London: Blackstone Press).

Walker, N. and Padfield, N. (1996), *Sentencing Theory, Law and Practice* (London: Butterworths).

Walklate, S. (1989), *Victimology: The Victim and the Criminal Justice Process* (London: Unwin Hyman).

Walsh, D. (1978), *Shoplifting: Controlling a Major Crime* (London: Macmillan).

Warner, S. (1992), *Making Amends: Justice for Victims and Offenders* (Aldershot: Ashgate).

Wasik, M. (1985), "The Grant of an Absolute Discharge" [1985] 5 O.J.L.S. 211.

Wasik, M. (1993), *Emmins on Sentencing* (London: Blackstone Press).

Wasik, M. and Taylor, R. (1994), *Blackstone's Guide to the Criminal Justice Act 1991* (2nd ed.) (London: Blackstone Press).

Watson, M. and Taylor, R. (1995), *Blackstone's Guide to the Criminal Justice and Public Order Act 1994* (London: Blackstone Press).

Watson, D., Boucherat, J. and Davis, G. (1989), "Reparation for Retributivists", in Wright M. and Galaway, B. (eds.), *Mediation and Criminal Justice.*

Weinberger, B. (1981), "The Police and the Public in Mid-Nineteenth Century Warwickshire", in Bailey, V. (ed.), *Policing and Punishment in Nineteenth Century Britain* (Beckenham: Croom Helm).

Westwood, D. (1991). "The Effects of Home Office Guidelines on the Cautioning of Offenders" [1991] Crim.L.R. 591.

White, R.M. and Willcock, I.D. (1993), *The Scottish Legal System* (London: Butterworths).

Wilkins, L. (1964), *Social Deviance* (London: Tavistock).

Wilkinson, C. and Evans, R. (1990), "Police Cautioning of Juveniles: the Impact of Home Office Circular 14/1985" [1990] Crim.L.R. 165.

Williams, G. (1984), *The Law and Politics of Police Discretion* (Westport, Ct.: Greenwood Press).

Willis, C. (1983), *The Use, Effectiveness and Impact of Police Stop and Search Powers* (Home Office Research and Planning Unit Paper No. 15) (London: HMSO).

Wilson, J.Q. (1968), *Varieties of Police Behaviour* (Cambridge, Mass.: Harvard University Press).

Wilson, J.Q. (1983), *Thinking About Crime* (New York: Basic Books).

Woolf, Lord Justice (1991), *Prison Disturbances, April 1990: Report of an Inquiry by Lord Justice Woolf and Judge Stephen Tumim*, Cm. 1456 (London: HMSO).

Worrall, A. and Pease, K. (1986), "The Reporting of Personal Crime Against Women: Evidence from the 1982 British Crime Survey" [1986] 26 *Howard Journal of Criminal Justice* 118.

Wright, M. (1991), *Justice for Victims and Offenders* (Milton Keynes: Open University Press).

Wright, M. (1995), "Victims, Mediation and Criminal Justice" [1995] Crim.L.R. 187.

Wright, M. and Galaway, B. (eds) (1989), *Mediation and Criminal Justice* (London: Sage).

Wrightson, K. and Levine, D. (1979), *Poverty and Piety in an English Village* (New York: Academic Press).

Young, R. and Sanders, A. (1994), "The Royal Commission on Criminal Justice: A Confidence Trick?" [1994] 14 O.J.L.S. 435.

Young, R. and Wall, D. (eds) (1996), *Access to Criminal Justice* (London: Blackstone).

Zander, M. (1993), "The 'Innocent' Who Plead Guilty" [1993] 143 N.L.J. 85.

Zedner, L. (1994), "Victims", Chap. 25 in Maguire, M., *et al.*, (eds.), *Oxford Handbook of Criminology.*

Index